ROOSEVELT *the* EXPLORER

★ ★ ★

ROOSEVELT *the* EXPLORER

T.R.'s Amazing Adventures as a Naturalist,

Conservationist, and Explorer

★ ★ ★

H. Paul Jeffers

TAYLOR TRADE PUBLISHING

LANHAM • BOULDER • NEW YORK • TORONTO • PLYMOUTH, UK

Published by Taylor Trade Publishing
An imprint of Rowman & Littlefield
4501 Forbes Boulevard, Suite 200, Lanham, Maryland 20706
www.rowman.com

10 Thornbury Road, Plymouth PL6 7PP, United Kingdom

Distributed by National Book Network

British Library Cataloguing in Publication Information Available

Library of Congress Cataloging-in-Publication Data

The hardback edition of this book was previously catalogued by the Library of Congress as follows:

Jeffers, H. Paul (Harry Paul), 1934–
    Roosevelt the explorer : Theodore Roosevelt's amazing adventures as a naturalist, con-servationist, and explorer / H. Paul Jeffers.—1st Taylor Trader ed.
      p. cm.
    Includes bibliographical references and index.
    ISBN 0-87833-290-1 (cloth : alk. paper)
      1. Roosevelt, Theodore, 1858–1919. 2. Roosevelt, Theodore, 1858–1919—Childhood and youth.
    3. Roosevelt, Theodore, 1858–1919—Journeys. 4. Hunting—United States. 5. Hunting—Africa, East
    6. Africa, East —Description and travel. 7. Natural history—Africa, East. 8. Presidents—United States—
    Biography. 9. Explorers—United States—Biography. 10. Naturalists—United States—Biography. 1. Title
    E757 .J444 2003
    973.91′1′092—dc21   2002010573

ISBN 978-0-87833-290-8 (cloth : alk. paper)
ISBN 978-1-58979-941-7 (pbk : alk. paper)
ISBN 978-1-4617-3437-6 (electronic)

♾ ™ The paper used in this publication meets the minimum requirements of American National
Standard for Information Sciences—Permanence of Paper for Printed Library Materials,
ANSI / NISO Z39.48-1992.

For my brother-in-law
Bill Detwiler,
the hunter in the family

★ ★ ★

"The free, self-reliant, adventurous life, with its rugged and its stalwart
democracy, the wild surroundings, the grand beauty of the scenery,
the chance to study the ways and habits of the woodland
creatures—all these unite to give to the career of
the wilderness hunter its peculiar charm."

THEODORE ROOSEVELT

1893

CONTENTS

★ ★ ★

ROOSEVELT *the* EXPLORER

★ ★ ★

INTRODUCTION

★ ★ ★

Right Stuff

NO AMERICAN PRESIDENT has been so associated with appreciation and conservation of the natural treasures of the wilderness and its creatures than the twenty-sixth. Being a man of his time, when he left the White House to spend a year on a big-game safari in Africa, he carried a rifle. Being a naturalist, he also took a camera. As a visionary and pioneer conservationist, he declared, "More and more, as it becomes necessary to preserve the game, let us hope that the camera will largely supplant the rifle." A prolific author, he recorded the experience in both illuminating detail and humor. The rhinoceros, he pointed out, "are truculent, blustering beasts, much the most stupid of all the dangerous game I know." When confronted by one of the lumbering animals, he was not sure if it was preparing to charge him or make a retreat. "I am not a rhinoceros mind reader," he wrote, "and its actions were such as to warrant my regarding it as a suspicious character." When it chose to attack, Roosevelt had no recourse but to shoot it.

In an earlier volume on his hunting experiences in the American wilderness the animal that came at him was a grizzly bear. Twenty-four years old and on his first trip into the Rockies, he sighted it unexpectedly. He fired a shot, but only wounded it in the flank. With "a harsh roar of fury and challenge, blowing the bloody foam from his mouth," and baring gleaming white fangs, the bear charged, "crashing and bounding through the laurel bushes." Hit again and again, the bear came steadily on. Leaping aside, Roosevelt saw a huge paw make a vicious blow close to his head. The rush of the charge carried the grizzly past him. Felled by the last of Roosevelt's cartridges, "leaving a pool of bright blood where his muzzle hit the ground," the bear recovered enough to make two or three jumps forward before collapsing and rolling over and over "like a shot rabbit."

Recalling an elk-hunting trip in the Bighorn Mountains, Roosevelt reported discovering a grizzly bear's "huge, half-human footprints." Alone in the silent, lonely woods, he gazed down at "the unmistakable proof that I was in the home of the mighty lord of the wilderness." Tracking the prints the next day in the company of other hunters, he found the grizzly in a "breastwork of fallen logs" in a "tangled thicket." The animal stood "not ten steps off." As the bear slowly rose from its bed among the young spruces, with shaggy hair seeming to bristle, it turned toward the intruders. When it sank down on his forefeet, Roosevelt raised his rifle and saw the grizzly's great head bent slightly down. Aiming between the "small, glittering, evil eyes," he pulled the trigger. Half-rising, the grizzly fell over on his side, dead.

"The whole thing was over in twenty seconds from the time I caught sight of the game," Roosevelt wrote. "Indeed it was over so quickly that the grizzly did not have time to show fight at all or come a step toward us." Standing by "the great brindled bulk, which lay out in the cool shade of the evergreens," he felt "not a little proud."

In recounting this kill in a book titled *Hunting Trips of a Ranchman*, Roosevelt could not resist an opportunity to educate his readers by pointing out "the name of this bear has reference to its character and not to its color, and should, I suppose, be properly spelt grisly—in the sense of horrible, exactly as we speak of a 'grisly spectre'—and not grizzly; but perhaps the latter way of spelling it is too well established by now." He also noted that a grizzly's brain "is about the size of a pint bottle," and that its coarse and not well-flavored flesh did not provide a tasty meal. The meat of a black bear, he instructed, was much better.

Comparing the black bear to the grizzly, Roosevelt found the former to be "not usually a formidable opponent, and though he will sometimes charge home he is much more apt to bluster and bully than actually to come to close quarters. I have myself shot one or two black bears, and these were obtained under circumstances of no special interest, as I merely stumbled on them while after other game, and killed them before they had a chance either to run or show fight."

While Roosevelt held the grizzly in higher esteem, calling it the most dangerous animal in the world, it's the black bear that is indelibly linked to his name. While on a black bear hunt in Mississippi in 1902 during a vacation from the

White House, the quarry proved scarce until a bedraggled one of roughly 230 pounds crashed out of the woods and was run down by hunting dogs. When it killed one of the hounds, a hunter roped it and invited the twenty-sixth president of the United States to shoot it. Deeming this unsportsmanlike, Roosevelt refused. The bear was let go. When news of this event reached Washington, a newspaper cartoonist drew a whimsical view of the president's refusal to shoot. The cartoon inspired a Brooklyn toy shop owner, Morris Michtom, to create a cuddly stuffed toy bear which he named "Teddy."

While the nickname was popular amongst the American people, journalists, and clever cartoonists, those closest to Roosevelt addressed him as "Theodore," "TR," or by the title he'd held as heroic leader of the Rough Riders in the Spanish-American War, "Colonel." As a child, his nickname was "Teedie."

Half a century before American astronauts leapt into space as explorers, Roosevelt wrote of his adventures in the wild, "If a man has the right stuff in him, his will grows stronger with each exercise of it."

Roosevelt proved that he had the right stuff in the lifetime of adventures as naturalist and explorer that are the subject of this book. A keen observer of nature who had to overcome childhood illnesses, he became an enthusiastic student of wild animal and plant life. In college he studied to be a natural scientist. As a young man, he sojourned west to become a rancher and cattleman when "the West" was still a wild and woolly place. Among his many escapades in Dakota were explorations of the Badlands and numberless hunts after deer, elk, moose, caribou, bears, and the always-fearsome grizzly.

Returning to New York, Roosevelt founded the Boone and Crockett Club, the nation's first group dedicated to conservation. When his chosen profession turned out not to be natural science, but politics, he championed the cause of conservation by using his executive power as president of the United States to decree by fiat that vast federal wetlands would henceforth be preserved as bird sanctuaries. He also persuaded the Congress to establish a system of national parks. As his time in the White House was running out, he announced that he intended to spend the first year of his retirement from public life by going exploring.

He set his mind on Alaska, but abruptly turned his sights to East Africa. With backing from the Smithsonian Institution and with a mandate from the National Museum in Washington, D.C., to gather wildlife specimens and other artifacts for the museum's collections, he took along his second son, Kermit, three professional naturalists, and a "Pigskin Library" of the world's great books for reading at night. Typically, he rode into "the Dark Continent" in 1909 on a special seat fitted to the cowcatcher of a train.

By foot, horseback, and boat, he explored, photographed, and hunted by pursuing the lion, elephant, rhino, hippopotamus, antelope, and buffalo until he had specimens of every kind of important game animal. Some of these adventures included hairbreadth escapes.

Employing his considerable proven talents as an author, he described his experiences in *African Game Trails*, adding it to a "Roosevelt shelf" at his Sagamore Hill home which held his previous best-sellers on life in the wild: *Hunting Trips of a Ranch-man*, 1885; *Ranch Life and the Hunting Trail*, 1888; *The Wilderness Hunter* and *American Big Game*, both in 1893; *The Deer Family* (co-author), 1902; and *Good Hunting*, 1907.

After losing a bid to become president again in 1912, as the candidate of the Progressive (Bull Moose) Party, the Roosevelt wanderlust revived. This time he looked southward. Deciding to explore some part of South America, he found himself invited to speak to learned societies in Argentina and Brazil. He then announced that he thought it would be "interesting" to come north "by way of the middle of the continent into the valley of the Amazon" to see what he could see.

Asked why a man of his age fifty-five would dare such a thing, he replied, "It's my last chance to be a boy again."

PART ONE

★ ★ ★

Enough Peril to Make It Exciting

1

★ ★ ★

Curious Teedie

THE FIRST FACT that Teedie Roosevelt noticed about the seal was that it was dead. The sight of it was still clear in 1913. "I was walking up Broadway," he recalled, "and as I passed the market to which I used sometimes to be sent before breakfast for strawberries I suddenly saw [it] laid out on a slab of wood. The seal filled me with every possible feeling of romance and adventure." At that moment, he wrote, "I started my career as a zoologist."

Questions gushed from his mouth. First, "Where was it killed?" He was told, "In the harbor." Not having a tape measure with him, he measured it with a folding pocket foot rule. "A difficult undertaking," it was accomplished with patience and excitement, with the findings set down in the first of a series of blank books in "simplified spelling, wholly unpremeditated and unscientific." Not only was a natural-historian being born, but a writer who during his lifetime would create an astonishing library of books on nature, hunting, exploration, naval warfare, the winning of the West, politics, government, civil service, manliness, virtue, the extolling of "the strenuous life," and pride in being an American.

Soon, his room in the house at Broadway and Fourteenth Street was given a name by his numerous cousins. They called it the "Roosevelt Museum of Natural History." Because of a "rebellion on the part of the chambermaid," and "the approval of the higher authorities of the household," the collection was moved up to a kind of bookcase in the back hall upstairs.

"It was the ordinary boy's collection of curios," Theodore Roosevelt remembered, "quite incongruous and entirely valueless except from the standpoint of the boy himself."

Sickly and delicate from birth, Teedie suffered with acute asthma and nearsightedness. Only when he got his first pair of eyeglasses did he realize "how beautiful the world was." Until then he'd been "a clumsy and awkward little boy." While much of the clumsiness and awkwardness was "doubtless due to general characteristics," a good deal of it was due to the fact that he could not see and "yet was wholly ignorant that I was not seeing."

Clear vision also resulted in the discovery of books on mammals and birds. Among the first was a volume of a "hopelessly unscientific kind" on mammals by Mayne Reid. This was followed by books on natural history by J.G. Wood, an English writer of popular volumes on the subject of nature. Presented with a copy of *Robinson Crusoe,* Teedie didn't care for the first part, but relished the marooned Crusoe's adventures with "the wolves in the Pyrenees, and out in the Far East." The young "embryo zoologist" also disliked *The Swiss Family Robinson* because of its "wholly impossible collections of animals met by that worthy family as they ambled inland from the wreck."

His sister Corrine would recall her younger brother excitedly making up stories about "jungles and bold, mighty, and imaginary fights with strange beasts" in which there was always "a small boy who understood the language of animals and would translate their opinions to us."

Among Teedie's early writings in notebooks were "The Foregoing Ant" and a "Natural History on Insects." Illustrated with his own drawings, it discussed his "observ-a-tion" of the tiny creatures' "habbits," along with what he'd been told about them by a friend. Although the title promised a treatise on small crawlers and flying things, the text also wandered off into the realms of water creatures and birds.

When the Roosevelts occupied a country summer house along the banks of the Hudson River, at Barrytown, the writing of scientific observations was augmented by keeping a diary. The first of the entries bore the headline:

BY THEODORE ROOSEVELT
MY LIFE
THREE WEEKS OF MY LIFE

AGE NINE YEARS
AUGUST '68

On that "Munday," he recorded, "A gentleman came here to day of whom I do not know the name and he told us that bears of both the brown and black species are still found on the catskills not ten miles from here." The gentleman reported that he had actually seen "a large brown bear emerge from the bushes, looking at him." Alone, unarmed, and "a good deal scared," the gentleman was fortunate "that the bear did not attack him but went close by the hill into thicker bushes."

Although no bears presented themselves for Teedie's personal study, on Saturday, August 21, he "went down to the brook" and discovered "wonders."

"It seemed as if all the inhabitants of the brook had got down to one point," he wrote. In a "small pond" were "crayfish, eels, minnows, salmanders (sic), water spiders, water bugs, etc."

A full register of observations was not possible, he continued, because he'd lost the book in which he'd recorded them. "I cannot remember what I have done," he inscribed in his diary, except getting nests of "robins and catbirds" by pushing them down from limbs with sticks. A swallows' nest located "high in the barn with a wasps nest near it" was obtained using a ladder.

After noting that nothing "now happened till the 4th of September," the diarist resumed with an account of being called from breakfast to "a room" and the "surprise" of seeing "on wall, curtains and floor about fourty swallows." The entry continued, "All the morning long in every room of the house (even in the kitchen) were swallows. They were flying south. Several hundreds were outside and about 75 in the house. I caught most of them. The others got out. One flew on my pants where he stayed till I took him off."

Later that day, a cousin arrived and brought Teedie "a christal and some stones from Niagara Falls." After an examination of them, the boys spent the rest of the day playing "Fort."

Sprinkled with a child's misspellings that were perhaps the origins of Roosevelt's life-long dedication to promotion of "simplified spelling," such as "tho" instead of "though," ten-year-old Teedie's diaries vividly and frequently painfully record a boy's sheer willpower in overcoming frail health and physical weakness, urged on by a father whom Theodore called "Great-heart," and would describe in his diary on the day of Theodore Roosevelt Senior's death as "the one I loved dearest on earth."

Crediting Teedie with having "the mind," the worried parent counseled that "without the help of the body the mind cannot go as far as it should. To see that this did not happen, he said, "You must *make* your body. It is hard drudgery to make one's body, but I know you will do it."

Teedie's answer was daily visits to Wood's gymnasium and exercises with chest-weights, then body-building routines in a second floor of the Roosevelt house equipped with all that was required to strengthen the body.

Born on October 27, 1858, Teedie had entered life with a tenuous hold and plagued from the start with asthma. "One of my memories," wrote the twenty-sixth president of the United States, and author of *The Strenuous Life,* "is of my father walking up and down the room with me in his arms at night when I was a very small person, and of sitting up in bed gasping, with my father and mother trying to help me."

Fondly recalling his father as "the best man I ever knew," the grown-up Theodore also noted in his autobiography that Theodore Senior "combined strength and courage with gentleness, tenderness, and great unselfishness."

"He never physically punished me but once," he noted, "but he was the only man I was ever really afraid of. I do not mean that it was a wrong fear, for he was entirely just, and we children adored him." To read Teedie's diary is to discover a foreshadowing of the character of the man his father endeavored to shape.

The introduction to the first publication of the boy's diary, found in a 1910 edition of the magazine *Personality,* noted, "Whatever the incidents described, and some of them were only the trivialities of play or sight-seeing, the journal entries fairly bubble with that energy and joy of life which were ever behind the magnetism of Theodore Roosevelt. Above all, the diaries bring to mind the man who fought at San Juan Hill [in the Spanish-American War], built the Panama Canal, and became for his country the embodiment of active and wholesome living. The reader of the diaries can understand how a child of such optimism and buoyancy succeeded in banishing health from his horizon."

When Teedie was ten years old, that horizon expanded beyond the house in New York City and the summer place of birds, insects, and fish to encompass a wider world. On May 12, 1869, he wrote, "We go to Europe today."

Looking back on the odyssey in his autobiography, he confessed, "I do not think I gained anything from this particular trip abroad. I cordially hated it, as did my younger brother [Elliott] and sister [Corinne, nicknamed Conie]. Practically all the enjoyment we had was in exploring any ruins or mountains when we could get away from our elders, and in playing in the different hotels. Our one desire was to get back to America, and we regarded Europe with the most ignorant chauvinism and contempt."

Young Theodore did not leave Teedie-the-naturalist at home. On the second day at sea aboard the English steamship *Scotia* he recorded seeing "several fish." On May 14, 1869, the view from the deck was of "a shoal of Porpoise." Five days later he observed "one shark, some fishe, several gulls and the boatswain (sea bird) so named because its tail feathers are supposed to resemble the warlike spike with which a boastmain (man) is usually represented."

Visiting the zoological gardens in London on June 22, 1869, he saw "a great maney animals, zebras, lions, camels, Elephants, monkeys bears, etc. etc., all common to other menageries but we also saw various kinds of wild asses etc. not common." Admitting being "a little disappointed," he returned to the zoo the next day to observe "some more kinds of animals not common to most menageries." They included "ixhrinumens, little earthdog queer wolves and foxes, badgers and raccoons and rattels with the queer antics" and "two she boars and a wildcat and a caracul fight."

Continuing on to the Netherlands in mid-July, the Roosevelts took in the botanic garden where the children "played at wild boars and hunting and being hunted." Although often "verry sick" and tormented by his asthma, he soldiered south to Switzerland. At Chanmouix on August 6, 1869, he experienced "pretty dangerous work" as he "found some specimen to keep" while climbing eight thousand feet to see the "great glacier called 'Mother of Ice.'"

After Switzerland came the south of France, then Italy. Of pausing on the border to sit with one leg in each country he wrote, "The sunset was splendid. No words can describe it. The stars now came out and with their's and the moons light shining on the palms and olives and the vilage and mountains it was very romantic."

He soon found that the "soft, balmy Italy of the poets" was "cold, dreary and smelly." Perhaps in part because of the chilly climate, he spent much of September "not well." On a Sunday evening in Saxony (October 17), feeling both ill and homesick (five months away, with seven to go before returning to the U.S.), he wrote:

I am by the fire with not another light but it. We went to church. It is now after 5. All was dark except the fire. I lay by it and listened to the wind and thought of the times at home in the country when I lay by the fire with some hickory nuts until like the slave who:

> "Again he is a king by the banks of the niger
> Again he can hear the wild roar of the tiger."

Again I was lying by the roaring wood fire (with the cold October wind shrieking outside) in the cheerful lighted room and I turned round half expecting to see it all again and stern reality forced itself upon me and I thought of the time that could come never, never, never.

In this remarkably thoughtful and poetic diary entry of a homesick, ten-year-old boy are inklings of the robust, ever-curious naturalist who would spend a lifetime seeking the tiger and other wildlife, but who, behind the famous, blustery, brash, self-confident, always-optimistic-about-his-country "Teddy" Roosevelt, frequently could be gloomy about himself and his future.

Christmas was in Rome. ("Christmas! Christmas!" he wrote, "hip, hip hurrah!") New Year's Eve found him walking up "amid the lava that still smoked" of snowy Mt. Vesuvius. Memorializing that "the ascent was the steepest I have ever made," and "being with snow it was verry slipprry," the asthmatic, but intrepid, diarist struggled to breathe as the "sulpher smoke now came sweeping down on us." Undaunted, he explored "a hole rather bigger than my arm round which came the smoke blindingly." Peering into the small crater, he saw "red flame and heard a roaring." When he poked his Alpine stick into the hole, "it caught fire right away."

Further sightseeing in Italy followed, including a glimpse of the Pope as he passed by in a procession. "We walked along and he extended his hand to me," wrote Teedie, "and I kissed it! hem!! hem!!" Finished with the museums, ruins, galleries, and other Italian attractions, the grand tour proceeded to Paris for three weeks, followed by a week in London before sailing home from Liverpool aboard the *Russia*, "a fine screw boat." On May 25, 1870, the diarist joyfully wrote, "This morning we saw land of America and swiftly coming on passed Sandy Hook and went in to the bay, New York!!! Hip! Hurrah!"

*   *   *

Two and a half years later, fourteen-year-old Teedie again peered from the deck of a ship as it sailed into a great harbor, but this seaport had been bustling with ships thousands of years before Henry Hudson had ventured into the mouth of the river that would be named for him. The port city coming into Teedie's view on November 28, 1872, bore the name of one of his favorite figures in history books that he'd read while illnesses often restricted him to bed. Of the moment he wrote, "How I gazed upon it! It was Egypt, the land of my dreams; Egypt, the most ancient of all countries! A land that was old when Rome was bright, was old when Troy was taken! It was a sight to awaken a thousand thoughts, and it did."

Four decades later, after serving almost eight years as president of the United States, and having returned to Egypt as "former president," at the end of a year's odyssey in Africa and a voyage down the Nile, Roosevelt said in his autobiography that his second visit to Europe, and especially his time in Egypt, "formed a really useful part of my education." The journey during the winter of 1872–73 began in Europe and would include the Holy Land, part of Syria, Greece, and Constantinople. But it was collecting along the Nile River that provided "the chief zest" of the odyssey. To prepare for the adventure the "directors of the 'Roosevelt Museum'" located in a house in mid-Manhattan "had printed a set of Roosevelt Museum labels in pink" for cataloging the treasures waiting to be gathered.

"I was old enough, and had read enough to enjoy the temples and the desert scenery and the general feeling of romance," Roosevelt recalled, "but this in time would have palled if I had not also had the serious work of collecting and preparing my specimens."

Although confident of his knowledge of the bird life of America from the "superficially scientific standpoint," Teedie had none concerning the ornithology of Egypt, but in Cairo he found a book about a trip up the Nile by an English clergyman. Had the volume not contained an appendix dealing with the region's birds the novice teenage student would have been collecting "entirely in the dark" about the winged denizens whose habits he was able to observe "quite well through my spectacles."

Before embarking up the Nile the Roosevelts set out to explore Cairo's museums, its bustling bazaars, and exotic mosques. Venturing to nearby Giza for the only remnant of the Seven Wonders of the Ancient World they gazed in awe at the Great Pyramid of Cheops. Not content with the view at its base, Teedie scrambled up the massive stones to its pinnacle and pronounced the vista from the peak "perfectly magnificent." Exploring the long, narrow and sloping tunnel leading to the King's Chamber, in a "perfectly stifling" atmosphere, he frequently lost his footing on the slippery stone floor while ducking bats that darted around him with "sharp cries that seemed literally to pierce the ear."

On December 12, 1872, the family boarded the *Aboo Erddan* (the *Ibis*) for a voyage up the Nile. The boy who would one day write a history of battles of great ships in the War of 1812, go on to prepare the U.S. fleet for the Spanish-American War as assistant secretary of the Navy, and as president dispatch a "Great White Fleet" of warships around the globe to demonstrate American sea power, found the river boat "the nicest, coziest little place you ever saw."

When the ruins of the temples of Karnak came into view, Teedie peered in wonder at its "grand, magnificent and awe-inspiring" panorama and felt drawn back "thousands of years, to the time of the Pharohs." Spelling the name "Harnak," he recorded seeing it by moonlight and feeling inspired to "thought which can never be spoken, a glimpse of the ineffable, of the unutterable." But admiration of these past glories was soon surpassed by flocks of egrets, cranes, kestrels, larks, doves, wild duck, kites, and every sort of wild bird listed in the appendix of the book he bought in Cairo. With intense delight he watched them wading and wheeling above and around the river, then recorded them in notebooks. By the close of one splendid day he'd jotted down fifteen species. These notes would eventually be augmented by actual specimens collected with the aid of a twin-barreled shotgun (a Christmas gift), then with his growing expertise as an amateur taxidermist, stuffed and carefully preserved to be added to the Roosevelt Museum of Natural History.

"Doubtless the family had their moments of suffering," wrote Roosevelt as he recalled these necessarily messy activities. The most important tool in his taxidermy outfit was an old toothbrush for applying arsenic soap to the skins. The work invariably left him looking grubby. Adding to this unkempt visage was a mop of untrimmed hair and clothing that he was rapidly outgrowing. "As there were no tailors up the Nile," Roosevelt explained many years later, "when I got back to Cairo I needed a new outfit. But there was one suit of clothes too good to throw away, which we kept for 'a change,' and which was known as my 'Smike suit,' because it left my wrists and ankles as bare as poor Smike himself [a bedraggled, marooned character in the Robert Louis Stevenson adventure *Treasure Island*]."

Brother Elliott came up with a teasing limerick:

There was an old fellow named Teedie,
Whose clothes at best looked so seedy
That his friends in dismay
Hollered out, "Oh! I say!"
At this dirty little fellow named Teedie.

Theodore Senior noted about his namesake in a letter home, "He is the most enthusiastic sportsman and infused some of this spirit into me. Yesterday I walked through the bogs with him at the risk of sinking hopelessly and helplessly . . . *but I felt I must keep up with Teedie.*"

In a burst of euphoria the object of his father's praise and a brother's rhyme wrote to a childhood friend, Edith Carow (a beautiful girl who was fated to be his second wife), "I think I have enjoyed myself more this winter than I ever did before."

Late in January 1873 the Egyptian explorations ended as the Roosevelts moved on to the Holy Land and the city that was the epicenter of Christianity, Judaism, and Islam. Teedie found Jerusalem "remarkably small." The place traditionally identified as the Calvary where Jesus was crucified instilled a sense of "awe." But the River Jordan, where Jesus was baptized by John the Baptist, Teedie noted, was "what we should call a rather small creek in America." To see the birthplace of Jesus in Bethlehem, he recorded, bribes had to be paid.

Temporarily abandoning his role as natural scientist for that of game hunter near Jaffa, he took aim on what he perceived to be a rabbit, only to find that he'd killed a cat.

Summing up the visit to Holy Land sites with the skepticism of a natural scientist, he wrote that "various other wonderful things" had left him with "the same impressions as when I saw Bones of Saints (or Turkeys) in Italy."

On horseback in the vicinity of Damascus, Syria, he spotted a pair of jackals. When they separated, he went after the largest, "thinking to ride over him and kill him with a club." But the animal was swift and elusive. It bounded over a cliff "some fifteen feet high, and while I made a detour he got in among some rocky hills where I could not get at him." The chase ended with the killing of "a large vulture."

Arriving in Athens, he was not profoundly moved by its advertised wonders. He found the Parthenon and other relics of ancient Greece lacking "the gloomy grandeur of Karnak." Nor was he overwhelmed by the city of Constantinople, possibly because he was "very sick" with a bout of colic. He noted being "very seasick" on the Black Sea and suffering from an asthma attack going up the Danube. Arriving in Vienna, Austria, on April 19, 1873, for a family visit to an international exposition, he began a period of "the most dreary monotony." The only bright spot for the impatient ornithologist was the purchase of "a block cock" on which he used up all his arsenic. If he had stayed much longer in Vienna, he noted, "I should spend all my money on books and birds *pour passer le temps.*" After nearly a month in the city of Mozart he happily left for Dresden, Germany, to spend the summer with his family in the home of Herr Minkwitz, a government official. The visit's purpose was acquisition of "some knowledge of the German language and literature." One of the most fascinating Germans he met was a famous swordsman who was called Herr Nasehorn (Sir Rhinocerous) because the tip of his nose had been cut off in a duel and sewn on again.

The hosts were hospitable, but drew a line on taxidermy. 'My scientific pursuits cause the family a good deal of consternation," he wrote in his diary. "My arsenic was confiscated and my mice thrown (with the tongs) out of the window."

Undaunted, he continued collecting "industriously" and enlivening the household with "hedgehogs and other small beasts and reptiles which persisted in escaping from partially closed bureau drawers."

After contracting mumps, he wrote in a letter to his mother of how he looked: "Picture to yourself an antiquated woodchuck with his cheeks full of nuts, his face well-oiled, his voice hoarse from gargling and a cloth resembling in texture and cleanliness a second-hand dustman's castoff stocking around his head." A wildlife comparison also described a "very slight attack of Asthma" that left him unable to speak "without blowing up like an abridged edition of a hippopotamus."

In late October 1873 he was home again. A world traveler and increasingly adept natural scientist who had just turned fifteen, he began preparing for enrollment at Harvard by studying with a tutor. With the family residing at the Long Island home of his grandfather at Oyster Bay, he prepped for college and "carried on the work of a practical student of natural history." His regimen of physical exercise and the process of growing from sickly boy to young manhood had produced a trim, athletic body that at the end of 1875 was recorded in a "Sporting Calendar" as:

Chest	34	in
Waist	26½	"
Thigh	20	"
Calf	12½	"
Neck	14½	"
Shoulders	41	"
Arms up	10½	"
" straight	9¾	"
Fore arm 10	"	
Weight	124 lbs	
Height	5 ft 8 in	

Entering Harvard in the fall of 1876, his chief interests remained scientific and his goal was "to be a scientific man" like ornithologist Charles Audubon. Fully intending to follow his heart, he established a small menagerie in his room (snakes, lobsters, and a large tortoise with a penchant for escaping from its pen). Ranking in the upper half of his class at the close of freshman year, he left Cambridge with a friend, Henry Minot, for an expedition into New York's Adirondack Mountains. Hunting for deer in the environs of Lakes St. Regis and Spitfire he heard a hermit thrush for the first time, then memorialized the moment in his diary:

The night was dark, for the moon had not yet risen, but there were no clouds, and as we moved over the surface of the water with the perfect silence so strange and almost oppressive to the novice in this sport, I could distinguish dimly the outlines of the gloomy and impenetrable pine forests by which we were surrounded. We had been out for two or three hours but had seen nothing; once we heard a tree fall with a dull, heavy crash, and two or three times the harsh hooting of an owl had been answered by the unholy laughter of a loon from the bosom of the lake, but otherwise nothing had occurred to break the death-like stillness of the night, not even a breath of air stirred among the tops of the tall pine trees. Wearied by our unsuccess we at last turned homeward when suddenly the quiet was broken by the song of the hermit thrush; louder and clearer it sang from the depths of the grim and rugged woods, until the sweet, sad music seemed to fill the air and to conquer for the moment gloom of the night; then it died away and ceased as suddenly as it had begun. Perhaps the song would have seemed less sweet in the daytime, but uttered as it was, with such surroundings, sounding so strange and so beautiful amid these grand but desolate wilds, I shall never forget it.

A result of this expedition, combined with two previous ventures into the region, was the compilation and self-publication with Minot of a four-page pamphlet, *The Summer Birds of the Adirondacks in Franklin County, N.Y.* Two years later, his second publication would be *Notes on Some of the Birds of Oyster Bay, Long Island.*

Although the Roosevelt family was well off financially because of Theodore Senior's successes in business, the Theodore who was now too big to still be called Teedie was instilled by his father with the expectation that he must work and make his own way in the world. "I had always supposed that this meant I must enter business," TR recalled. But in his sophomore year Theodore Senior declared that if he wished to become "a scientific man" he could do so, but that he must be sure that he "really intensely desired to do scientific work, because if I went into it I must make it a serious career." Theodore Senior had made enough money to enable his son to take up such a career "and do nonremunerative work of value *if I intended to do the very best work there was in me;* but that I must not dream of taking it up as a dilet-tante."

With requirements of freshman year behind him and free to select some of his courses, Roosevelt discovered to his dismay that the curriculum "utterly ignored the possibilities of the faunal naturalist, the outdoor natu-ralist and observer of nature." Biology was treated "as purely a science of the laboratory and the microscope, a science whose adherents were to spend their time in the study of the minute forms of marine life, or else in section-cutting and the study of tissues of the higher organisms under the micro-scope."

With no "taste" in that direction, he "abandoned all thought of being a scientist." Later analyzing why he'd so easily given up on the ambition, he wrote, "Doubtless, this meant that I really did not have the intense devotion to science which I though I had; for, if I had possessed such devotion, I would have carved out a career for myself somehow without regard to discourage-ments."

Looking back on the Harvard educational experience with the perspec-tive of his 1913 autobiography, he found "very little in my actual studies which helped me in later life." A diary entry in the fall of 1878 indicated a young man at loose ends with "absolutely no idea what I should do when I leave college." Then came devastating news of his father's death. "Oh Father, my Father," he wrote, "no words can tell how I shall miss your counsel and advice." Finding no direction from family, friends and classmates, he returned to Harvard determined to "study well" and comport himself "like a brave Christian." By "grinding like a Trojan" he ended sophomore year with an overall average of 89, garnering honors in six of his eight subjects, and returned to New York for a summer of frenzied rowing and swimming in the Bay and long hard rides on his horse Lightfoot. Yet no amount of such strenuous activity could blot out memories of good times with his father found in "every nook and cranny."

Believing that what the tormented youth needed was a change of scenery, and perhaps a father figure, his former tutor, Arthur Cutler, proposed a respite in the form of a hunting trip to the wilds of Maine in the company of a Cutler friend named Bill Sewall. The burly, bearded backwoodsman's rustic home on Lake Mattamakeag at Island Falls, near the Canadian border, Cutler informed his ex-student, was a kind of open house for hunters. Reaching the domain of this "man to know" would require traveling two days, the last 36 miles by buckboard.

Accompanied by cousins Emlen and West Roosevelt and Dr. W. Thompson, Theodore arrived on September 7 suffering "a pretty bad attack of asthma." To Sewall he appeared to be "a thin, pale youngster with bad eyes and a weak heart." But the guest quickly proved the host wrong about his heart by keeping up with Sewell on a 25-mile trek that Roosevelt deemed "a good fair walk for any common man."

Discerning "a good deal of force" in Theodore, the veteran outdoorsman and city boy, in Sewall's words, "hitched well, somehow or other, from the start." He found not "a single thing that wasn't fine in Theodore," no qualities that he didn't like. Warned that Theodore could be "headstrong and aggressive," Sewall discovered that while Theodore "was not remarkably cautious about expressing his opinion," he "never found him so except when necessary; and I've always thought being headstrong and aggressive, on occasion was a pretty good thing."

Tramping through the woods, they might have been a pair of hardy characters in a fairy tale, a frontier father and his son from the pages of an adventure yarn, or two Norsemen out of Viking myths and legends, except for their hunting guns. Four inches taller and 33 years older than Theodore, and with a lush, rust-colored beard, Bill Sewall fascinated his eager student not only because of his knowledge of Maine's wilderness, but for his familiarity with literature and epic poetry. So indelibly inscribed within Theodore Roosevelt's esteem was Bill Sewall that President Theodore Roosevelt would appoint him collector of customs in Aroostook County, then write that Sewall represented the "self-respecting, duty-performing, life-enjoying" Americanism "which is the most valuable possession that one generation can hand to the next."

But in that autumn of grieving for a father, Sewall was a needed mentor and every inch "a man to know," as Arthur Cutler had predicted. Raised to value hardiness and heroism in brave, strong men in books and in real life, Theodore saw in Sewall the very man he longed to become. Proudly keeping up with Sewall as they ventured into the woods in search of game, he delighted in joining Sewall in reciting Longfellow verses and swapping passages of Sir Walter Scott in the warming glow of campfires.

After one 33-mile tramp through the woods, "keeping near the Mattawamkeag river most of the time," Theodore wrote, "Except for half an hour for lunch we were on the go steadily from 8 A.M. till 7 P.M. I got four shots and saw no game whatever during the last twenty miles, but enjoyed the walk greatly."

Despite having been "disgusted with myself" for "as many consecutive bad shots" in a week of hunting, Theodore deemed his time in Maine "a great success." Writing *The Wilderness Hunter* in 1893, he mused, "In hunting the finding and killing of the game is after all but a part of the whole. The free, self-reliant, adventurous life, with its rugged and stalwart democracy; the wild surroundings, the grand beauty of the scenery; the chance to study the ways and habits of the woodland creatures—all these unite to give the career of the wilderness hunter its peculiar charm. The chase is among the best of all national pastimes; it cultivates that vigorous manliness for the lack of which in a nation, as in an individual, the possession of no other qualities can possibly atone."

The man whom historian Stephen E. Ambrose places "in the first rank of twentieth-century American presidents by every criterion of greatness," and who earned a reputation as an outdoorsman and big-game hunter, engaged in a bit of self-evaluation in his autobiography. He placed himself in "the mass of men of ordinary ability" who, if they choose to practice, can by sheer industry and judgment "raise themselves to the second class of respectable rifle shots, and it is to this class that I belong." Believing that the prime requisites were "cool judgment and that kind of nerve which consists in avoiding being rattled," he explained that this was attained only by actual practice.

"If the man has the right stuff in him," he wrote, "his will grows stronger and stronger with each exercise of it—and if he has not the right stuff in him he had better keep clear of dangerous game hunting, or indeed of any form of sport or work in which there is bodily peril."

Describing youthful Theodore Roosevelt and Bill Sewall "tramping through the wood together," TR biographer Edmund Morris pictured Sewall as just such a "right stuff" figure, "large and powerful, advancing with bearlike tread," and Theodore "wiry and nervous, cocking his gun at any hint of movement in the tress, stopping every now and again to pick up bugs."

Reluctantly leaving Maine in late September 1878, Theodore returned to Harvard. For his junior year he was required to take logic, metaphysics, and forensics. For elective studies he chose German, Italian, philosophy, zoology, and geology. At the end of the year he would stand thirteenth in a class of 166, and first in natural history. Amid all this studying he found time to begin writing a naval history of the War of 1812.

He also fell in love with seventeen-year-old Alice Hathaway Lee of the Boston suburb of Chestnut Hill. Finding her "beautiful in face and form, and lovelier still in spirit," he discovered as he ardently courted her during the fall and early winter that she did not share his enthusiasm for natural science. This revelation, he noted, "brought about a change in my ideas as regards science" as a career. The result was that he began contemplating post-graduate law studies and possibly going into politics. Perhaps to ponder this prospect, he chose to take a short vacation in Maine in the company of Bill Sewall and Sewall's nephew, twenty-three-year-old Wilmot Dow.

After tramping on snow shoes to a lumber camp at Oxbow, he was introduced to "the roughest human beings" he'd ever met. Illiterate Aroostook County lumbermen who had spent their whole lives in the rugged work of felling trees, they enthralled him with firsthand accounts of their backwoods experiences. The awed college junior "enjoyed every minute of it."

Back at Harvard in mid-March, he did "double work to make up for my holiday," passed semiannual exams with flying colors, resumed courting Alice Lee, and took up boxing, as much to impress Alice as to find out if he had the right stuff in the ring. Harvard freshman and future novelist Owen Wister, who would become Roosevelt's lifelong friend, provided this account of a bout with lightweight collegiate champion C.S. Hanks:

We freshmen on the floor and the girls in the gallery witnesses more than a spirited contest; owing to an innocent mistake of Mr. Hanks, we saw that prophetic flash of the Roosevelt that was to come.

Time was called on a round, Roosevelt dropped his guard, and Hanks landed a heavy blow to his nose, which spurted blood. Loud hoots and hisses from the gallery and floor were set up, whereat Roosevelt's arm was instantly flung out to command silence, while his alert and slender figure stood quiet.

"It's all right," he assured us eagerly, his arm still in the air to hold the silence; then, pointing to the time-keeper, "he didn't hear him," he explained, in the same conversational but arresting tone. With bleeding nose he walked up to Hanks and shook hands with him.

Although Roosevelt lost the fight, another observer bubbled with admiration. "You should have seen that little fellow staggering about, banging the air," he exclaimed. "Hanks couldn't put him out and Roosevelt wouldn't give up. It wasn't a fight, but, oh, he showed himself a fighter."

Many years later in an address at the Sorbonne in Paris, the former collegiate pugilist, hero of the battle of San Juan Heights in the Spanish-American War, ex-president, winner of the Nobel Peace Prize, and leading proponent of the strenuous life provided the Roosevelt definition of the right stuff:

It is not the critic who counts, not the man who points out how the strong man stumbled or where the doer of deeds could have done better. The credit belongs to the man who is actually in the arena; whose face is marred by dust and sweat and blood; who errs and comes short again . . . who knows the great enthusiasms, the great devotions, and spends himself in a worthy cause; who at least knows in the end the triumph of high achievement; and who, at worst, if he fails, at least fails while doing greatly; so that his place shall never be with those cold and timid souls who know neither victory nor defeat.

Motivated by this credo in late August 1879, Roosevelt left romancing Alice Lee behind and again ventured north to Maine with his will set on climbing the highest peak in the state. Rising a mile, Mount Katahdin was reachable only by an arduous eight-day trudge from Bill Sewall's rustic cabin at Island Falls. In the company of Sewall, Wilmot Dow, Arthur Cutler, and cousin Emlen Roosevelt, he carried a forty-five-pound backpack through thick forests, then up an increasingly steepening, rocky, and slippery climb in drenching rain. A challenge for even experienced climbers, the ascent proved too daunting for Cutler and Emlen. As they remained behind in a small tent camp, their defiant friend fought his way to the peak. That night, feeling proud of his achievement, he boasted on a page of his diary, "I can endure fatigue and hardship pretty nearly as well as these lumbermen."

Compared to the conquest of Mount Katahdin, the next adventure on this excursion was "absolute luxury." The destination of the six-day, fifty-mile trip up the Aroostook River in a large dugout canoe was the Munsungen Lakes region. Much of the journey was spent out of the boat and hip-deep in icy torrents, dragging the boat through rapids and around beaver dams and other obstructions. His description of the struggle was provided in a letter to his mother:

> The current more than once carried us off our feet, and swept us into the pools of black water; now we would lift the boat over ledges of rock, now unload and carry everything around waterfalls, and then, straining every muscle, would by main strength drag her over shoal places. . . . So we plodded wearily on till nightfall, when we encamped, and after dinner crept under our blankets drenched through, but too tired to mind either cold or wet.

The next day was a repetition of this, he continued, as "hour after hour" they waded on in perfect silence. "But, oh how we slept at night!" he joyfully recorded. "And how we enjoyed the salt pork, hardtack and tea which constituted our food!"

Not content with having scaled a mile-high peak and the conquest of a raging stream, he badgered Sewall for more in the form of a three-day, 110-mile outing by wagon and foot. "As usual, it rained," he noted, "but I am enjoying myself exceedingly, am in superb health and as tough as a pine knot."

In another diary note he exclaimed, "Am feeling strong as a bull. By Jove, it sometimes seems as if I were having too happy a time to have it last. I enjoy every minute I live, almost." [The "almost" is a reference to continuing bouts of asthma.]

In a mood of self-examination, the twenty-year-old, soon-to-be-a-Harvard-senior, love-stricken suitor of Alice Lee discerned a pattern of behavior that would run through all his years. The future politician who would at the same time be a Dakota rancher and hunter, the man of letters who spent the time between books to venture into the wilds, and president of the United States who would leave the White House after two terms and promptly pack his bags for a year on safari in Central Africa, then explore a jungle river in Brazil wrote, "My life has such absurd contrasts. At one time I live in the height of luxury; and then for a month will undergo really severe toil and hardship—and I enjoy both extremes almost equally."

Shedding his woodsy wardrobe for the fashionable "Dude" style of clothing favored by well-dressed young men of his age, he returned to Harvard and resumed his courtship of Alice Lee. Although she had deferred accepting several proposals of marriage, he was delighted in January 1880 when she agreed to become Mrs. Theodore Roosevelt.

"At last everything is settled," he wrote exultantly in his diary, "but it seems impossible to realize it." The entry continued, "Oh, how bewitchingly pretty she looked! If loving her with my whole heart and soul can make her happy, she shall be happy."

Turning twenty-one on October 27, 1879, the intrepid conqueror of Mount Katahdin was a whirlwind of campus activity: librarian of the elite Porcellian society, secretary of the Hasty Pudding club, president of the Natural History Society, and editor of the *Advocate*. Hard work at his studies placed him nineteenth in a class of 120. While squeezing in time to pursue his history of the naval engagements of the War of 1812, he was a handsome, dapper young man-about-town and, some observers noted, somewhat of a snob whose date book became so crammed with dinners, suppers, and evenings at the theater that he noted in his diary, "I find I don't get to bed too early."

Having given up being a professional natural scientist and determined to study law "and work hard for my little wife," he informed a friend of an intention to "help the cause of better government in New York City," although he didn't "know exactly how." In a senior thesis on the "Practicality of Giving Men and Women Equal Rights" he shocked the Victorian Era men of Harvard with an assertion that in marriage, there should be "absolute equality" of the sexes.

Engaged to be married, with a "cup of happiness almost too full," ranked twenty-first in the 1880 graduating class of 177, he received his Bachelor of Arts degree *magna cum laude*. Proudly wearing a Phi Beta Kappa key, he was on that day, wrote future biographer Edmund Morris, "rich, pleasant-looking, and, within a limited but growing circle, popular; he was the author of two scholarly pamphlets, a notable thesis, and two chapters of what promised to be a definitive naval history."

The only cloud in his sky was a warning from the college physician that if he did not restrain his physical activities, such as running up stairs and climbing mountains, he would not live long. "Doctor," he replied, "I'm going to do all the things you tell me not to do. If I've got to live the sort of life you have describe, if I've got to live the short life you described, I don't care how short it is."

Leaving Harvard, he wrote in his diary, "My career at college has been happier and more successful than that of any man I have ever known."

After spending a few weeks of hiking, playing tennis, swimming, and rowing on Oyster Bay, he departed with friends for Bar Harbor, Maine, and long treks in the woods and enjoying "perfectly magnificent scenery" while scaling mountains. When stricken by an attack of *cholera morbus,* he griped to his sister Corinne, "Very embarrassing for a lover isn't it? So unromantic, you know, suggestive of too much ripe fruit."

Expecting that a long-planned, six-week hunting trip to Illinois, Iowa, and Minnesota with his younger brother Elliott "will build me up," he boarded a night-train on August 16 bound for Chicago. In a parting letter to Alice Lee he wrote, "I hope we have good sport."

2

★ ★ ★

Back-East Dude

ORE THAN THREE DECADES after Theodore Roosevelt partnered with his brother Elliott for a first venture into the heartland of America, he wrote in his autobiography, "I owe more than I ever can express to the West, which of course means to the men and women I met in the West."

Arriving in western Illinois, the first leg of the hunting expedition, he found "the farm people are pretty rough, but I like them very much; like all rural Americans they are intensely independent." Among them were "a canny, shrewd Scotchman; a great, strong, jovial, blundering Irish boy; a quiet, intelligent yankee"; and a "reformed desperado" who was "very silent but when we can get him to talk his reminiscences are very interesting—and startling." There were also a "good natured German" who was delighted to discover that the Roosevelts understood and spoke "hochdeutch," and "a clumsy, giggling, pretty Irish girl, and a hard-featured backwoods woman who sings Methodist hymns and swears like a trooper on occasion."

Trying to fit in, the brothers "dressed about as badly as mortals could be." With "cropped heads, unshaven faces, dirty gray shirts, still dirtier yellow trousers and cowhide boots," they soon proved that a pair of easterners could shoot as well as the locals and could stand as much physical fatigue. On August 22, Theodore wrote, "We have three days good shooting, and I feel twice the man for it."

Because Elliott had gained hunting experience during an earlier, year-long expedition for game in Texas, Theodore tried hard to at least match Elliott's prowess and found great delight on any day that he outdid him. When chasing the small game of Illinois farm country lost its appeal, they moved on to Iowa, then joined a cousin, Jack Elliott, at his home on the banks of the Red River at Moorehead, Minnesota. Just east of the Dakota Territory, the region afforded Theodore his first view of the wide open plains that maps labeled "the Great American Desert."

"Nowhere, not even at sea," he wrote, "does a man feel more lonely than when riding over the far-reaching, seemingly endless plains."

Not many years before he marveled at the panorama of clear skies and broad horizons, the vast, open land would have been teeming with buffalo. But because of unrestrained hunters the only quarry coming into the sights of the guns of brothers and cousin were birds. Despite the vexations of the occasional asthma attack and an often upset stomach, homesickness, missing Alice, being bounced out of a wagon when it struck a hole, getting lost in an early snow squall, and breaking two of his guns, he ended the adventure with a score sheet showing that he had bagged two more trophies than Elliott (203–201). Heading home at the end of September 1880, he declared, "The trip has been great fun, but how glad I am it is over and I am to see Alice!"

They married on his twenty-first birthday in the Unitarian Church in Brookline, Massachusetts, spent their wedding night in Springfield, and had their honeymoon at Oyster Bay in the Roosevelt house, temporarily vacated by his mother and siblings. "I am living in dreamland," he wrote, "how I wish it could last forever."

Taking up residence in the family's Manhattan house on Fifty-fifth Street, the brand new husband was also now a law student at Columbia with a plan to find some role for himself that would allow him to proceed with his nebulous idea of civic reform. He soon discovered that law, for the most part, "did not make for fair social dealing."

At the end of his first term, longing for "a proper honeymoon," he whisked his bride to Europe for a fortnight that began with Alice being "awfully" seasick. After visiting uncles and cousins in London, they crossed the English Channel. "The two innocents are now on foreign soil," he noted. Like countless Americans who ventured to France, Alice did not care for the French and appeared to regard being addressed in any language but English "an impertinence." Tarrying briefly in France, they proceeded to Switzerland and the challenge, to Theodore, of conquering mountains named Jungfrau and Matterhorn. Of the second, he wrote, "I was anxious to go up it because it is reputed very difficult and a man who has been up can fairly claim to have taken his degree as, at any rate, a subordinate kind of mountaineer." Finding "some English climbers" there, he had another reason to make the climb: "to show them that a Yankee could climb just as well they could."

Hiring guides, he began a two-day journey that made Mount Katahdin seem like a mole hill. "The mountain is so steep," he noted, "that the snow will not remain on crumbling, jagged rocks, and possesses a certain somber interest from the number of people that have lost their lives on it. Accidents, however, are generally due either to rashness, or else a combination of timidity and fatigue; a fairly hard man, cautious but not cowardly, with good guides, has little to fear. Still, there is enough peril to make it exciting, and the work is very laborious being as much with the hands and feet, and (very unlike the Jungfrau) as hard coming down as going up."

Sailing down the Rhine, he found the German river's scenery "lovely, but no more so than the Hudson except for the castles." He enjoyed Holland. Paris was "mainly devoted to the intricacies of dress buying." Deeply moved after seeing the "grandly simple" tomb of Napoleon, he wrote, "I do not think there is a more impressive sepulchre on earth."

Writing to Bill Sewall from London, the future president of the United States noted, "This summer I have passed travelling through Europe, and though I have enjoyed it greatly, yet the more I see, the better satisfied I am that I am an American, free born and free bred, where I acknowledge no man my superior, except for his own worth, or as my inferior, except for his own demerit."

On evenings during the European excursion he'd frequently tried to work on his book on the naval aspects of the War of 1812, but made so little progress that he said in a gloomy note to his sister, "I have plenty of information, but I can't get it into words. I am afraid it is too big a task for me." He then wrote a line that a reader today, knowing the triumphs that were in store for Theodore Roosevelt, finds difficult to believe that he'd penned it: "I wonder if I won't find everything in life too big for my abilities."

Back in New York in the fall of 1881, twenty-three-year-old Roosevelt basked in the joys of marriage, resumed his law studies, continued struggling with the writing of the book, and explored the mysteries of politics in the form of the only party that "a young man of my bringing up and convictions could join." That his father's son would favor the Republicans came as no surprise to the men he knew best "in the clubs of social pretension and the men of cultivated taste and easy life." But when he announced his intention to actually seek membership in the Twenty-First District Republican Association, and to try to take an active part in the club's work, his friends were aghast. To them politics was considered "low," political clubs were no place for "gentlemen," and the men who controlled them were "saloon-keepers, horse-car conductors, and the like" who "would be rough and brutal and unpleasant to deal with."

Perhaps recalling his experiences with the rough woodmen of Maine and the leathery men he'd met out West, and with his conquests of Mount Katahdin, the Jungfrau, and Matterhorn fresh in his memory, Roosevelt replied that he intended to be one of "the governing class." He would not flinch from the challenge, he vowed, "until I had made the effort and found out whether I really was too weak to hold my own in the rough and tumble."

He would later write, "The man with the university education is in honor bound to take an active part in our political life, and to do his full duty as a citizen by helping his fellow citizens to the extent of his power in the exercise of the rights of self-government."

The Republican Association he sought to join held its meetings in Morton Hall, a large, barnlike room over a saloon. Its furniture consisted of dingy benches, spittoons, a dais at one end with a table and chair, and a stout pitcher for iced water. Walls were adorned by pictures of President Ulysses S. Grant and Levi P. Morton, for whom the hall was named. To join a party club in those days a man had to be proposed for membership. This required getting known. To do so, Roosevelt recalled, "I went around there often enough to have the men get accustomed to me and to have me get accustomed to them, so that we began to speak the same language, and so that each could begin to live down in the other's mind what Bret Hart has called 'the defective moral quality of being a stranger.'"

As he had won over and proved himself to Maine lumbermen, Great Plains hunters, and dubious English mountain climbers in the Alps, he "soon became on good terms with a number of the ordinary 'heelers' and even some of the minor leaders."

Among the latter group was Joe Murray. Irish-born and having grown up tough on the streets of New York, he was by nature "as straight a man, as fearless and as stanchly loyal" as anyone Roosevelt had ever met, and "a man to be trusted in any position demanding courage, integrity and good faith."

The liking and respect proved mutual. The result in the autumn of 1881 was Murray's proposal that Roosevelt go up against a veteran Republican heavyweight, Jake Hess, for the party's nomination for a seat in the New York Legislature. To the surprise of everyone, except Joe Murray, Roosevelt won the nomination in an Assembly district in which the Republican was almost always the victor in the general election. When the ballots were tallied, he found himself "triumphantly elected," making him the youngest member of the legislature and representative in Albany of the wealthiest district in Manhattan.

Arriving in the capital in stylish clothes and carrying a gold-headed walking stick, he was initially viewed by veteran lawmakers and newspaper reporters as a New York City version of outlandishly foppish Irish playwright Oscar Wilde, a wet-behind-the-ears and lowly freshman, and, worse, a Republican in a house controlled by Democrats. Feeling like "a boy in a strange school," but finding life in the New York Legislature "always interesting and often entertaining," he recognized that if he were to accomplish anything, he had to be "a thoroughly practical man of high ideals who did his best to reduce those ideals to actual practice."

A problem with claiming to be a man of high ideals, the novice politician who boasted that he'd "risen like a rocket" soon learned, was that such a man can come across, as an Albany newspaper pointed out, as "patronizing those who agree with him and abusing those who do not." Another paper called him "silly and sullen and naughty." He was ridiculed in an editorial for keeping "a pulpit concealed on his person."

Years later, he admitted that he had "immediately proceeded to lose my perspective," with the result being that he "came an awful cropper and had to pick myself up after learning the lesson that I was not all-important and that I had to take account of many different elements in life." Like most young men in politics, he confessed, "I went through various oscillations of feeling before I 'found myself.' At one period I became so impressed with the virtue of complete independence that I proceeded to act on each case purely as I personally viewed it, without paying any heed to the principles and prejudices of others."

The result was that he "speedily and deservedly lost all power of accomplishing anything at all." He learned the "invaluable lesson" that in the practical activities of life "no man can render the highest service unless he can act in combination with his fellows, which means a certain amount of give and take between him and them."

As the work of the legislature continued amid a flurry of barbed criticisms in the press and within the state capitol, the young Assemblyman from Manhattan who dressed like a "dude" began longing for an escape in the form of a few weeks of shooting at a spot out in the Dakota Territory. This attractive idea came from a young naval officer, W.W. Gorringe. The spot that he proposed was the town of Little Missouri. On a river of that name it would be, Gorringe said, an ideal jumping-off point for a summer of chasing deer, antelope, and buffalo.

Although Gorringe was ultimately unable to make the trip, Roosevelt went. In doing so, he began a romance with the West and a career as hunter and explorer that forever established the image of Theodore Roosevelt as a rugged individual, tireless proponent of the "strenuous life," prolific writer on the subjects of hunting and the outdoor life, champion of conservation, and an ardent believer that "life is a great adventure, and the worst of all fears is the fear of living."

En route to the Dakotas, he wrote to the wife he'd left behind, "I have been miserably home-sick for you all the last forty-eight hours; so home-sick that I think, if it were not that I had made all the preparations, I should have given up the journey entirely. I think all the time of my little laughing, teazing beauty, and how pretty she is, and she goes to sleep in my arms, and I could almost cry I love you so. You sweetest of all little wives! But I think my hunting will do me good; and I am very anxious to kill some large game—though I have not much hopes of being able to do so."

Reaching the Little Missouri on a Northern Pacific train about three in the morning of a cool September day in 1883, Roosevelt entered the still Wild West of Owen Wister stories and Frederic Remington drawings, the West of the Indian and the buffalo-hunter, the soldier and the cow-puncher. Aside from the railway station, the only building was the ramshackle Pyramid Park Hotel. Dragging a duffle bag, he hammered at the door until a frowsy proprietor opened it, muttering oaths. Ushered upstairs, the newcomer was given one of fourteen beds in a room that constituted the entire upper floor. Exploring an abandoned army post the next day, he met Joe Ferris, a Canadian and owner with a brother, Sylvane, and a partner, William J. Merrifield, of the Maltese Cross Ranch.

With a dirt roof the one-room log cabin had an attached chicken house near a corral for horses. The scene that enfolded as Roosevelt appeared would appear in countless movies about the frontier in future decades in which suspicious westerners gazed dubiously at a youngster from Back East whose pince-nez spectacles were viewed in the Badlands as a sure sign that the wearer was an individual of defective moral character. Playing cards that evening with the wary partners in the ranch hands, Roosevelt heard "a frightful squawking" of a bobcat raiding the chicken coop. Abandoning the cards and grabbing guns, the Ferris brothers and Merriwether dashed outdoors with their guest hurrying after them. Although a brisk chase failed to catch the marauding cat, the pursuit broke the ice between ranchers and guest.

Back at the cabin, Roosevelt blurted out the dream that had drawn him to the Dakotas. What he desired intensely, he explained to Joe Ferris, was to hunt buffalo. Ferris agreed to act as his guide, but reluctantly. Too excited to sleep, Roosevelt wrapped himself in blankets on a dirt floor and awaited daybreak. When it came at last, he mounted a horse that he'd purchased from Ferris and named Nell. On that early morning, riding southwest behind Ferris's rattling wagon, he gloried in the beauty of the landscape of the Little Missouri and majestic buttes of the Badlands. From a plateau reached around noon the view to the west was of Montana and, below, the valley of the meandering Little Missouri River. To reach that day's destination, the crude home of Gregor Lange, a friend of Ferris, they would have to ford the Little Missouri seventeen times.

As they approached the cabin at the mouth of Little Cannon Creek, Lange's sixteen-year-old son, Lincoln, peered through the door at Ferris's familiar figure and gazed in wonder at a slender young rider who wore "large conspicuous-looking glasses." When the stranger neared, the fascinated frontier youth noted "a pair of twinkling eyes" and an "expansive grin overspreading his prominent, forceful lower face," plainly revealing a set of large, smiling teeth that "are made to hold anything once they close upon it." Introduced to "Mr. Roosevelt," Lincoln found his hands "in the solid double grip of our guest."

"Dee-lighted to meet you, Lincoln," Roosevelt boomed.

"Young and all, as I was," Lincoln recalled, "the consciousness was instantly borne in upon me of meeting a man different from any I had ever met before. I fell for him strong."

The elder Lange explained that he was employed by a British financier to look into the prospect of investing in Little Missouri Land and Stock Company, owned by the naval officer, Commander W.W. Gorringe, who had urged Roosevelt to join him on a hunting trip to the Little Missouri, then was unable to make the journey. Although he was unenthusiastic about recommending that his employer put money into Gorringe's venture, Lange had thought enough of the land around Little Cannonball Creek to start his own ranch there. As Lange and Roosevelt sat up late talking, rain began. When Lange warned Roosevelt that footing on the clay slopes of the region would be "too greasy" to climb, and Joe Ferris proposed waiting for improved weather, Roosevelt exclaimed that he'd "come after buffalo, and buffalo he was going to get, in spite of hell or high water."

A week of searching for buffalo proved so disappointing that Roosevelt wrote to Alice, "For eight days my bad luck was steady." But on the ninth day, "it culminated." Leaving early in the morning, the hunting party crossed the Little Missouri and got only a quarter of a mile when a rattlesnake struck at one of the horses and barley missed him. Killed and with its rattles cut off as a prize, it was the fourth Roosevelt had seen on the trip. Two had been seen from horseback. The third had been a closer encounter. While crawling on all fours after an antelope, Roosevelt had "almost crawled on him." Warned "by the angry, threatening sound of the rattle," he'd shot the snake before it could attack.

With the fourth rattler dead, the buffalo hunters threaded through narrow defiles and along tortuous divides of a great tract of Badlands. Black-tail deer appeared, but were too far off to be in shooting range. A couple of hours later, they discovered the fresh track of a bull buffalo in the soft creek bottom, but soon the trail tuned up a winding coulee that branched out in several directions. Following the buffalo on such hard ground proved futile. But late in the afternoon the party saw three black specks in the middle of a large plain. The specks were bull buffalo. Because the hunters' horses had come a great distance without water and were in no condition for running, the men dismounted, determined to creep up on their quarry. Although the ground was unfavorable, they started off on hands and knees, using sagebrush as cover.

To his chagrin, Roosevelt wrote of lying flat on their bellies and wriggling forward like snakes, he "blundered into a bed of cactus and filled my hands with spines." Pressing onward while taking advantage of every hollow, hillock, or sagebrush, he lay "within a hundred and twenty-five yards of the bulls." With bare ground between him and the buffalo, he "drew up and fired." But confused "by the bulk and shaggy hair of the best," he "aimed too far back at one that was standing nearly broadside to me."

Roosevelt's account continued:

> The bullet told on his body with a loud crack, the dust flying up from his hide. Away went all three, with their tails up, disappearing over a light ride in the ground.
>
> Much disgusted, we trotted back to where the horses were picketed, jumped on them, out of breath, and rode after the flying game. We thought that the wounded one might turn out and leave the others, and so followed them, though they had over a mile start. For seven or eight miles we loped our jaded horses along at a brisk pace, occasionally seeing the buffalo far ahead. Finally, when the sun has just set, all three came to a stand in a gentle hollow. There was no cover anywhere near them and, as a last desperate resort, we concluded to try to run them on our worn-out ponies.
>
> As we cantered toward them they faced us for a second and then turned round and made off, while with spurs and quirts we made the ponies put on a burst that enabled us to close in with the wounded one just about the time that the lessening twilight had almost vanished. The pony I was on could barely hold his own, after getting up within sixty or seventy yards of the wounded bull. My companion, better mounted, forged ahead a little to one side. The bull saw him coming and swerved from his course, and by cutting across I was able to get nearly up to him. When within twenty feet I fired my rifle, but the darkness, and especially the violent labored motion of my pony, made me miss. I tried to get in closer, when suddenly up went the bull's tail, and, wheeling, he charged me with lowered horns. My pony, frightened into momentary activity, spun round and tossed up his head. I was holding the rifle in both hands, and the pony's head, striking it, knocked it violently against my forehead, cutting quiet a gash, from which, heated as I was, the blood poured into my eyes. Meanwhile, the buffalo, passing me, charged my companion, and followed him as he made off, and, as the ground was very bad, for some little distance his lowered head was unpleasantly near the tired pony's tail. I tried to run in on him again, but my pony stopped short, dead beat, and by no spurring could I force him out of a slow trot. My companion jumped off and took a couple of shots at the buffalo, which

missed in the dim moonlight, and, to our unutterable chagrin, the wounded bull labored off and vanished in the darkness. I made after him on foot, in hopeless and helpless wrath, until he got out of sight.

At dusk the hunters settled down for the night with the horses tethered to saddles that became pillows. "As we were in a lonely part of the wilderness," Roosevelt explained in his account of the adventure, "we knew we were in the domain of both white and red horse thieves, and that the latter might, in addition to our horses, try to take our scalps."

Around midnight the men were rudely awakened by having their pillows whipped out from under their heads. Bolting up in bright moonlight, Roosevelt saw the horses galloping off with the saddles dragging behind. Thinking that the horses had been stampeded by thieves, he and Joe Ferris rolled over and crouched in the grass with their rifles ready. Realizing that their mounts had bolted after being alarmed by wolves, they pursued the horses and found them in a glade, "standing close together and looking intently round when we came up."

In a fine drizzling mist at dawn, after a breakfast of biscuits, the hunters rode over a formless, shapeless plain, drenched through and thoroughly uncomfortable. Rising over a low divide as the fog lifted, they spotted several buffalo slowly crossing the rolling country. Leaving the horses, the hunters edged closer. In a moment that Roosevelt would recall with "wonder and regret" he fired and missed. As the buffalo plunged down a hollow, he left Roosevelt wet and sullen. Roosevelt wrote of the start of his first buffalo hunt, "So far the trip had not been a success." Joe Ferris phrased it more colorfully. "Bad luck," he said, "followed us like a yellow dog follows a drunkard."

Fortune took a favorable turn the next day. Skirting a ridge of broken buttes and moving through a dry creek bottom, Roosevelt studied soft bottom soil and found the round prints of a bison's hoofs. A moment later, he caught a glimpse of the buffalo as he fed slowly up the course of the ravine some distance ahead. The wind was right, and the ground could not have been better for stalking. Hardly needing to bend down, he walked up behind a small sharp-crested hillock, peeped over, and there below him, not fifty yards away, was a great bison bull. Grazing as he walked, his full glossy coat in fine trim and shining in the rays of the sun, while his pride of bearing showed him to be in the lusty vigor of his prime. As Roosevelt rose above the crest of the hill, the buffalo held up his head and cocked his tail to the air.

Pointing to a yellow spot just back of the animal's shoulder, Joe Ferris whispered to Roosevelt. "If you hit him there, you'll get him right through the heart."

Roosevelt's bullet struck the spot, but with surprising agility for so large and heavy an animal, and seemingly oblivious to two more wounds in his flank, he bounded up the opposite side of the ravine to disappear over the ridge at a lumbering gallop, the blood pouring from his mouth and nostrils. Certain that the quarry could not go far, Roosevelt and Ferris mounted their horses and trotted leisurely along the bloody trail. They found the bull dead in the next gully, lying almost on his back.

Joe Ferris recalled Roosevelt's reaction, "I never saw any one so enthused in my life," he exclaimed, "and, by golly, I was enthused myself for more reasons than one. I was plumb tired out, and, besides, he was so eager to shoot his first buffalo that it somehow got into my blood; and I wanted to see him kill his first one as badly as he wanted to kill it."

To "Darling Wife," Roosevelt wrote exultantly, "Hurrah! The luck has turned at last."

After describing getting his first buffalo, he concluded the letter to Alice with assurances that he was "in superb health, having plenty of game to eat, and living all day in the open air."

In his senior years he would write of hunting as a youth in the Badlands of Dakota in 1883 that "the romance of my life began."

How the history of the United States might have been written differently had Theodore Roosevelt not fallen in love with the frontier is one of the unanswerable questions that arise in the annals of human events, but there is no room for disputing that if Roosevelt hadn't ventured into the Badlands he would not have become the monumental figure of his time in politics, nor a successful historian, biographer, authoritative and prolific writer on all facets of hunting, the exponent of the strenuous life, and unabashed enthusiast for all things American. Who other than Theodore Roosevelt could have declared, in a speech in the town of Dickinson in the Dakota Territory on July 4, 1886, "Like all Americans, I like big things; big prairies, big forests and mountains, big wheat fields, railroads—and herds of cattle, too—big factories, steamboats, and everything else."

Eight years later, in the April 1894 edition of the magazine *Forum*, he wrote, "To bear the name of American is to bear the most honorable of titles; and whoever does not so believe had no business to bear the name at all."

As president on December 2, 1902, he used "the bully pulpit" of the White House to say that a nation "seated on a continent flanked by two great oceans" was composed of people who "are the descendants of pioneers, or, in a sense, pioneers themselves, of men winnowed out from among the nations of the Old World by the energy, boldness, and love of adventure found in their own eager hearts."

Upon his return from the Dakotas in the fall of 1883, with the preserved head of his first buffalo as a trophy, he told a reporter from the New York *Tribune*, "I would strongly recommend some of our gilded youth to go West and try a short course of riding bucking ponies, and assist at the branding of a lot of Texas steers."

Always a man to back up words with deeds, he came back to New York as co-owner of a cattle ranch. His partners were William Merrifield and Sylvane Ferris. That a member of the New York Legislature who was up for re-election, and with a beautiful young wife, returned with the news that he was now in the cattle business came as a shock to his city friends, and to politicians with visions of Theodore Roosevelt going as far in government as he might wish. A further befuddlement over news of the ranching enterprise for family, friends, and politicians was the fact that Alice was pregnant, with the baby due in February 1884.

Handily chosen by the voters of the mostly Republican district, he continued representing them in the State Assembly. Although disappointed that he was not picked by party members to preside as Speaker of the Assembly, a job he'd held in the previous session, he rationalized the setback by asserting that he had fought hard and efficiently for the post, and that he had made the victory "single-handed, with no machine back of me." His defeat, he declared, "strengthened my position, and enabled me to accomplish far more than I could have accomplished as Speaker."

As the session began, he wrote to Alice on January 22, 1884, "I feel much more at ease in my mind and better able to enjoy things since have gotten underway. I feel now as though I have the reins in my hand." He added, "How I long to get back to my own sweetest little wife."

In the ninth month of her pregnancy and looked after by Roosevelt's sister, twenty-two-year-old Alice saw him only when he came home on weekends. After one such visit he wrote in a letter dated February 6, "How I did hate to leave my bright, sunny little love yesterday afternoon! I love you and long for you all the time, and oh so tenderly, doubly tenderly now, my sweetest little wife. I just long for Friday evening when I shall be with you again."

Although Republicans in the Assembly had denied him election as Speaker, he found himself appointed to three of the most important committees: banks, militia, and cities. Of the three, the one that attracted him most was the latter. Having campaigned against corruption in the government of New York City, he lost no time in introducing a resolution to establish a Special Committee to Investigate Local Government and County of New York. With expected vigor, he questioned evasive corrupt officials and exposed a system of bribery, malfeasance, misfeasance, and nonfeasance.

"There was enough to investigate," wrote newspaperman Jacob Riis, "but the public had not yet grown a conscience robust enough to make the facts tell."

In the midst of this probe of corruption in the city of his Dutch ancestors and his birth, Roosevelt worried about the two most important women in his life. His beloved mother was ill, possibly with typhoid fever. His darling wife, in the final weeks of her pregnancy, was suffering from an illness that her doctor was not able to explain.

Concerned about him, Alice wrote to him on Monday, February 11, 1884, "I don't think you need feel worried about my being sick, as the Dr told me this afternoon that I would not need my nurse before Thursday. I am feeling well tonight." She closed with a wish "that I could have my little baby soon." At half-past eight the next evening she gave birth to a girl.

Notified by telegram in Albany, her beaming father rushed to finish legislative business in order to take the next train to New York. But as he was about to leave, he received a second message, informing him that Alice's condition had taken a turn for the worse. Reaching the city on the thirteenth, he was met at the door of his Fifty-seventh Street house by his brother Elliott with the exclamation, "There is a curse on this house." He reported that Alice was experiencing kidney failure and their mother was dying from typhoid fever. Their parent passed away in the predawn hours of Thursday, February 14. Alice died in the afternoon. "Seldom, if ever, has New York society received such a shock as yesterday," noted the New York *World* on Friday. "The loss of his wife and his mother in a single day is a terrible affliction."

Roosevelt wrote in his diary, "The light has gone out of my life." Following the burials on the sixteenth, he inscribed, "For joy or sorrow, my life has now been lived out."

The day after the funerals, the baby girl was christened Alice Lee. With the child put in the care of his sister Anna, Roosevelt returned to Albany and answered his crushing grief by throwing himself into his work of eliminating government corruption in New York City in the form of seven "Roosevelt reform bills," and earning a journalistic nickname: "Theodore, the Cyclone Hero of the Assembly."

Despite the praise and a general expectation that Roosevelt would be "a name" to be reckoned with in the future of New York and national politics, he wrote to a Utica, New York, newspaper that he had "little expectation of being able to keep on in politics." He added, "I shall probably be in Dakota, and I think I shall spend the next two to three years in making shooting trips, either in the Far West or in the Northern Woods."

The plan was delayed so that he could serve as a delegate to the Republican National Convention. Dismayed that the party nominated Speaker of the U.S. House of Representatives James G. Blaine, a politician with a reputation for corruption, the reform-minded Assemblyman from New York City blurted to a newspaper reporter, "I am through with politics."

The next day, he was back at the Little Missouri, eager to immerse himself in hunting and owning two cattle ranches, Elkhorn and Chimney Butte. After a week he wrote, "I have been having a glorious time here, and am well hardened now. I have just come in from spending thirteen hours in the saddle. For every day I have been here I have had my hands full. First and foremost, the cattle have done well, and I regard the outlook for making the business a success as being very hopeful."

To help run the ranches he enticed Bill Sewall and Wilmot Dow to leave the Maine woods for "the virtues that ought to come from life in the open country." The cattle were branded with a triangle and elkhorn. After the first year a long, row ranch house of hewn logs (most of them cut by Sewall and Dow) was built for the Elkhorn ranch. It had a large sitting room with a fireplace, a rubber bathtub, plenty of books, and a veranda with a rocking chair.

The house stood on the brink of a low bluff overlooking the broad, shallow bed of the Little Missouri, twisting down in long curves between narrow bottoms bordered by sheer cliff walls, "for the Badlands, a chaos of peaks, plateaus, and ridges, rose abruptly from the edges of the level, tree-clad, or grassy, alluvial meadows." In front of the veranda was a row of cottonwood trees with gray-green leaves which quivered all day long if there was a breath of air.

"I do not see how anyone could have lived more comfortably," he recalled. "We had buffalo robes and bearskins of our own killing." Meals were "game of our own killing, usually an antelope or deer, sometimes grouse of ducks, and occasionally, in the early days, buffalo or elk." Noting that getting the meat for the ranch fell mostly to him, he described riding with a rifle either across the saddle pommel or in a scabbard under his thigh. Admitting that he was never more than a fair hunter, he sometimes found himself "either failing to see game which I ought to have seen, or committing some blunder in the stalk, or failing to kill when I fired."

Within the combination of cattle rancher and game hunter that was Theodore Roosevelt there was still room for a boy called Teedie whose dream was to become a natural scientist. It was Teedie who would lie awake in the still fall nights by the Little Missouri, listening to "the clanging cries of water fowl, as their flocks sped southward," the "uncanny wailing" of coyotes," and larger wolves joining in with "a kind of deep, dismal howling."

A large measure of Teedie was also expressed in the clothing worn by the ranchman and hunter. The outfit consisted of "a sombrero, silk neckerchief, fringed buckskin shirt, sealskin chaparajos or riding-trousers, and alligator-hide boots." In this garb, he wrote his sister, "and with my pearl-hilted revolver and beautifully finished Winchester rifle, I feel able to face anything."

He was also armed with keenly observant eyes, although they peered out from behind glasses that at first garnered giggles from local characters who found sport in referring to him as "Four Eyes." But these dubious denizens of the town of Medora quickly learned, as had equally derisive Maine woodsmen and English Alps climbers, that Theodore Roosevelt possessed the right stuff. In one such instance when he was searching for lost horses, he sought refuge from a cold night in an establishment calling itself a hotel. Its sleeping accommodations were a loft with fifteen or twenty beds. Below this were a dining room, a lean-to kitchen, and a saloon. As he rode up to the hotel, he heard two gunshots from within. With nowhere else to go, he went in and found that "several men, including the bartender, were wearing the kind of smile worn by men who are making believe to like what they don't like." A shabby individual in a broad hat and holding a cocked gun paced the floor, "talking with strident profanity." He'd been shooting at a clock that now had two or three holes in it. Roosevelt saw "an objectionable creature, a would-be bad man, a bully who for the moment was having all his own way."

Glaring at the bespectacled intruder, the gunman blared, "Four eyes! Four eyes is going to treat!"

Joining in a burst of laughter from the other men, Roosevelt "got behind a stove and sat down, thinking to escape notice." The gunman followed him and stood leaning over the object of his bullying, a gun in each hand, and blaring "very foul language."

"He was foolish to stand so near," Roosevelt recalled in his autobiography. Moreover, "his heels were close together, so that his position was unstable."

As the gunman repeated his demand that Four Eyes treat the customers to a round of drinks, Roosevelt replied, "Well, if I've got to, I've got to."

As Roosevelt rose, he struck a quick, hard blow with his right fist just to one side of the point of the jaw, followed by a quick left, and another right. The two guns went off, evidently in a convulsive reaction. Stumbling backward, he fell against a corner of the bar, knocked senseless. Taking away the prostrate man's guns, Roosevelt heard from the men a loud "denunciation" of the gunman. Lifting him, they hustled him out of the saloon and put him a shed. After a sleepless night in which he feared he might be shot, Roosevelt learned that when his assailant came to, he went down to the railway station and hopped aboard a passing freight train.

"There were bad characters in the Western country at that time, of course," Roosevelt declared in his memoirs, "and under the conditions of life they were probably more dangerous than they would have been elsewhere." To avoid them, he avoided going into saloons and small hotels with barrooms and did so only when he had no other recourse. Twenty-four years after his encounter with the gunman, when Teddy Roosevelt formed the Rough Riders to wrest Cuba from Spain, he found himself leading "just such men."

A bullying drunk in a saloon was not the only nuisance to be dealt with by a fledgling rancher. Roosevelt found himself vexed by wolves. The "natural foes" of cattlemen frequently lurked around outbuildings to pounce on their prey at night by seizing a cow by the haunch or flank, then tearing out the entrails. If spotted, they were unrelentingly shot at and chased. Many were killed by poisoning.

Unlike wolves, cougars were rarely seen around the ranch. The big cats wreaked havoc by lying in wait for single heifers or young steers in the mountains. As the prey came down to water, the cougar attacked in a couple of bounds and gripped the animal by the neck. "It is a beast of stealth and rapine," wrote Roosevelt in a tone of disgust with an animal that he saw as cowardly. "Its great, velvet paws never make a sound," he continued contemptuously, "and it is always on the watch whether for prey or for enemies, while it rarely leaves shelter even when it thinks itself safe. Its soft, leisurely movements and uniformity of color make it difficult to discover at best, and its extreme watchfulness helps it; but it is the cougar's reluctance to leave cover at any time, its habit of slinking off through the brush, instead of running in the open, when startled, and the way in which it lies motionless in its lair even when a man is within twenty yards, that render it so difficult to still-hunt."

Noting that he'd seen a wild cougar alive but twice, and then only by chance, Roosevelt regarded the cougar as "a more skillful hunter than any human rival." On one occasion a cougar was found eating a skunk in a mulberry patch. Frightened by Roosevelt's approach, it scurried away from its unsavory repast before Roosevelt could get off a shot. The second encounter was while he was on a hunt for deer for supper. The spot he chose to wait was behind a breastwork of rotten logs, with a few evergreens for cover, on a steep, pine-clad slope leading down to a little mountain lake. After lying quietly for about an hour, listening to the murmur of the pine forests, and the occasional call of a jay or woodpecker, and gazing eagerly along a frequently traveled deer trail, a cougar suddenly appeared before him.

"The unlooked for and unheralded approach of the beast," Roosevelt recalled, "was fairly ghost-like." With its head lower than its shoulders, and its long tail twitching, it slouched down the path, treading as softly as a kitten. Waiting until it passed, Roosevelt aimed for its short ribs. Throwing its tail up in the air, and giving a bound, the big cat galloped off over a slight ridge. It didn't go far. Roosevelt found it within a hundred yards, stretched out on its side, its jaws still working convulsively as it died.

Although Roosevelt appreciated that it was next to impossible to successfully hunt the cougar without the use of dogs or bait, he grabbed his rifle on a snowy December evening to track a cougar that had killed a heifer and a deer, thereby thwarting Roosevelt's hunt for venison by driving off all the remaining deer. Following the cougar's tracks in the snow in the morning, he found its freshly deserted bed among some cedars in a dark, steep gorge. When an afternoon tracking the cougar proved fruitless, Roosevelt trudged wearily homeward, determined to take up the chase in the morning. Setting out, he discovered the cougar's rounded footprints, "as clear as writing in the snow."

The cougar had evidently observed Roosevelt abandon the pursuit of the previous day, then, "according to the uncanny habit sometimes displayed by his kind, cooly turned likewise, and deliberately dogged" his stalker's footsteps to within a mile of Roosevelt's ranch house.

"This was the best chance of the kind I ever had," Roosevelt noted in his account of the episode, "but again and again I have found fresh signs of cougar, such as a lair which they had just left, game they had killed, or one of our venison caches which they had robbed, and have hunted for them all day without success. My failures were doubtless due in part to various shortcomings in hunter's craft on my own part, but equally without doubt they were mainly due to the quarry's wariness and its sneaking ways."

Far less menacing around the ranch was the skunk. The smelly black-and-white night stalkers appeared with dismaying regularity. On one memorable occasion, one of them made its way into a hut where Roosevelt and others were sleeping. Among the men, Roosevelt recorded, was "a huge, happy-go-lucky Scotchman who went by the name of Sandy." Hearing the skunk moving about among the tin pans, Sandy struck a light, then took a shot at the intruder. When he missed, the skunk "retired promptly without taking any notice of the attack." Half an hour later, he was back. This time, Sandy's bullet found its target. The result, Roosevelt recalled, "was a frantic rush of all hands from the hut" to escape the blasted skunk's powerful odor.

A "dangerous and disagreeable neighbor" was the rattlesnake. Plentiful along the river bottoms, on the broken, hilly ground, and on the prairies and the great desert wastes, they were killed by the dozens. The rattlers exhibited an annoying fondness for crawling into a hut or taking refuge among the blankets left on the ground.

When venturing away from the ranch to hunt for food, the quarry was one of seven kinds of plains game—bear, buffalo, elk, bighorn, antelope, and blacktail or whitetail deer. But to the man who had fancied becoming a natural scientist, these treks across the Badlands were also opportunities to observe and study a rich variety of wildlife, and to use his skills as a writer, proven in the successful publication of *The Naval War of 1812*, to share his findings with the countless people for whom a book would be as close as they would ever come to the wonders of the West. The title of the volume Roosevelt decided to write would be straightforward: *Hunting Trips of a Ranchman*. He worked on it in fits and starts, then briefly left the tasks of authorship and cattle ranching behind to return to New York to vote in the 1884 presidential election, and to see the little daughter he'd left in the care of his sister. With James G. Blaine roundly defeated by the Democratic candidate, Grover Cleveland, he gladly returned to the Little Missouri with a contract for his book from the publisher of the 1812 naval warfare book, G.P. Putnam's Sons, in which Roosevelt was also an investor.

Back on the ranch in the snow-deep Badlands, he joined a cattle drive from his ranch in the south of the Badlands to the northern Elkhorn ranch. In mid-December he found time to write a prose poem titled "Winter Weather":

> When the days have dwindled to their shortest, and the nights seem never-ending, then all the great northern plains are changed into an abode of iron desolation. Sometimes furious gales blow down from the north, driving before them the clouds of blinding snow-dust, wrapping the mantle of death round every unsheltered being that faces their unshackled anger. They roar in a thunderous bass as they sweep across the prairie or whirl through the naked canyons; they shiver the great brittle cottonwoods, and beneath their rough touch the icy limbs of the pines that cluster in the gorges sing like the chords of an aeolian harp. Again, in the coldest midwinter, not a breath of wind may stir; and then the still, merciless, terrible cold that broods over the earth like the shadow of silent death seems even more dreadful in its gloomy rigor than is the lawless madness of the storms. All the land is like granite; the great rivers stand still in their beds, as if turned to frosted steel. In the long nights there is no sound to break the lifeless silence. Under the ceaseless, shifting play of the Northern Lights, or lighted only by the wintry brilliance of the stars, the snow-clad plains stretch out into the dead and endless wastes of glimmering white.

In an introduction to a 1998 Modern library reprint of *Hunting Trips of a Ranchman*, historian Stephen E. Ambrose depicted a Theodore Roosevelt at his two ranches in the Dakota Badlands who "never stopped looking around through the day, nor listening at night around the fire." The amateur naturalist "absorbed impressions, details, and stories like a giant sponge," Ambrose continued. "Observing, listening, and research are sedentary occupations, the opposite of action. They are receiving rather than giving, taking, or leading. They form the basis on which action can be effective, by providing knowledge, breadth of vision, and understanding. TR was a great observer, listener, and scholar, as well as a man of action."

Although Roosevelt began writing the book in the heart of the West, he completed it in a flood of words during the first nine weeks of 1885 at his home in New York, proving, in the words of biographer Edmund Morris, "that writers write best when removed from the scene they are describing." On March 8, Roosevelt triumphantly informed his friend and political mentor, Henry Cabot Lodge, "I have just sent my last roll of manuscript to the printer."

The book was dedicated to "that keenest of sportsmen and truest of friends, my brother Elliott Roosevelt." An introductory note informed the reader that most, "although by no means all, of my hunting has been done on the Little Missouri River, in the neighborhood of my two ranches, the Elkhorn and Chimney Butte."

The frontispiece was a photo of the author as game-hunter of the West with Winchester rifle at the ready and finger on the trigger, a silver dagger tucked into his belt, bedecked with cartridges, and shod in moccasins. The backdrop for the picture was a scene of flowers and ferns in a photographer's studio. But the rifle in the subject's hand was not just a prop. A 45-75 half-magazine Winchester, stocked and sighted to suit its owner, Roosevelt wrote in chapter 1 of the book, "is by all odds the best weapon I ever had, and I now use it almost exclusively, having killed every kind of game with it, from a grizzly bear to a big-horn."

An endorsement that must have thrilled the gun's manufacturer continued, "It is as handy to carry, whether on foot or horseback, and comes up to the shoulder as readily as a shotgun; it is absolutely sure, and there is no recoil to jar and disturb the aim, whole it carries accurately quite as far as a man can aim with any degree of certainty'; and the bullet, weighing three quarters of an ounce, is plenty large enough for any thing on this continent."

While the photo of the author showed no pistol, Roosevelt noted in the text, "Of course every ranchman carries a revolver, a long 45 Colt or Smith & Wesson." Roosevelt's preference was the former, as indeed it was for many men who were the gun-slinging heroes and villains in dime-novels that provided Easterners with a romanticized depiction of life out in the wild and woolly West. It was a portrait that Roosevelt reinforced as he described rugged figures wearing buckskin tunics and pants for keeping out wind and cold, and the "best possible color for the hunter." Alligator boots were "of service against the brambles, cacti, and rattlesnakes." For use in the woods, heavy moccasins were recommended, while light alligator-hide shoes were best to cross rocks and open ground. Protection in wet weather was in the form of an oilskin "slicker or waterproof overcoat and a pair of shaps (sic)."

While writing, often poetically, about his experiences, Roosevelt looked ahead and saw that the life he and others like him had enjoyed would shortly pass away. "The free, open-air life of the ranchman, the pleasantest and healthiest life in America," he wrote wistfully, "is from its very nature ephemeral. The broad and boundless prairies have already been bounded and will soon be made narrow. It is scarcely a figure of speech to say that the tide of white settlement during the last few years has risen over the west like a flood; and the cattlemen are but the spray from the crest of the wave, thrown far in advance, but soon to be overtaken."

Nine chapters of the book covered the business of cattle ranching in the Badlands, his thoughts and experiences hunting water-fowl, the grouse of the northern cattle plains, the deer of the river bottoms, black-tail deer, a trip on the prairie seeking the prong-horn antelope, a trip after mountain sheep, the "lordly buffalo," elk-hunting, and the most dangerous of all the game, the grizzly bear.

Of all the game that roamed the territory around his ranches, Roosevelt most enjoyed hunting elk. Of the "whistling" call of elk bulls in the rutting season, he wrote, "It is a most singular and beautiful sound, and is very much the most musical cry uttered by a four-footed beast. When heard for the first time it is almost impossible to believe that it is the call of an animal. It consists of quite a series of notes uttered continuously, in a most soft, musical, vibrant tone, so clearly that they can be heard half a mile off."

He'd killed his first elk in the summer of 1884 in the Bighorn Mountains on a hunting trip in the company of Bill Merrifield. They reaped several, but Roosevelt regarded one that he killed in the midst of "very beautiful and grand surroundings" was a "great bull, beating and thrashing his antlers against a young tree, about eighty yards off." Facing the hunters with his mighty antlers thrown in the air, and holding his head aloft, he gazed at them for a second, then turned to run. When Roosevelt's shot struck him just behind the shoulder, he staggered gamely for a few yards into the forest before Roosevelt's second shot drilled through his lungs, dropping him to the ground.

Describing the kill in *Hunting Trips of a Ranchman*, Roosevelt declared, "No sportsman can ever feel much keener pleasure and self-satisfaction than when, after a successful stalk and good shot, he walks up to a grand elk lying dead in the cool shade of the great evergreens, and looks at the massive antlers which are to serve in the future as the trophy of his successful skill."

Publication of *Hunting Trips of a Ranchman* was limited to five hundred copies that were printed on expensive, heavy, hand-woven paper with elegant engravings, and bound in gray, gold-lettered canvas. Priced at an unprecedented $15 in the first edition, it was highly praised by literary critics in the U.S. and in England, quickly became available in quantity, and came to be regarded as the definitive volume on big-game hunting in the United States.

An author with two best-sellers to his credit (*Hunting Trips* and *Naval War of 1812*), Roosevelt returned to the Little Missouri in May 1885 in time for an annual ritual. Organized for the branding of calves, spring and early-summer roundups, Roosevelt wrote in his autobiography in a chapter titled "In Cowboy Land," meant hard work and some risk, "but also much fun."

Gathering at a designated meeting point, lean and sinewy men who were accustomed to riding half-broken horses at any speed over any country by day or night wore flannel shirts, with loose handkerchiefs knotted round their necks, broad hats, high-heeled boots with jingling spurs, and sometimes leather chaps. "There was a good deal of rough horse-play," Roosevelt wrote, "and, as with any other gathering of men or boys of high animal spirits, the horse-play sometimes became very rough indeed; and as the men usually carried revolvers, and as there were occasionally one or two noted gun-fighters among them, there was now and then a shooting affray."

Although Roosevelt knew most of the men on the roundup, he occasionally encountered strangers who poked fun at him because he wore glasses. His policy was to remain "judiciously deaf" to remarks about "four eyes" or "storm windows," unless it became evident that staying quiet was "misconstrued and that it was better to bring matters to a head at once."

Moving down the Little Missouri Valley, the spring roundup of 1886 spread out to the east and west. For five weeks, sixty men riding three hundred horses gathered more than four thousand cattle and calves spread out among creeks, coulees, ravines, and gorges. On a roundup, "as with all other forms of work," Roosevelt noted, "a man of ordinary power, who nevertheless does not shirk things merely because they are disagreeable or irksome, soon earns his place."

Admitting that he was never a great rider and expert cow-roper, Roosevelt held his own for nearly a thousand miles. He was in the saddle for thirty-two days, more than most of the veteran cowboys with whom he'd started out. When he left the roundup on June 20, 1885, to return to New York for the summer, he exclaimed, "It is certainly a most healthy life. How a man does sleep, and how he enjoys the coarse fare!"

Drawn back east by personal matters, including seeing his daughter and checking on the progress being made in the finishing of a house he'd built at Oyster Bay with the intention of living there with Alice's mother, and in answer to the imploring of reform-minded friends that he get back into politics, Theodore Roosevelt was twenty-six. In his own description he was, "as brown and tough as a hickory nut." A sturdy physique was no longer plagued by maladies that had vexed an inquisitive boy called Teedie. Easily transforming himself from a buckskin-clad westerner to a well-off, well-tailored easterner who had published two well-received books, he slipped into the role of a Long Island squire who played polo. The rugged Badlands character who had come face to face with rattlesnakes and grizzly bears now joined in chasing foxes at the Meadbrook Hunt. There, on the eve of his twenty-seventh birthday, the western horseman who had occasionally been thrown by bucking bronco and come through relatively unscathed found himself pitched to the ground with his fallen horse rolling on top of him. With a broken arm, he remounted and finished the hunt looking "pretty gay, with arm dangling, and my face and clothes like the walls of a slaughterhouse."

In a letter to his friend Henry Cabot Lodge, he exclaimed, "I don't grudge the broken arm a bit. I am always willing to pay the piper when I have a good dance; and every now and then I like to drink the wine of life with brandy in it."

Presiding over a hunt ball at his new house, named Sagamore Hill, after an Indian chief, he had the arm in a splint when he asked a childhood friend, Edith Carow, for a dance. Although he knew that she was in love with him, and had been all her life, only to lose him to Alice Lee, Roosevelt lived by the social strictures and mores of the Victorian Age that required a man so recently widowed to observe a lengthy period of mourning. But youth and longing proved more compelling. Becoming engaged, they agreed to keep their plan to marry a secret for a year.

In the meantime, Edith would join her mother in London.

Theodore would return to the West.

Five days after leaving New York, he was again at the Elkhorn Ranch and reporting in a letter to his sister, "I got out here all right, and was met at the station by my men; I was really heartily glad to see the great, stalwart, bearded fellows again, and they were as honestly pleased to see me."

Arriving in the bitter cold, snowy, and frozen of mid-March in the Badlands, he began a new book, a biography of U.S. Senator Thomas Hart Benton. A champion of western expansion, he'd promoted policies to enable poor men to obtain western lands easily and had made a run for president in 1848 on a Free Soil ticket.

What Roosevelt admired in Benton was that, while at times "prone to attribute to his country a greatness she was not to possess for two or three generations to come, he nevertheless had engrained in his very marrow and fiber the knowledge that inevitably and beyond all doubt, the coming years would be hers. He knew that, while other nations held the past, and shared with his own the present, yet that to her belonged the still formless and unshaped future. More clearly than almost any other statesmen he beheld the grandeur of the nation to loom up, vast and shadowy, through the advancing years."

Two days after completing the writing, Theodore Roosevelt found himself invited to speak in the little prairie town of Dickinson to mark the 110th anniversary of the Declaration of Independence. Asserting his American's love of "big things," he warned that "we must keep steadily in mind that no people ever benefitted by riches if their prosperity corrupted their virtue."

Declaring "I am, myself, at heart as much as Westerner as an Easterner," he told the largest crowd ever assembled in Stark County, "I am proud, indeed, to be considered one of yourselves, and I address you in this rather solemn strain today, only because of my pride in you, and because your welfare, moral as well as material, is so near my heart."

Listening to the speech, and later in a conversation with Roosevelt on a train back to Medora, a young newspaper editor, Arthur Packard, pondered "the bigness of the man," and that one "could not help believing he was in deadly earnest in his consecration to the highest ideals of citizenship." When Roosevelt said that he had been offered the presidency of the New York City Board of Health, but that Henry Cabot Lodge felt he could do his best work "in a public and political way," Packard blurted out, "Then you will become President of the United States."

Roosevelt replied, "If your prophecy comes true, I will do my part to make a good one."

In the meantime, he was still a cattle rancher, but one with growing apprehensions about the Badlands as a place that was really suitable for that endeavor. He'd invested a great deal of his inherited money in the two ranches without earning a profit. While on an almost month-long hunting trip to the Coeur d'Alene mountains in search of the "problematic bear and visionary white goat," he worried about the future of the ranching enterprise and, as a result, "never felt less enthusiastic" about being on a hunt.

Always on his mind as he ventured across the Badlands was the reality that he was in an unforgiving land populated not only by dangerous animals, but by men with six-guns and hair-trigger tempers, "in regard to which laws of morality did not apply."

And there were Indians.

"When I went West, the last great Indian wars had just come to an end," he wrote in his autobiography, "but there were still sporadic outbreaks here and there, and occasionally bands of marauding young braves were a menace to outlying and lonely settlements."

Discussing Indians in *Hunting Trips of a Ranchman*, he dismissed talk about "our taking the Indians' land" as "sentimental nonsense." This did not mean, he said, that "gross wrong has not been done the Indians, both by government and individuals." Where "brutal and reckless frontiersmen are brought into contact with a set of treacherous, vengeful, and fiendishly cruel savages," he continued, "a long series of outrages by both sides are sure to follow. But as regards taking the land, at last from the Western Indians, the simple truth is that the latter never had any real ownership of it at all."

When his cattle came to the Little Missouri, he noted, the region was only inhabited by a score or so of white hunters whose title to the land was "quite as good as that of most Indian tribes to the lands they claimed, yet nobody dreamed of saying that these hunters owned the country." He believed that Indians should be treated in the same way as white settlers. "Give each his little claim; if, as would generally happen, he declined this, why, then let him share the fate of thousands of white hunters and trappers who have lived on the game that the settlement of the country has exterminated [a Roosevelt reference to what he saw as the foolhardy mass-hunting of game for fun, rather than for food], and let him, like these whites, perish from the face of the earth which he cumbers."

Yet the plain fact was that Indians were in the Badlands, and some of these "parties of savage young bucks" were "burning to distinguish themselves" by selecting the white man as a target. In Theodore Roosevelt's case, the encounter occurred on a day in early autumn as he set out for a solitary

ride into what he deemed "debatable territory" on his favorite horse, Manitou, "a wise old fellow, with nerves not to be shaken at anything."

The instant five young braves saw the lone horseman, they whipped out
guns and raced at full speed toward him. As they charged, yelling and flog-
ging their ponies, Roosevelt leapt off Manitou and stood with rifle ready. It
was possible, he thought, that the Indians were merely making a bluff and
intended no mischief. But he didn't like what he saw. Thinking that if he
allowed them to get hold of him they would at least steal his horse and rifle,
and possibly kill him, he waited until they were a hundred yards off, then
drew a bead on the first.

"Indians—and for the matter of that, white men—do not like to ride in
on a man who is cool and means shooting," Roosevelt wrote in explaining
his reaction, "and in a twinkling every [Indian] was lying over the side of his
horse, and all five had turned and were galloping [away]."

When one of the Indians slipped from his horse, made the peace sign,
and advanced toward him with an open hand, Roosevelt "halted him at a fair
distance and asked him what he wanted. The Indian exclaimed, "How! Me
good injun, me good injun," as he tried to show Roosevelt a "dirty piece of
paper" on which a government Indian agency official had written a pass,
allowing the Indian to be off the federal reservation.

Roosevelt said that he was glad the Indian was "good," but that he must
not come closer.

The Indian asked for tobacco and sugar. As Roosevelt said he had none,
another Indian began slowly drifting forward. Roosevelt raised his rifle and
warned him to stop. With that, both Indians got on their mounts and galloped off, yelling oaths that "did credit to at least one side of their acquain-
tance with English."

Back on Manitou, Roosevelt pushed over a plateau, mindful that the five
Indians were trailing him. Making for the open prairie beyond the plateau,
he felt confident because, as he later wrote, "In those days an Indian,
although not as good a shot as a white man, was infinitely better at crawling
under and taking advantage of cover, whereas out in the open if he kept his
head [a white man] had a good chance of standing off even half a dozen
assailants."

Reaching open country, Roosevelt resumed his northward ride unmo-
lested, but with a tale to tell of what must have been a scary encounter, but
that he dismissed as "trifling."

Other non-game-hunting stories that would be recounted in parlors and drawing rooms of New York and Washington involved adventures in pursuing desperadoes and other miscreants during Roosevelt's brief tenure as a deputy sheriff. Little of this was included in the pages of his memoirs, but he wrote of being impressed with the advantage the officer of the law has over ordinary wrong-doers, provided the law officer "thoroughly knows his own mind." But in the pursuit of "exceptional outlaws, men with a price on their heads and of remarkable prowess, who are utterly indifferent to taking a life, and whose warfare against society is as open as that of the savage on the warpath, the law officer "has no advantage whatever over these men save what his own prowess may—or may not—give him."

Although men committed crimes of "revolting baseness and cruelty" that could never be forgiven, Roosevelt believed as deputy sheriff, and years later when he was president, in the case of ordinary offenses, the man who had been caught, tried, and served his prison term, and who tried to make good, should be given a fair chance to make a new life.

"On the frontier," he wrote, "if the man honestly tried to behave himself there was generally a disposition to give him fair play and a decent show. Several of the men I knew and whom I particularly liked came in this class."

Affirming that "punishment is an absolute from the standpoint of society," and that reformation of the criminal must be secondary to the public welfare, he believed that the man or woman who has paid the penalty and who wishes to reform be given a helping hand. "Every one of us who knows his own heart must know that he too may stumble," he wrote, "and should be anxious to help his brother or sister who has stumbled. When the criminal has been punished, if he shows a sincere desire to lead a decent and upright life, he should be given the chance, he should be helped and not hindered; and if he makes good, he should receive that respect from others which so often aids in creating self-respect—the most invaluable of all possessions."

When a possibility of a war with Mexico arose, Roosevelt envisioned forming a regiment consisting of "as utterly reckless a set of desperadoes as ever sat in the saddle." But the crisis was resolved diplomatically, leaving the organization of a group of Roosevelt rough riders for another decade, and its eager would-be leader to do battle with the myriad problems of running two cattle ranches in a territory that he felt was becoming too crowded and overgrazed.

Also vexing his thoughts at this time was his impending marriage to Edith

Carow. He felt tormented by a feeling that he was marrying too soon after the death of Alice Lee. He blamed himself for "no constancy."

To make matters worse, he was informed by Bill Sewall and Wilmot Dow that they wanted to terminate their contract and return to Maine. Disappointed by a failure to get a decent price for their cattle at the Chicago market, and pessimistic about the viability of the Dakotas as cattle country, they felt that they were throwing away money, and that the quicker Roosevelt got out of cattle ranching, as well, the less Roosevelt would lose.

Sharing their gloomy outlook, and longing to go back to New York, to take a bride, and to see his little girl, but saddened by their decision, he responded, "How soon can you go?"

They were gone in early October 1886, and Roosevelt along with them.

While Sewall and Dow were calling it quits as cattlemen, their partner, having too much money invested to give up on the ranches, left them in the care of Merrifield and Ferris for the coming winter. But not before having a last talk with Sewall about the Roosevelt future. The choice was between going into law or politics. As to the latter, he noted, he found himself being urged by friends in New York to run for mayor.

Sewall pondered the question, then answered, "If you go into politics and live, your chance to be president is good."

Roosevelt replied, "Bill, you have a good deal more faith in me than I have in myself."

3

★ ★ ★

Danny, Davy, and Teddy

WHEN THEODORE ROOSEVELT returned to his newly built home at Oyster Bay to adorn its walls with heads of game as trophies and the floors with rugs made of pelts, he also came back to the East with a cause that would remain a passion for the remainder of his life. He'd become an outspoken champion of conservation. This may have seemed odd to friends who were proudly shown the prizes of so many hunts. But, as all of Theodore Roosevelt's biographers point out, he'd never engaged in a "one-man slaughter of big game."

In the introduction to the 1998 Modern Library edition of *Hunting Trips of a Ranchman,* Stephen E. Ambrose wrote that "politically correct readers will find much of Roosevelt's writing objectionable" because of his vivid accounts on stalking, killing, and the pride Roosevelt found in his successes. But the game he hunted as a rancher was not for sport. All of it ended up in the cooking pot, to be eaten around the campfire, or was an effort to eliminate predators that pillaged cattle. "It is always lawful to kill dangerous or noxious animals, like the bear, cougar and wolf," Roosevelt wrote, "but other game should only be shot when there is need of the meat, or for the sake of an unusually fine trophy." Men who did otherwise were "swinish" game-butchers. "No one who is not himself a sportsman and lover of nature," he insisted, "can realize the intense indignation with which a true hunter sees these butchers at their brutal work of slaughtering the game, in season and out, for the sake of the few dollars they are too lazy to earn in any other and more honest way."

But in the autumn and winter of 1886, hunting and ranching were left behind so that he could engage in the even more perilous endeavor of New York City politics. Two years had passed since he had declared himself done with politics as a means of championing civic virtue. For reform-minded New Yorkers who had been heartened by Assemblyman Roosevelt's attacks on the entrenched corruption of Tammany Hall and its lackeys in the police department, the news of his departure in 1884 had been a crushing disappointment. With Roosevelt suddenly back in their midst, Republicans envisioned him taking up the cause as their candidate for mayor in a three-sided race.

The Tammany candidate was Representative Abram S. Hewitt, an industrialist with a relatively enlightened attitude toward the working man. The other contender, carrying the banner of something new, the United Labor Party, was Henry George. A brainy social critic, he was the author of a popular book, *Progress and Poverty*. Published in 1897, the book had proposed a system of taxation of land related directly to speculation in real estate.

Surprised that the Republicans wanted him to run, Roosevelt saw "a perfectly hopeless contest." Calculating that there were "over forty thousand majority against me," and seeing his "chance of success being so very small that it may be left out of the account," he shook off the gloomy prospect and promised a "rattling good" campaign. True to his word, he put in eighteen-hour days, sometimes addressing three or four meetings a night. He did so, he told Henry Cabot Lodge, "on the score of absolute duty," and in the hope that after the election the Republicans would have a "better party standing."

So impressed with Roosevelt were the Democrat editors of the New York *Sun* that they praised "his accustomed heartiness." Noting, "Fighting is fun for him, win or lose," the paper continued, "It cannot be denied that his candidacy is attractive in many respects, and he is able to get votes from many sources. He has a good deal at stake, and it's no wonder that he is working with all the strength of his blizzard-seasoned constitution. It is not merely the chance of being elected Mayor that interests him. There are other offices he might prefer. To be in his youth the candidate for the first office in the first city in the U.S., and to poll a good vote for that office, is something more than an empty honor."

Roosevelt can not be mayor, the *Sun* declared, "but who knows what may happen in some other year? Congressman, Governor, Senator, President?"

When the ballots were tallied, Hewitt defeated George by 90,552 votes to 68,110, with Roosevelt garnering 60,435. Roosevelt cabled Henry Cabot Lodge (who'd won election to the Congress), AM BADLY DEFEATED. WORSE THAN I FEARED.

On Saturday, November 8, 1886, Theodore Roosevelt borrowed the name of his ranching partner Bill Merrifield to board the Cunard liner *Erturia*, to join Edith Carow in London. They married in St. George's Church in Hanover Square on December 2. The honeymoon was spent in Europe. After a fifteen-week tour, the newlyweds returned to New York City on March 28, 1887. Awaiting the groom was a letter from Merrifield and Ferris containing a shocking report on the devastation inflicted by a winter of blizzards on their cattle. The letter pleaded with Roosevelt to hurry to the Little Missouri to see for himself.

Calculating the losses in April, he found his surviving herds "a skinny sorry-looking crew." Shocked, dejected, and demoralized, he wrote to his sister, "I am bluer than indigo about the cattle. It is even worse than I feared. I wish I was sure I would lose no more than half the money I invested here. I am planning to get out."

A letter to Henry Cabot Lodge on April 20 reported, "The losses are crippling. For the first time I have been utterly unable to enjoy a visit to my ranch. I shall be glad to get home."

A discouraged rancher with no expectation of a bright political future after his defeat in the 1886 mayoral contest, married, and with the happy news that Edith was pregnant, the author of *The Naval War of 1812, Hunting Trips of a Ranchman*, and the biography of Thomas Hart Benton decided that he would be "a literary feller." Because of the success of his life of Benton, his publisher, Houghton Mifflin, had been urging him to write another biography of a historical figure. His subject would be one of the most colorful and dashing figures of the Revolution and the formation of the Republic, Gouverneur Morris.

Assessing why his brilliant subject had not ascended to the status of esteemed statesman, Roosevelt wrote, "His keen, masterful mind, his farsightedness, and the force and subtlety of his reasoning were all marred by his incurable cynicism and deep-rooted mistrust of all mankind."

These were traits not to be found in Morris's biographer. While Roosevelt disapproved of Morris's avowal of a "disbelief in all generous and unselfish motives," he lauded Morris as a champion of a strong national government and "thoroughgoing nationalism," but faulted him for favoring a system of class-based representation, "leaning toward aristocracy."

Working intensely on the book for three months, Roosevelt took occasional breaks to row on Oyster Bay with Edith, play tennis and polo, and chop wood (a pastime that he enjoyed all his life, including the White House years). A century would pass before Americans tuned in television news broadcasts and found President Ronald Reagan similarly whacking away at shrubbery, underbrush, and trees on Reagan's ranch in California, and then scenes of George W. Bush doing the same on his ranch in Texas.

Two years before becoming president after the assassination of William McKinley, in a speech to the Hamilton Club in Chicago (April 10, 1899) Theodore Roosevelt declared, "I wish to preach, not the doctrine of ignoble ease, but the doctrine of the strenuous life." As president in the summer of 1904 he was discovered at Sagamore Hill, cutting away brush and chopping down trees. "We're not building anything this afternoon," he cheerfully announced. "Something is coming down. It's bully exercise."

The subject of physical activity was still on his mind in his 1913 autobiography. "A man whose business is sedentary," he wrote, "should get some kind of exercise if he wishes to keep himself in as good physical trim as his brethren who do manual labor."

On September 13, 1887, all outdoor activity paused when Theodore Roosevelt became a father again. A few hours after Edith gave birth to an eight-and-a-half-pound boy, Roosevelt wrote to a friend to announce the blessed event and proudly added to his signature the word "Senior." This was despite the fact that the father of the Theodore who penned the announcement had also been named Theodore, thus entitling the newborn Theodore to put "III" after his name. To avoid any confusion, Theodore Roosevelt Jr. would be called Ted.

With the birth of a half-brother, perky, blonde Alice plunked herself next to his crib in her little rocking chair and would not be moved. She told their father she thought the little boy's squeals and cries made him sound like "a howling polly parrot." When Ted reached the crawling stage, his beaming father wrote to one of the child's aunts that he was "just like one of Barnum's little seals" and that he "plays more vigorously than anyone I ever saw."

Two years later, Alice and Ted gained a brother called Kermit, his mother's middle name. During the next decade, Kermit would be followed by Ethel, Archibald and Quentin. To their father they were "my bunnies." He enjoyed frolicking with them not only in the fields and woods, but throughout the house with rooms crammed with souvenirs of adventures in a land of cowboys and Indians. Most of these thrilling objects were kept in a large room on the top floor which the architect's plan designated as "the den." Ted called it "the gun room," a name that stuck. In it, Ted recalled, were "relics of the time when Father as a young man wished to dress as well as act the part of a dashing young cattleman" in the rugged hills of Dakota. Among the artifacts were a pair of dueling pistols in a mahogany box, a brace of six-shooters with ivory grips, cartridge boxes, leather cases, and ramrods. Behind glass in big cases were three shotguns, several rifles, six-shooters with ivory handles, a brace of dueling pistols, swords and scimitars from Roosevelt's sojourn to Egypt when he was eleven years old. Displayed on the walls of the room which filled the western gable of the house were heads of game shot on numerous hunting trips, each with an exciting tale to be told. The floor was scattered with rugs of animal hide.

Bookcases held volumes whose pages brimmed with stories of gallant soldiers, intrepid sailors, and fighters in the American Revolution and the Civil War, including relatives. Among them in Edith Carow Roosevelt's family tree were four ancestors who'd sailed to America on the *Mayflower*. Among the exciting volumes in the Sagamore Hill library were Ted's father's book of the naval war of 1812, the Benton biography, and *Hunting Trips of a Ranchman*. But more impressive to Ted than his father's shelves of books was the man to whom they belonged.

"His knowledge," Ted recalled, "stretched from babies to the post-Alexandrian kingdoms and, what was more, he could always lay his hands on it. It made little difference in what channels the conversation turned. Sooner or later he was able to produce information which often startled students of the theme under discussion."

Education of a son extended beyond the walls of library and the gun room to the woods surrounding the house. The house was for sharpening the mind. The outdoors was for honing the body. Determined to toughen Ted, Roosevelt took him on tramps that tested both strength and spirit. On these outings the father became, in the words of TR biographer Hermann Hagedorn, "a combination of deity and friend, his mystical heroes brought to life, King Arthur and Daniel Boone rolled into one."

After observing the father and son one day, Edith noted in a letter, "Ted is such a piece of quicksilver that I am in constant anxiety about his life and limb. Theodore thought his neck was broken the other day and declares he will never live to grow up."

When Roosevelt watched the bunnies frolicking each summertime with the numerous Roosevelt cousins who lived nearby in Cove Neck, he called the noisy tableau "the seventh heaven of delight." Edith joyously observed her husband full of "life and energy" as he acted as their guiding spirit. The inventor of these activities and games intended to provide fun, along with a strengthening of bodies and a character based on self-esteem and courage.

Doting on the children without spoiling them, he saw himself as "their special friend, champion and companion." He was beside them when they rode horseback, raced, hiked, swam, hunted and climbed. As their role model, he presented a straightforward example. His message was that if they wished to be like him they had to be enthusiastic about life, physically active and brave. "Don't let anyone impose on you," he lectured. "Don't be quarrelsome, but stand up for your rights. If you've got to fight, fight hard and well."

The children of a father who advocated "the strenuous life" were expected to take part in all kinds of sports, both individual and team. As a family they competed at tennis. "We had a dirt court near Sagamore," Ted remembered. "It was in a hollow. The moles traversed it regularly, which gave it an uneven surface. In addition, it was so well shaded that moss grew over it. The branches of the trees were so low that we had a special rule that when a ball hit a branch and might have gone in it was a 'let.' There were no professionals in those days, so we batted the ball in whatever fashion seemed best to us. Father played with us whenever he had the time, and was always welcome. His method of playing was original, to say the least. He gripped the racquet halfway up the handle with his index finger pointed back. When he served he did not throw the ball into the air, but held it in his left hand and hit it from between his fingers. In spite of this, and in spite of his great weight, he played a surprisingly good game."

In winter the children's strenuous life included hikes through the snow, sledding, and snowball fights. When their father came home one day with "snowshoes" which had been given to him by a Norwegian diplomat, they were introduced to skiing.

That "Father" was an important man was evidenced by guests who called at Sagamore Hill. Some came only for a dinner. Others spent a day or weekend. A few stayed for a week or month. Men and women with brilliant minds and animated spirits, they talked about politics and the great issues of the day. As they assessed the characters of the leading personalities in the government in New York, city and state, and in the national capital, Ted proudly observed that the person who shaped and dominated the lively conversations was his father. Nor was it lost on him that most visitors were confident that one day Theodore Roosevelt would be president of the United States.

Less than two months after Ted's birth Roosevelt again heard the call of the wilds of the West. He persuaded a cousin with an appropriate name, West Roosevelt, and a friend to join him for five weeks of hunting at his ranches. Discovering after ten days that they were not cut out for the strenuous life, the companions decamped. As they retreated to the civilities and comforts of New York, Roosevelt was actually pleased. He wrote his sister, "I really prefer to be alone while on a hunting trip."

He believed that only the hunter could understand that the keen delight of finding and killing of game was only part of the adventure. For him the joys were the horse well ridden and the rifle well held, and long days of toil and hardship resolutely endured that were crowned at the end with triumph. In later years would come memoirs of "endless prairies shimmering in the bright sun; of vast snow-clad wastes lying desolate under gray skies; of the melancholy marshes; of the rush of mighty rivers; of the breadth of the evergreen forest in summer; of the crooning of ice-armored pines at the touch of the winds of winter; of cataracts roaring between hoary mountain masses, of all the innumerable sights and sounds of the wilderness; of its immensity and mystery; and of the silences that brood in its still depths."

Pleased to be a solitary venturer, he spent the next three weeks on an odyssey in search of these delights. Instead, he found as he roamed that the once wildlife-rich valley of the Little Missouri River and the adjoining lands around the lower Powder and Yellowstone Rivers had changed. Long-gone were the mighty herds of bison. To him the extermination of the buffalo had been "a veritable tragedy of the animal world." No sight was more common on the plains than a bleached buffalo skull. Their countless numbers attested to the abundance of the animal. They lay over ground "so thickly that several score could be seen at once."

Other game had also been pillaged by relentless hunters. Trapping of beavers had left so few of the enterprising dam-builders that the resulting ponds and backwaters that once teemed with fish had largely vanished. Ground that had been usurped for the benefit of cattle had been so overly grazed that the grassless top soil was eroded by winds and rains.

"What had once been a teeming natural paradise, loud with snorts and splashings and drumming hooves," wrote biographer Edmund Morris in describing Roosevelt's solitary sojourn in November of 1887, "was now a waste of naked hills and silent ravines."

Deeply disturbed by this devastation of nature by men, Roosevelt returned to New York on December 8, 1887, with his mind, heart, and soul afire with a new cause, and an idea as to how to enlist others in what for him was suddenly an exciting and important calling. From his Manhattan house at 689 Madison Avenue flowed invitations to twelve distinguished gentlemen who shared his enthusiasm for nature and the joys of the hunt for game.

At the top of the guest list was George Bird Grinnell. Editor of the magazine *Forest and Stream,* and already a crusader against the very pillaging of wildlife that galvanized Roosevelt, he had become a close friend following his publication of an enthusiastically approving review of *Hunting Trips of a Ranchman.* With considerably more experience in the West, Grinnell was well acquainted, and alarmed, by unrestrained assaults on the region's wildlife. After receiving a doctorate in paleontology in 1880, he'd taken over *Forest and Stream* and had used the weekly publication to channel the growing dissatisfaction of outdoor enthusiasts with dwindling game populations and disappearing habitat into a crusade to conserve natural resources. To accomplish his goal of ensuring effective enforcement of game laws he advocated a game warden system to be financed by small fees from all hunters. The notion that traditionally free and unstructured activity of hunting must be financially supported by sportsmen themselves and regulated on the state level was a revolutionary concept that would become a cornerstone of game management.

Realizing that the enforcement of game laws was the solution to only half a problem, he turned his attention to habitat conservation. Although it was invariably a subject of conversation between him and the author of *Hunting Trips of a Ranchman,* Grinnell recalled, "We did not comprehend its imminence and the impending completeness of the extermination." Nor did they know "what they could most effectively do, how they could do it, and what dangers it was necessary to fight first."

With the dozen dinner guests assembled, Roosevelt proposed that the men organize an association of amateurs devoted to "manly sport with a rifle." Their purpose was to work for "the preservation of the large game of this country," passage of laws to attain that objective, and to assist in enforcing existing laws. Other activities would include inquiry into and recording of observations about natural history of wild animals, preservation of forest regions as nurseries and reservations for woodland creatures "which else would die out before the march of settlement," encouragement of explorations of the continent's wilderness, and publications of books and articles on conservation.

Roosevelt also proposed naming the association after a pair of hardy heroes of Teedie Roosevelt, and the inspirations for Theodore Roosevelt's adventures in the wild. Daniel Boone of Kentucky was to Roosevelt the "archetype of the American hunter." The "quaint, honest, fearless" Davy Crockett, the Tennessee rifleman and congressman, was "perhaps the best shot in our country, whose skill in the use of his favorite weapon passed into proverb." How better to honor them, and to state the purpose of an association of conservationists, Roosevelt asked, than by naming the group the Boone & Crockett Club?

And who better to serve as its first president, the founding members agreed during a formalizing meeting in January 1888, than Theodore Roosevelt?

Soon counting ninety members, including prominent scientists, lawyers, and political leaders, the organization promptly adopted Roosevelt's proposal to form a Committee on Parks to promote creation of a National Zoo in Washington, D.C. Acting on his own, Roosevelt set up another committee with orders to work with the Secretary of the Interior "to promote useful and proper legislation towards the enlargement and better government of the Yellowstone National Park." Created by Congress in 1872, Yellowstone in 1888 was a victim of exploitation by the westward-reaching railroads, greedy logging enterprises, resort-builders, and other noisome commercialization, and wanton slaughtering of its buffalo and elk. The plight of Yellowstone had long been a passionate crusade of George Bird Grinnell. In large measure because of the efforts of the Boone & Crockett Club, Congress would pass the Park Protection Act of 1894 to save Yellowstone. Legislation was also crafted to establish zoos in New York and an island reserve in Alaska for the propagation of seals, salmon, and sea birds. Boone & Crockett efforts also led to passage of the Forest Reserve Act, empowering the president of the United States to designate protected national forests.

In pursuit of the goal of publishing books and articles on wilderness themes, members of the club contributed to volumes titled *American Big-Game Hunting, Hunting in Many Lands,* and *Trail and Campfire.*

Declaring that he probably would never be in politics again, Roosevelt wrote to a friend from his days in the New York Assembly, "My literary work occupies a good deal of my time; and I have done fairly well at it; I should like to write some book that would really rank in the very first class." Although he added, "I suppose this is a mere dream," he was actually giving a great deal of thought to realizing a *"magnum opus"* on the history of the westward spread of the United States, from Daniel Boone crossing the Allegheny Mountains in 1774 to Davy Crockett's heroic demise at the Alamo in 1836. The title would be *The Winning of the West*. In mid-March 1888, he had a contract with his publisher, Putnam's, with a spring 1889 delivery date for the first two volumes.

As he was researching and writing, the magazine *Century* published six essays on his western adventures that were revised and published in December 1888 as a book with the title *Ranch Life and the Hunting Trail,* with illustrations by Frederic Remington. Among the essays was the story of the theft of a duck-hunting boat. There was little doubt about that it had been taken by a triumvirate of "bad men" led by a notorious red-headed cattle and horse rustler named Finnegan. To go after them, Roosevelt, Sewall, and Dow spent three days constructing a flat-bottomed scow, then outfitting it with warm bedding, mess kits, and a two-week supply of flour, coffee, bacon, and other victuals. Shoving off on a bitterly cold March morning, the pursuers were "thickly dressed, with woolen socks and underclothes, heavy jackets and trousers, and great fur coats." There was a double-barreled shotgun for augmenting their food with duck and deer. Each man had a rifle.

Fighting ice in the river for three days, with the air temperature hovering around zero, they were, Roosevelt wrote, "always on the alert, keeping a sharp lookout ahead and around us, and making as little noise as possible." The watchfulness paid off on the afternoon of the third day. As they rounded a bend, they spotted their purloined boat, together with a scow belonging to the thieves, moored against a bank of the stream. Among bushes "some little way back," a plume of smoke from a campfire curled up through the frosty air. Looking at Sewall and Dow, Roosevelt was struck by the grim, eager look in their eyes.

"Our overcoats were off in a second," he wrote, "and after exchanging a few muttered words, [our] boat was hastily and silently shoved toward the bank. As soon as it touched the shore ice I leaped out and ran up behind a clump of bushes, so as to cover the landing of the others, who had to make the boat fast."

Feeling "a thrill of keen excitement," they crept toward the fire, but found only one of the boat thieves in the camp. His gun was on the ground. Taken "absolutely by surprise," the man "gave in at once," and was quickly secured. Roosevelt, Sewall, and Dow then sat down to wait for their other quarry to return to the camp.

"In an hour or so they came in," wrote Roosevelt. "We heard them a long way off and made ready, watching them for some minutes, as they walked toward us, their rifles on their shoulders an the sunlight glinting on the steel barrels. When they were within twenty yards we straightened up from behind a bank, covering them with our cocked rifles, while I shouted to them to hold up their hands."

Only Finnegan hesitated to obey, "his eyes wolfish."

Taking a few paces closer, his rifle covering the center of Finnegan's body "so as to avoid overshooting," Roosevelt repeated his demand of hands-up. With a curse, Finnegan let his rifle drop and held his hands up beside his head.

"Having captured our men," Roosevelt's account continued, "we were in a quandry how to keep them. The cold was so intense that to tie them tightly hand and foot meant freezing both hands and feet off during the night, and to tie tightly was no good at all. So nothing was left to us but to keep perpetual guard over them. Our next step was to cord their weapons up in some bedding, which we sat on while we took supper. Immediately afterward we made the men take off their boots—it was cactus country—and go to bed, all three lying in one buffalo robe and covering with another, in the full light of the blazing fire."

The captors took turns guarding, with Roosevelt taking the first watch, while Sewall and Dow slept, "revolver under head, rolling up in their blankets on the side of the fire opposite that on which the three captives lay, while I, in fur cap, gauntlets, and overcoat, took a position in which I could watch my men with absolute certainty of being able to stop any movement, no matter how sudden."

The next eight days, making their way back down river, were to Roosevelt "as irksome and monotonous as any I ever spent." But at one point, Finnegan had obviously been thinking back to having been caught with his rifle unready. Glaring at Roosevelt, he growled, "If I'd had any show at all, you'd have had a fight, Mr. Roosevelt, but there wasn't any use making a break when I'd only have got myself shot, with no chance of harming any one else."

In Roosevelt's capacity as a deputy sheriff, his reward for making three arrests, plus a fee per mile for the three hundred or so that he'd covered in tracking the thieves and bringing them in, came to fifty dollars. Asked to explain why he hadn't invoked frontier justice and just shot them on the spot, he replied, "I didn't come out here to kill anybody. All I wanted to do was to defend myself and my property. There wasn't anyone around to defend me for them, so I had to do it myself."

Subscribers to *Century* who read of this adventure in man-hunting may have found its bloodless ending a welcome diversion from the author's descriptions of the killing wildlife that filled the pages of the series. Many also wondered how the author of lyrical descriptions of killing animals was able to take up the cause of wildlife preservation as a founder and president of the Boone & Crockett society. It is a contradiction that runs throughout Roosevelt's life that Roosevelt historians have been challenged to explain.

Biographer Edmund Morris wrote in *The Rise of Theodore Roosevelt*, "The overwhelming impression after reading *Hunting Trips of a Ranchman* is that of love for, and identity with all living things." Nathan Miller opined in *Theodore Roosevelt: A Life* that Roosevelt's hunting was more than blood and slaughter; he "enjoyed the totality of the wilderness experience." In an introduction to an account of Roosevelt's lifetime of hunting expeditions, historian Elting E. Morison observed that Roosevelt "was obviously proud to bring back a big bag of game," but that Roosevelt hastened to explain, "The mere size of the bag indicates little as to the man's prowess as a hunter and almost nothing as to the interest or value of his achievement."

The things derived from the hunt were not the number of animals killed, the quantity of species gathered for scientific study, the memories persisting after a lion's charge or a buffalo "sullen under his helmet of horn," nor the truculent and stupid rhinocerous in bright sunlight on the empty plains. These things could be told, but there were no words to relate the "hidden spirit of the wilderness—its mystery, its melancholy, its charm." To a non-hunter there could be no adequate language to capture "the awful glory of sunrise and sunset in the wide waste spaces of the earth, unworn of man."

Again feeling the tuggings of the lure of open spaces, Roosevelt suspended work on *The Winning of the West* at the end of August 1888 and headed for big-game country around Idaho's Kootenai Lake, headwaters of the Columbia River. His companions were an old hunting partner, John Willis, and an impassive-looking Indian named Ammal. Hired because Roosevelt felt that Indians of the West were hard and willing workers, he had little knowledge of English, so that conversations were carried on in a Chinook jargon. Roosevelt often tried to talk with him about game and hunting, but they undersood each other too little to exchange much more than the most rudimentary ideas.

Although Ammal was initially reluctant to leave the neighborhood on the lake, he made the first day's journey willingly, only to grow increasingly difficult and eventually sulky. When Roosevelt asked why Ammal was less and less enthusiastic about going on, Ammal managed to explain that up in the high mountains there were "little bad Indians" who would kill him if they caught him alone, especially at night.

At first the white hunters thought he was speaking about stray warriors of the Blackfeet tribe, Roosevelt wrote, "but it turned out that he was not thinking of human beings at all, but of hobgoblins." Musing that indeed "night sounds of these great stretches of mountain woodland were very weird and strange," and noting that "I have often and for long period dwelt and hunted in the wilderness," Roosevelt admitted that until talking to Ammal about the Indian's fear of the little bad Indians he had "never before so well understood why the people who live in lonely forest regions are prone to believe in elves, wood spirits, and other beings of an unseen world."

Roosevelt's quarry was the caribou, but ever the naturalist, he delighted in pausing beside a little brook for a bite of "a chunk of cold frying-pan bread" and watching a water wren.

"This strange, pretty water-thrush," he wrote, "was to me one of the most attractive and interesting birds to be found in the gorges of the great Rockies. Its haunts are romantically beautiful, for it always dwells beside and in the swift-flowing mountain brooks. It spend half of its time under the water, walking along the bottom, swimming and diving, and flitting through as well as over the cataracts."

When this interlude ended, the hunters resumed their march, "toiling silently onward through the wild and rugged country." An hour or two before sunset, as they traversed an open wood of great hemlock trees, Willis suddenly dropped down in his tracks, pointing forward. As Roosevelt peered ahead, the head and shoulders of a bear popped up from the brush in search of branches or berries. As the bear rose, Roosevelt lifted his gun and fired, meaning to shoot him through the shoulders, but instead, in a hurry to shoot, he struck him in the neck.

Surprised that the wounded bear uttered no sound, Roosevelt raced forward, with Willis close behind, while Ammal "danced about in the rear, very much excited." Judging by the sway of tall plants that the bear was coming toward them, Roosevelt feared for Willis's safety.

As the bear came to almost within an arm's length of Willis, it presented Roosevelt "a beautiful shot." When it struck between an eye and ear, the bear fell "as if hit by a poleaxe."

With that, Ammal "began jumping about the body, uttering wild yells, his impassive face lighted up with excitement," while Roosevelt and Willis stood at rest, leaning on their rifles and laughing. "It was a strange scene," Roosevelt recalled, "the dead bear lying in the shade of the giant hemlocks, while the fantastic-looking savage danced around him with shrill whoops, and the frontiersman [Willis] looked quietly on."

Then, in a passage that was typical of writings in which historian Stephen E. Ambrose found "an unmatched description of a time and a place," Roosevelt described the "prize" as a large black bear with two curious brown streaks down his back, one on each side of the spine that became part of a fine meal of frying-pan bread and sugarless tea. Leaping sheets of flames of their campfire "lighted the tree-trunks round about, causing them to stand out against the cavernous blackness beyond, and reddened the interlacing branches that formed a canopy overhead. The Indian sat on his haunches, gazing steadily and silently into the pile of blazing logs, while Willis and I talked."

Determined to find caribou, they trudged for miles across sharp rocks that threatened to shred their shoes. With Willis setting "such a brisk pace, plunging through thickets and leaping from log to log, and from boulder to boulder," the three men had several bad falls, barely saving their rifles. As the food supply dwindled, and with aching feet, Roosevelt began to fear that he would have to call off the hunt, until they emerged from a hemlock forest one day and Willis pointed to a game trail with fresh caribou footprints. Following the trail to a high, bare alpine valley, with snow lying in drifts along the side, then onward to another forest which widened out and crept up the mountainsides. After descending a steep incline, they came within fifty yards of three bull caribou, grazing "so greedily" that they were unaware of the hunters.

Demonstrating a remarkable ability to recall details as he described his adventures many months, and often years after experiencing them, Roosevelt wrote of hunting caribou that September day:

The largest, a big bull with a good head, was nearest. As he stood fronting me with his head down I fired into his neck, breaking the bone, and he turned a tremendous back somersault. The other two halted a second in stunned terror, then one, a yearling, rushed past us up the valley down which we had come. The other, a large bull with small antlers, crossed right in front of me, at a canter, his neck thrust out, and his head turned toward me. There was a spur a little beyond, and up this he went at a swinging trot, halting when he reached the top, and turning to look at me once more. He was only a hundred yards away and, though I had not intended to shoot him, the temptation was sore. I was glad when, in another second, the stupid beast turned again and went off up the valley at a slashing run.

We hurried down to examine with pride and pleasure the dead bull. His massive form, sleek coat, and fine antlers made it one of those moments that repay the hunter for days of toil and hardship.

The hunt had taken four days. After a night on which they "feasted royally" on caribou steak, and with Ammal carrying the caribou's skull and antlers on his head, they returned to the base camp, welcoming the sight of their boat and their white tent among the trees, while "the glassy mirror of the lake reflected the outlines of the mountains opposite." On their way out of the woods, the confirmed naturalist recorded, "there was a slight warm spell, followed by rain and then by freezing weather, so as to bring about what is known as a silver thaw," during which every twig "was sheathed in glittering ice, and in the moonlight the forest gleamed as if carved out of frosted silver."

After a visit to the ranch on the Little Missouri to oversee the sale of his remaining cattle, and with the head and antlers of his first caribou to become a trophy on a wall, he returned to Sagamore Hill on October 5, 1888, to hear the beckoning siren song of presidential politics on behalf of James G. Blaine, the Republican opponent of President Grover Cleveland, a maverick Democrat who had vaulted from being of mayor of Buffalo, New York, to the governorship of the Empire State, and into the White House in less than three years.

Because of unpopular policies on tariffs, Cleveland was deemed vulnerable, even to a former Civil War general, ex-U.S. Senator, and grandson of president, William Henry Harrison, with a premature white beard and an austere, cold, and off-putting personality. In order to bolster his chances,

Republican leaders turned to a bevy of surrogates to take to the hustings and do all the necessary hand-shaking, a task for which the colorful and boisterously engaging Theodore Roosevelt was perfectly suited. Enlisted in the cause, he spent one day at Oyster Bay, then went westward again to campaign in Illinois, Michigan, and Minnesota. Increasingly confident of a Republican victory, he marked his thirtieth birthday and, nine days later, welcomed not only a Harrison victory, but the capture by the Republicans of a majority in both houses of Congress.

As Harrison took the reins of government on March 4, 1889, Roosevelt was working to complete volume two of *The Winning of the West* while his publisher, George Haven Putnam, was supervising the binding of volume one. While this was going on, Roosevelt's friend, Henry Cabot Lodge, was busy in the nation's capital on behalf of finding a position for Roosevelt in the Harrison administration. The post Roosevelt desired was Undersecretary of State. The offer that came was membership on the United States Civil Service Commission, at an annual salary of $3,500. Expecting Roosevelt to decline such paltry pay for a rather insignificant job, Lodge did his duty to the new president, conveyed the proposal, and was surprised that Roosevelt accepted.

Before moving to Washington, he squeezed in another outing in the Badlands with the hope of hunting buffalo around the head of the Wisdom River. After a few days of a fruitless search for "these great wild cattle," but now rapidly vanishing former lord of the prairies, he and his guide, an old hunter with rheumatism and carrying a long walking staff instead of a rifle, found themselves south of the Montana boundary. About twenty-five miles west of the Wyoming line, in what Roosevelt supposed was Idaho, he and the aging hunter discovered "unmistakable hoofmarks of a small band of bison, apparently but a few hours old." Heading toward a little lake, the tracks were those of half a dozen buffalo, including one bull and two calves. Following the trail, they walked on ground covered with pine needles and soft moss, allowing them to walk noiselessly. Peering through the safe shelter of a glade of young trees, the hunters spotted three bison, a cow, a calf, and a yearling grazing greedily on the other side of a glade. Soon another cow and calf appeared. Expecting a big bull to present himself, Roosevelt waited with "the eager excitement of the hunter" and "a certain half-melancholy feeling" as he gazed on the buffalo, "themselves part of the last remnant of a doomed and nearly vanished race."

"Few indeed," he mused, "are the men who now have, or ever more shall have, the chance of seeing the mightiest of American beasts, in all his wild vigor, surrounded by the tremendous desolation of his far-off mountain home."

When the bull appeared on the edge of the glade, he stood with out-stretched head and scratched his throat against a young tree, which shook violently. Raising his rifle, Roosevelt aimed low, behind the shoulder, and pulled the trigger. At the crack of the rifle, all the bison, "without the momentary halt of terror-struck surprise so common among game, turned and raced off at headlong speed." As they bolted, the fringe of young pines cracked and swayed "as if a whirlwind were passing," and in another moment they reached the top of a steep incline, thickly strewn with boul-ders and dead timber.

"Their surefootedness was a marvel in such seemingly unwieldy beasts," Roosevelt recalled. "A column of dust obscured their passage, and under its cover they disappeared in the forest. The trail of the bull was marked by splashes of frothy blood, and we followed it at a trot. Fifty yards beyond the border of the forest we found the stark black body stretched motionless. He was a splendid old bull, still in his full vigor, with large, sharp horns, and heavy mane and glossy coat. I felt the most exulting pride as I handled and examined him, for I had procured a trophy such as can fall henceforth to few hunters indeed."

With no remorse at having contributed to the obliteration of the Amer-ican bison that he, as president of the Boone & Crockett Club, so eloquently deplored, Roosevelt continued with his hunt, fueled by the meat of his trophy. As he trekked onward to the headwaters of the Salmon and Snake Rivers and along the Montana line from Big Hole Basin, to the head of the Wisdom River, Red Rock Pass, and north and west of Henry's Lake, Roo-sevelt found his guide growing increasingly sullen, reluctant to continue and complaining about "trundling a tenderfoot." The situation came to a resolu-tion over a flask of whiskey. While Roosevelt was not an imbiber, he carried the liquor for emergencies. Discovering that the guide had gotten drunk by consuming it to the last drop, Roosevelt confronted him.

The guide's reply was to ask Roosevelt what he was going to do about it. Roosevelt answered that he would "part company" with the guide and go on alone.

The guide grabbed his rifle, cocked it, and retorted that Roosevelt could go alone "and be damned," but that he couldn't take a horse.

Adopting the compliant attitude he'd adopted in handling the gunman who'd tried to humiliate him in the barroom of a hotel, Roosevelt said, "All right. If I can't take a horse, I can't take a horse."

Moving around the camp to gather flour and salt pork, Roosevelt noted that the surly, inebriated guide was sitting with the cocked rifle across his knees, the muzzle to the left, and that Roosevelt's rifle was leaning against a tree near cooking gear to the guide's right. Whipping up the gun, Roosevelt aimed it at the guide and shouted, "Hands up!"

"Oh, come on," said the guide, thrusting up his arms, "I was only joking."

"Well, I am not," replied Roosevelt. "Now straighten your legs and let your rifle go to the ground."

The guide "remonstrated, saying the rifle would go off."

"Let it go off," Roosevelt snapped.

The rifle slid gently to the ground. Roosevelt ordered the guide to move away from the gun, then picked it up. By this time the guide appeared quite sober. He gazed at Roosevelt not in anger, but quizzically, and said that if he could have his rifle back, they would call it quits and go on together. In no mood to trust the man, Roosevelt said that their hunt was "pretty well through, anyway," and that he intended to go on alone.

Pointing to a distant pine tree, Roosevelt said that he would leave the gun by the tree, if he could see that the guide was still in the camp. If the guide came after him, he warned, he would assume that it was with "hostile intent," and would shoot. The guide said that he had no intention of following. "As he was very much crippled with rheumatism," Roosevelt recalled, "I did not believe he would do so."

Taking a little mare, with nothing but some flour, bacon, tea, and his bed roll, Roosevelt departed the camp. Looking back from the pine tree, he saw the guide still seated in the camp, left the rifle, and traveled till dark. When he made camp, he adopted "a trick of the old-time trappers in the Indian days." Choosing caution over trust in the guide's promise and physical condition, he left a campfire burning, repacked the mare, and pushed ahead until it became so dark that he could barely see. Choosing a new camp site, he settled down for the night without making a fire. In describing the adventure, he explained, "No plainsman needs to be told that a man should not lie near a fire if there was danger of an enemy creeping up on him, and that above all a man should not put himself in a position where he could be ambushed at dawn."

Happy to be alone, as always, Roosevelt completed his hunt by killing a grizzly, but had a difficult time in getting the skin of "fine fur" on a little mare that "cared nothing for bears or anything else." The man without experience, he noted, "can hardly realize the work it was to get that bearskin off the carcass and then to pack it, wet and slippery, and heavy, so that it would ride evenly on the pony."

The feat of killing the bear sank into nothing, he noted, "compared to the feat of making the bearskin ride properly as a pack on the following three days."

Although friends had warned that if he joined the civil service commission he would find it a political graveyard in which he would be "buried, never to be heard from again," Roosevelt plunged into the job with the same vigor and tenacity of any big-game hunt. The commission's purpose was to eliminate political favoritism in government employment, and that people who got federal jobs were qualified to hold them. In the New York Assembly Roosevelt had made civil service reform one of his causes and had helped enact the first such law in the nation. The story of his reform work on the U.S. Civil Service Commission has been detailed at length in many Roosevelt biographies, but Roosevelt succinctly summarized his record in a letter to one of his previously dubious friends on June 23, 1889. Boastfully but rightly, he declared, "I have made this Commission a living force."

He also had good reason to be pleased with himself as author of the first two volumes of *The Winning of the West*. Published soon after he joined the commission, the work was warmly praised in newspaper reviews. An especially laudatory critic for the New York *Tribune* found "literary ability and skill" and "remarkable dramatic and narrative power" in "an admirable and deeply interesting book [that] will take its place with the most valuable and indispensable works in the library of American history."

The reviewer for the *Atlantic Monthly*, esteemed scholar Dr. William F. Poole, wrote, "Mr. Roosevelt's style is natural, simple and picturesque, without any attempt at fine writing, and he does not hesitate to use Western words which have not yet found a place in the dictionary. He has not taken the old story as he finds it printed in Western books, but has sought for new materials in manuscript collections. . . . Few writers of American history have covered a wider or better field of research, or are more in sympathy with the best modern method of studying history from original sources. . . . It is evident from these volumes that Mr. Roosevelt is a man of ability and great industry."

With good reason to be pleased with his return to the arena of government and with his continuing success as an author, Roosevelt confessed to worrying that he was "rapidly sinking into fat and lazy middle age," and that his life seemed to "grow more and more sedentary." With this on his mind, along with onset of the national capital's notoriously steaming and unhealthy summer weather, and his wife and family (Alice, Ted, and Kermit) settled down in the cooler conditions of Sagamore Hill, he again longed for the West. But he did not go alone. He set off in September 1891 for his ranch in the company of Edith, two sisters, a brother-in-law, and Henry Cabot Lodge's teenage son. The adventure included introductions to people Edith had only heard about, Bill Merrifield and the Ferris brothers, and places she had tried to imagine as he'd spun pictures of their beauty—the valley of the Little Missouri, the Badlands, the Rockies, and the wonders of Yellowstone's bubbling mud pools, hot springs, and gushing geysers. At the end of the odyssey, he noted that Edith "looks just as well and young and pretty as she did four years ago when I married her."

He wrote to his mother-in-law, "I have rarely seen Edith enjoy anything more than she did the six days at my ranch, and the trip through Yellowstone Park."

Back in the nation's capital, Theodore Roosevelt, the Westerner who happily wore rain-soaked hunting outfits and slept on blankets on the ground, was again a government official who felt just as comfortable dressing up for Washington social life. The rugged plainsman who had faced down a bullying gunman in a hotel barroom, who'd grabbed a rifle to stave off a pack of trouble-seeking Indians, and who'd gotten the drop on a surly and drunken hunting guide found himself discussing literature with the philosopher and author Henry Adams, talking politics with Henry Cabot Lodge and Speaker of the House Thomas B. Reed, and being the host at dinners for ambassadors. "Washington is just a big village," he explained in a letter to his sister, "but it is a very pleasant big village."

Between evenings of socializing and his duties as the leading, and often controversial, member of the Civil Service Commission, he found little time to work on the third volume of his history of the West. Having published a history of New York City, he'd found himself taken to task for being preachy on the subject of municipal corruption. Part of the problem with the book was that it was hastily written. "I am trying to hurry up my accursed history of New York City," he'd admitted in a letter to his sister. "How I regret ever having undertaken it." But a worrying complication in his life at this time involved his beloved brother.

Because of Elliott's problems with drinking, squandering his inheritance, an unfortunate marriage, and family concerns about Elliott's mental stability, Roosevelt applied to a court to appoint a commission to decide if a committee should be appointed to care for Elliott's "person and for his estate." Roosevelt told their sister, "It is all horrible beyond belief. The only thing to do is go resolutely forward."

There was one happy event during the summer of 1891. On August 31, Mr. and Mrs. Theodore Roosevelt of Sagamore Hill and Washington, D.C., became parents of "a jolly naughty whacky" daughter named Ethel. But Roosevelt's delight in becoming a father for a fourth time was shadowed by the death of his ranching partner Wilmot Dow.

Satisfied that mother and baby were doing well, and grieving over Dow, Roosevelt again headed West to visit his ranch and experience shooting in Wyoming's Shoshone Mountains. To accompany him, he chose two hunters who were familiar with the territory, Tazewell Woody and Elwood Hofer, plus a packer who acted acted as cook, and a boy to herd the horses. The pack train consisted of six for riding and fourteen "half-broken, tough, unkempt, jaded-looking beasts of every color" to tote the packs.

On the second day of an otherwise "uneventful" journey they encountered the camp of a "squaw man." A white man with an Indian wife, Beaver Dick was an old mountain hunter living in a skin teepee with her and their "half-breed children." The next morning, the sky was gray and lowering. Gusts of wind blew in his face as the hunters plodded up a valley beside a rapid brook running through narrow willow flats. The dark forest crowded down on each side when the call of an elk came echoing down through the wet woodland on the right. The call was answered by a faint, far-off call from a rival elk on the mountain beyond.

Instantly halting the pack train, Roosevelt and Woody slipped off their horses, crossed a brook, and began a hunt for wapiti elk. While still at some distance, they listened to the bull elk's pealing notes, like those of a bugle, delivered in two bars, first rising then abruptly falling. As they drew nearer, the call took on a harsh squealing sound. "Each call made our veins thrill," Roosevelt remembered. "It sounded like the cry of some huge beast of prey."

Stealing forward, Roosevelt saw the tips of the elk's horns through a mass of dead timber and young growth. Poised to make a clean shot, he watched the elk step boldly toward him with a swinging gait, then stand motionless, facing the two hunters, barely fifty yards away, with his handsome twelve-tined antlers held aloft. As the elk held his head with lordly grace, Roosevelt fired into its chest, then into the flank. But the second shot was not needed. Mortally wounded by the first, the elk managed to run barely fifty yards before dying. After admiring the beautiful dark brown color of its strong, yet slender, clean and smooth legs, and contrasting their tone with the yellowish body, Roosevelt and Woody cut off the head as a trophy. They harvested the loins for food, although, Roosevelt noted, "bull elk in the rutting season is not very good."

On a later all-day tramp in wind and rain squalls as Roosevelt and Woody paused to rest at the edge of a deep, wide gorge, with numb fingers and their feet icy-wet, to await what might turn up, "the love-challenge of an elk came pealing across the gorge, through the fine, cold rain, from the heart of the forest opposite."

After an hour's climb, down and up, they came near enough to observe the elk lying on a point of a cliff shoulder, surrounded by his cows. When the elk spotted the men, he made off, leaving them to seek a prize elsewhere. Their chance came an hour later. Trudging up a steep hillside dotted with grove of fir and spruce, they found a young bull. Roused by their approach, some sixty yards off, he was a "fat and tender young ten-pointer." Taking aim, Roosevelt pulled the trigger just as the elk came to a small gully. The shot felled him in a heap with a resounding crash. Remembering that the date was his son Ted's fourth birthday, Roosevelt collected the antlers to present to his firstborn son "for his very own."

After a week of hunting at Two-Ocean Pass, the party crossed the summit of Wolverine Pass and camped at Wolverine Creek. Roosevelt killed two elk and collected a set of twelve-point antlers that he deemed "the finest I ever got."

At the start of 1892, with a burgeoning family straining finances that had been dealt a crippling blow from the losses incurred by the downturn in the cattle market, Roosevelt split his writing time between his duties as Civil Service Commissioner, working on his history of the winning of the West, and earning money with a flurry of articles for magazines. Added to these demands on his time were expectations that he take a role in the Republican politics of a year in which President Harrison would seek a second term. His Democratic opponent was likely to be the man he'd defeated in 1888. Turned out of office after one term, Grover Cleveland had been biding his time as a corporate lawyer in New York, but with plans to make history by becoming the first president in history to win election to two non-consecutive terms.

Although Roosevelt and Cleveland had been allies in the cause of governmental reform when Cleveland was governor of New York, Roosevelt faulted Cleveland's presidential record in the area of civil service reform. As the presidential campaign got under way in the summer of 1892, Roosevelt found himself in the West again, but this time on government business in the form of a tour of Indian reservations and schools, with time out to do some politicking on behalf of President Harrison. Upon his arrival in South Dakota, he was invited to speak to a gathering of Theodore Roosevelt admirers at Deadwood. In a letter to Henry Cabot Lodge he reported, "I was enthusiastically received, and opened the Republican campaign by speaking to a really large audience in the fearful local opera house."

Gritting his teeth for the "tedious but important" official business of inspecting Indian reservations at Pine Ridge and Crow Creek as the personal emissary of President Harrison, he had never embraced the idea of some romanticizing Americans who considered the Indian a "noble savage." His experiences as a rancher and the solitary hunter who had felt threatened by a party of five young braves had felt no sympathy for the original claimants of the lands of the West. In *Hunting Trips of a Ranchman* he'd dismissed a century of talk about the taking of Indians' land as "a good deal of sentimental nonsense" because, he wrote, the simple truth was that Indians never had a right to claim its ownership. "Where the game was plenty," he wrote, "there they hunted; they followed it when they moved away to new hunting grounds, unless they were prevented by stronger rivals, and to most of the land on which we found them had no stronger claim than that of having a few years previously butchered the original occupants."

By the time Roosevelt arrived in the Dakotas, whatever claims the Indians professed to the land had been brushed aside by the U.S. Army in a series of "Indian Wars" that ended with the tribes restricted to "reservations," the kind that the Civil Service Commissioner, and author of two out of a proposed four-volume story of the winning the West, had been sent by the "Great White Father in Washington" to survey in the late summer of 1892.

After a few eye-opening days of seeing the squalid living conditions at the Pine Ridge and Crow Creek reservations, and how the Indians were victimized by their white overseers and forced to make "contributions" to the Harrison re-election campaign, the ardent proponent of civil service reform called a press conference in Sioux City to berate the "infamy of meanness that would rob women and Indians of their meager wages." In irate tones, he announced, in his official capacity, that Indians classified as civil servants could not be compelled to "contribute a single penny." Furthermore, he declared, Republican officials who made such demands ought to be prosecuted.

Still fuming at what he'd witnessed, he later said in a speech summing up his service as Civil Service Commissioner under Harrison, "Here we have a group of beings who are not able to protect themselves; who are groping toward civilization out of the darkness of heredity and ingrained barbarism, and to whom, theoretically, we are supposed to be holding out a helping hand. They are utterly unable to protect themselves. They are credulous and easily duped by a bad agent, and they are susceptible of remarkable improvement when the agent is a good man, thoroughly efficient and thoroughly practical. To the Indians the workings of a spoils system is a curse and an outrage [that] must mean that the painful road leading upward from savagery is rendered infinitely more difficult and infinitely more stormy for the poor feet trying to tread it."

How much Roosevelt's blast at the policies of Indian agents of Harrison's administration, and calling for prosecutions of the "bad" ones, helped to undermine Harrison's chances of re-election can't be known. But there is no doubt that Roosevelt expected, no matter who won in November, there was no likelihood of him being kept on as a civil service commissioner. In the face of this reality, he spoke to a friend of the "profound gratification" of knowing there was no man more bitterly disliked by many men in his own party. "When I leave on March 5th," he said, "I shall at least have the knowledge that I have certainly not flinched from trying to enforce the law during these four years, even if my progress has been at times a little disheartening."

When Cleveland won, the man who would go into history books as the twenty-second and twenty-fourth president surprised Roosevelt by asking him to stay on for "a year or two." With this announcement, Harrison's Secretary of the Navy, Benjamin F. Tracy, sidled up to Roosevelt and declared, "Well, my boy, you have been a thorn in our side during four years. I earnestly hope that you will remain to be a thorn in the side of the next administration."

Being a Republican in a Democrat government, and occupying the same post, Roosevelt described the experience as "a little like starting to go through Harvard again after graduating." While fighting the same old battles against the spoils system and political patronage, he resumed work on *The Winning of the West* and found himself balancing the tasks of author, government official, husband, and father. On evenings when he had no appointments, he sat in his parlor with Edith, reading. He also found time on Sundays to take his "bunnies" for hikes in Rock Creek Park, where Alice, Ted, Kermit, and Ethel were encouraged to climb the rocks, banks, and low cliffs.

On many evenings he was a much-sought-after guest in the capital's society whirlwind of dinners and receptions. During one of these occasions, he met the world's greatest writer on the subjects of manly adventures, beginning a lifelong friendship with Rudyard Kipling with a hot debate on the topic of America's Indians. When Kipling took the United States to task for its treatment of the native population, Roosevelt retorted by thanking God that he, Roosevelt, did not have "one drop of British blood." Soon, the renowned author of *Plain Tales from the Hills, Soldiers Three,* and *Gunga Din* was introduced to grizzly bears at the Washington zoo, built at the urging of the Boone & Crockett Club. Following an evening of conversation at the Cosmos Club on Madison Place, Kipling reported, "I curled up on the seat opposite and listened and wondered until the universe seemed to be spinning around and Theodore was the spinner."

Laboring on through 1893 and into 1894 in the causes of civil service reformation and reconstructing the westward tide of white Americans in their quest to win the West, and vexed by dwindling funds, Roosevelt found himself drawn again into New York politics as friends urged him to run for mayor. He was inclined to do so, but Edith was concerned about the state of their finances. The prize was very great, the expense of running would have been "trivial," and "the chances of success very good," Roosevelt wrote to his sister. "But it is hard to decide when one has the interests of a wife and children to consider first."

While weighing ambition against family responsibilities, he learned of the death of his sister-in-law, Anna, followed by that of her husband, his brother Elliott. Gripped by delirium tremens, he'd attempted suicide by leaping from an upper window and died during a convulsive attack. Wracked by these disasters, and torn between ambition and Edith's deep misgivings about a bid for the mayoralty, Roosevelt again looked longingly westward.

He arrived in Dakota on September 4, 1894, but stayed only two weeks. On the last day at the ranch he left the ranch house early in the afternoon on his favorite pony, Muley, in the company of foreman Sylvane Ferris. They forded a shallow river and rode up a long, winding coulee, with a belt of timber running down its bottom. After going a couple of miles, by sheer good luck, they spotted whitetail deer—a buck, a doe, and a fawn. When they saw them the deer were trying to sneak off. As Ferris galloped toward one end of the belt of timber, Roosevelt urged Muley forward to intercept the fleeing quarry.

Dismounted, Roosevelt heard a cracking in the brush that meant the deer were close. A moment later, he saw the shadowy outlines of the doe and fawn as they scudded through the woods. Then the buck appeared at the edge of the trees, "running like a quarter-horse." One shot felled the "fine fellow with a handsome ten-point head, and as fat as a prize sheep."

Back at the ranch house, Roosevelt sat on the veranda in a rocking chair, looking across the wide, sandy river bed at the strangely shaped buttes and the groves of shimmering cottonwoods until the sun went down and the frosty air forced him into the house. As he packed his belongings for the trip back to New York, he did so having made two wrenching decisions.

Believing he was throwing away "one golden chance, which never returns," he acceded to Edith's request that he put his family first and not run for mayor. And he had faced up to the sad reality that his cattle ranching enterprise had proved to be a costly business failure.

He had lost about half his inheritance, close to eighty thousand dollars. Yet, as historian Elting E. Morison would write of the experience, "The money spent, wherever it had gone, had given to him glorious fun and adventure. It had brought him a companionship that was genuine and vital, and friends that remained loyal to his death."

Ironically, he made more money writing about his experiences in the Badlands than he earned ranching. Ranking Roosevelt "alone, unchallenged by any other twentieth-century president as writer and scholar," historian Stephen E. Ambrose, in an introduction to a one-volume reprint of *Hunting Trips of a Ranchman* and *The Wilderness Hunter*, found in the books "sharp observation, revealing details, charming and illuminating anecdotes, an overview, and honesty." Going West had taught Theodore Roosevelt lessons that he could have learned nowhere else. They shaped a character that would capture the imaginations of the Americans of his era and those of fascinated succeeding generations to this very day.

In the West he discovered in himself the spirit that would motivate him as hunter, husband, father, author, reforming politician, war hero, governor of New York, president of the United States, and intrepid explorer in Africa and South American jungles. It was a spirit that took nothing for granted, that insisted on the constructing of one's life "from the raw materials," and met life head-on with "knowledge, faculties and native genius."

"One of the chief attractions of the life of the wilderness," he wrote, "is its rugged and stalwart democracy. There every man stands for what he actually is and can show himself to be."

For him the measure of outdoor adventuring required "enough peril to make it exciting."

★ ★ ★

Strong as a Bull Moose

M Y FATHER was an ardent sportsman," wrote Theodore (Ted) Roosevelt Jr. with amusing understatement in a book of family memoirs. Consequently, Ted noted, he and his siblings were brought up
to be sportsmen. More important to the energetic figure whom they called
"Father," he continued in *All in the Family* (1929), even if the children did not
become experts with the rifle, "we got the right spirit, which is what counts."

Evidence of Father's "spirit" abounded in a large space beneath the
slanting roof of the house at Oyster Bay. Named the Gun Room, it was a
"sort of overflowing library where odds and ends of all kinds were gathered." Facing a gun case, a closet that was tucked under the eaves of the roof
seemed to Ted like a robber's cave. "Fraught with every possibility," it held
boxes of cartridges, leather cases, ramrods, old pistols, and all the parapher-
nalia of a sportsman, with "an entrancing musty smell like a shop in an
Eastern bazaar."

Among Father's souvenirs displayed on and between bookcases were a
couple of "very meritorious Arab scimitars in frayed plus scabbards" that
Teedie had collected in Egypt. On a cabinet stood two glass-covered groups
of birds, killed and stuffed by Teedie when he'd ventured up the Nile at the
age of eleven. More fascinating than these artifacts were Roosevelt's tales of
his ranch and the West. Shuddering with delicious excitement, the children
heard of cattle thieves and grizzly bears. Nearby, a shelf held a brace of hand-
somely inlaid dueling pistols in a mahogany box. Two "gorgeous old six-

shooters with carved ivory butts" were relics of his father as a young man who wished "to dress as well as act the part of a dashing cattleman."

The idea that Roosevelt liked to play a part to the hilt was not lost on his friends. Henry Adams once declared that Roosevelt was "pure act."

Another literary friend, Owen Wister, who contributed to the lore of the wild and woolly West with the novel *The Virginian* and *When West Was West,* wrote of Roosevelt, "He was his own limelight, and could not help it; a creature charged with such voltage as his, became the central presence at once, whether he stepped on a platform or entered a room—and in a room the other presences were likely to feel crowded, and sometimes displeased."

Having met Roosevelt when both were students at Harvard, and having gone to Wyoming after graduation, while Roosevelt chose to explore Dakota, Wister enjoyed being in "the full sunshine" of Roosevelt's attention. He wrote, "Not many golden strokes of fortune equal the friendship of a great man."

Convinced that any chance to achieve significance beyond that of a controversial Civil Service Commissioner had slipped through his fingers, Roosevelt returned from Dakota in the autumn of 1894. Having spent his last day on the ranch, and "with the last bullet fired" from his rifle, he was back at Sagamore Hill, thronged by his adoring "bunnies" and with Edith relieved that he had chosen not to run for mayor of New York.

The honor and responsibility of leading a "fusion" ticket went to businessman William Lafayette Strong. He was swept into office on a tide of public revulsion at revelations of corruption and scandals in every aspect of a city government controlled by Democrat political bosses. Ruling and pillaging public coffers from their "Wigwam" headquarters at Tammany Hall, they shared in millions of illicit dollars extorted by a graft-sodden police department that was more interested in strong-arming the illegal businesses of gambling and prostitution than arresting criminals. As a result of public demands that the crooks of the Mulberry Street police headquarters be cleaned out, Mayor Strong came under increasing pressure to appoint an incorruptible individual to lead a four-member Board of Police Commissioners. The name at the top of nearly everyone's list for the post was Theodore Roosevelt.

On accepting the appointment in May 1895, followed immediately by his election to be president of the police board by the other three members, Roosevelt said, "The public may rest assured that so far as I am concerned, there will be no politics in the department, and I know that I voice the sentiment of my colleagues in that respect. We are all activated by the desire to so regulate this department that it will earn the respect and confidence of the community. Every man in the force will have to stand on his merits and all appointments will be made for merit only, and without regard to political or religious considerations."

To show that he meant what he'd promised, he launched "midnight rambles," during which he prowled the city streets at night looking for slacking cops, then hauled them before a tribunal for punishment. The day after one of these trials the New York *World* offered readers this lively portrait:

Sing, heavenly muse, the sad dejection of our poor policemen. We have a real police commissioner. His name is Theodore Roosevelt. His teeth are big and white, his eyes are small and piercing, his voice is rasping. When he asks a question, Mr. Roosevelt shoots at the poor trembling policeman as he would shoot a bullet at a coyote. He shows a set of teeth calculated to unnerve the bravest of the Finest. His teeth are very white and almost as big as a colt's. They are broad teeth, they form a perfectly straight line. The lower teeth look like a row of dominoes. They do not lap over or under each other, as most teeth do, but come together evenly. They seem to say, "Tell the truth to your commissioner, or he'll bite your head off!"

Generally speaking, this commissioner's face is red. He has lived a great deal out of door, and that accounts for it. His hair is thick and short .Under his right ear is a long scar. It is the opinion of all the policemen who have talked to him that he got that scar fighting an Indian out West. It is also their opinion that the Indian is dead.

Following a lunch with Roosevelt at police headquarters, Owen Wister thought that his friend was putting on weight and impressiveness. The jaw was "acquiring a grimness which his experience of life made inevitable; and beneath the laughter and the courage of his blue eyes, a wistfulness had begun to lurk which I had never seen in college; but the warmth, the eagerness, the boisterous boyish recounting of some anecdote, the explosive expression of some opinion about a person, or a thing, or a state of things— these were unchanged. And even to the end still bubbled up unchanged."

During the two years as head of the police department, Roosevelt wrote, "I have been so absorbed by my own special work and its ramifications that I have time to keep very little in touch with anything outside of my own duties; I see but little of the life of the great world; I am but little in touch even with our national politics." Declaring that work of the police board had "nothing of the purple in it," he described it as "grimy" and "inconceivably arduous, disheartening, and irritating." Often attending to his duties seven days a week, he found no time for respite and relief in outdoor pursuits, and no room on his calendar for grabbing a gun and going after game. Consequently, when he was able to spare a few weeks in August of 1896, he headed West for the first time in two years.

He arrived in North Dakota carrying a new small-bore Winchester rifle that fired 30-166 smokeless ammunition in the form of a half-jacketed bullet with a naked lead point and the butt plated with hard metal. With "the greatest satisfaction" he wrote his sister, it was "as wicked-shooting weapon as I ever handled, and knocked the bucks over with a sledgehammer."

Three years earlier, in *The Wilderness Hunter*, he'd expressed himself on the subject of rifles. Noting that there was "an endless variety of opinion" on them, he wrote, "It is the man behind the rifle that counts." Musing on the topic in his autobiography (1913), he wrote, "There are men whose eye and hand are so quick and so sure that they achieve a perfection of marksmanship to which no practice will enable ordinary men to attain. There are other men who cannot learn to shoot with any accuracy at all. In between come the mass of men of ordinary abilities who, if they choose resolutely to practice, can by sheer industry and judgment make themselves fair rifle shots." He ranked himself in "the second class of respectable rifle shots."

Eager to introduce ten-year-old Ted to the sport of shooting, he bought him a Flaubert rifle. The presentation was made just after dark at Sagamore Hill. "I wanted to see if it fired to make sure it was a real rifle," Ted recalled, "but Father was not dressed to go outside at the moment."

Picking up the rifle and slipping a cartridge into the chamber, Roosevelt whispered, "You must promise not to tell Mother." Ted gave his word and Roosevelt fired into the ceiling.

"The report was slight, the smoke hardly noticeable," Ted reported, "and the hole in the ceiling so small that our sin was not detected."

Practice in using the gun was on a makeshift firing range set up across a gully with the butts of logs as targets. The shooting was performed while lying in a shallow pit. "It was almost as exciting to be snuggled in the pit and to hear the bullets strike the butts as it was to shoot," Ted wrote. "We used to dig the spent bullets out of the bank and keep them as treasures."

Of learning how to handle firearms Ted wrote in *All in the Family*, "If I got on the target at fifty yards I was happy. Above two hundred yards the element of luck plays the greatest part in shooting. The rifle may be accurate but the sportsman is not."

Three or four years after receiving the rifle, an admirer of Roosevelt presented Ted with a 16-gauge Scott shotgun. In order to "christen fittingly this new possession" Roosevelt took Ted hunting for ducks. Up before daylight on a cold winter morning and fortified by "gulping some coffee," they tramped through woods to Eel Creek. With a gray dawn breaking they paddled out from shore in a small boat, and "with numb fingers" set wooden decoys.

"Soon the ducks began to flight," Ted recalled. "After much expenditure of ammunition I succeeded, more by good luck than good management, in killing one female oldsquaw. Meanwhile, Father had practically duplicated my performance by killing one male. In triumph we returned to the house in time for a regular breakfast. In spite of their very fishy taste and leathery toughness we had the birds cooked and ate them for dinner."

With Ted and the other children left at Sagamore Hill with their mother, and glad to be liberated, however briefly, from the New York police department, Roosevelt ventured West in a bittersweet mood. He was happy to have a rifle in hand, but keenly aware of the changes that a decade had brought since he'd taken up cattle ranching. Where the buffalo and the Indian had ranged, along the Little Missouri, branded herds of cattle grazed. Settlers and miners invaded the ground where he'd killed bear and moose. The winning of the West that he chronicled in four thick volumes had been largely achieved. In a burst of exercising the "manifest destiny" of the United States to populate the land between the Atlantic and Pacific Oceans, a continent had been conquered and its cities linked by railroads.

America had become, he would write in June 1897 to his friend John Hay, the American ambassador to Great Britain, the "young giant" standing on a continent and clasping the crest of an ocean in either hand. "Our nation, glorious in youth and strength," he wrote, "looks into the future with eager eyes and rejoices as a strong man to run a race."

But the part of America that captured his heart in 1880 and drew him there to take up ranching in 1886 no longer existed. Looking back in his 1913 autobiography at what had been lost, he wrote:

We had a free and hardy life with horse and rifle. We worked under the scorching midsummer sun, when the wide plains shimmered and wavered in the heat, and we knew the freezing misery of riding night guard around the cattle in the late fall roundup. In the soft springtime the stars were glorious in our eyes, each night before we fell asleep; and in the winter we rode through blinding blizzards, when the driven snowdust burned out faces. There were monotonous days, as we guided the trail cattle, or the beef herds, hour after hour at the slowest of walks; and minutes or hours teeming with excitement as we stopped stampedes or swam the herds across rivers treacherous with quicksand, or brimmed with running ice. We knew toil and hardship and hunger and thirst; and we saw men die violent deaths as they worked among the horses and cattle, or fought in evil feuds with one another, but we felt the beat of hardy life in our veins, and ours was the glory of work and the joy of living.

In the fall of 1896 he was Owen Wister's man of "weight and impressiveness" with a jaw acquiring a grimness and wistfulness which his experience made inevitable, but with boisterous boyishness still bubbling up. He was a husband, father, city official, and a politician whom his friends expected to one day, as Henry Cabot Lodge predicted, "inherit a larger kingdom." No one had to explain that Lodge envisioned Theodore Roosevelt as president of the United States.

But as Roosevelt ranged far and wide, hunting game, and with what biographer Edmund Morris lyrically called the "oily perfume of sage in his nostrils," the Republican candidate for that office was William McKinley. Regarding his fitness for the presidency, Roosevelt expressed such grave misgivings that he told Henry Cabot Lodge that McKinley's nomination would be "a great misfortune." But once the grandfatherly looking governor of Ohio was chosen by the party, the always-loyal Roosevelt threw himself into the campaign with all the vigor he'd shown in the pursuit of game in a series of speeches in midwestern states by aiming rhetorical bullets at the Democrat candidate, William Jennings Bryan.

Following McKinley's lopsided victory, Roosevelt employed friends to convey his wish to the president-elect that McKinley award his campaign efforts with appointment to the post of assistant secretary of the navy. Keenly aware of Roosevelt's desire to see the United States aid a rebellion in the Spanish colony of Cuba by lending military and naval assistance, McKinley was worried that Roosevelt would prove "too pugnacious" and try to "drive through" his war policy "the moment he got in." One McKinley aide went so far as to say that the new president "hates Roosevelt like poison." But politics is politics, and therefore, on April 6, 1897, McKinley gave in and nominated Roosevelt. The U.S. Senate voted to confirm him two days later.

By mid-August, the New York *Sun* was able to report on Roosevelt's vigorous efforts to build up the fleet that "the liveliest spot in Washington" was the Navy Department. With "decks are cleared for action" and "the whole Navy bordering on a war footing," said the newspaper, all that remained was "to sand down the decks and pipe to quarters for action."

Men such as Roosevelt who urged intervention in Cuba were known as "jingoes." The word came from an English music hall song about Great Britain's resistance to Russian designs on the Turkish port of Constantinople. The song asserted:

> We don't want to fight yet by Jingo!
> if we do
> We've got the ships, we've got the men,
> and got the money too.

No individual embodied the definition of jingo more than Theodore Roosevelt. In 1886 as newspapers had been filled with predictions of a war with Mexico, he had offered to organize a cavalry battalion made up of cowboys from the Dakota territory. On July 4 of that year he told an audience that he hoped to see the day "when not a foot of American soil will be held by any European power." In 1894 he'd been the first to call for annexation of the Hawaiian Islands and had endorsed building of an ocean-linking canal through Nicaragua, whether Nicaraguans agreed or not. Speaking to the National Republican Club on May 28, 1895, he had called for a navy "that will sustain the honor of the American flag" and ensure that the Monroe Doctrine would be "upheld in its entirety." Writing on that subject in March 1896, he declared, "The United States ought not to permit any great military powers, which have no foothold on this continent, to establish such a foothold; nor should they permit any aggrandizement of those who already have possessions on the continent. Every true patriot, every man of statesmanlike habit, should look forward to the day when not a single European power will hold a foot of American soil."

When Great Britain had sought settlement of a boundary dispute with Venezuela without considering the interests of the United States, he all but welcomed a war. If it should come, he predicted, Canada would be "wrested from England" and never restored. In a letter to his friend and political mentor Henry Cabot Lodge he exclaimed, "This country needs a war."

Espousing his opinion that the United States had not only the right to take the side of the Cuban rebels, but a duty to do so, he called anyone who disagreed "anti-American." Claiming they were "too short-sighted or too unimaginative to realize the hurt to the nation that would be caused by the adoption of their views," he dismissed such persons as timid individuals "who undervalue the great fighting qualities, without which no nation can ever rise to the first rank."

Debate over whether the United States should to go to war in Cuba took a dramatic turn on the night of February 15 in the harbor of Havana, Cuba. Lying at anchor in Havana harbor on the twenty-first day of a "friendly call," in keeping with McKinley's interest in averting entry into strife between the Spanish colonial government and the Cuban rebels, the U.S. battleship *Maine* exploded. Outraged Americans who believed the ship had been blown up by Spaniards screamed "Remember the *Maine*" and demanded an immediate declaration of war. A reluctant McKinley asked for it from Congress on April 11, 1898—the day after Easter. Eight days later at three o'clock in the morning Congress granted it in a resolution demanding that the government of Spain withdraw its land and naval forces from Cuba at once and "directing the President of the United States to use the entire land and naval forces of the United States" to force the Spaniards from Cuba.

As war fever swept the nation, the phenomenon also touched Sagamore Hill. After seeing an operetta in Manhattan, Ted and Alice paraphrased one of the songs in the show. As they cavorted on the lawn, they sang:

> *Unleash the dogs of war!*
> *The enemy will find us unrelenting,*
> *When our cannons roar,*
> *The little King of Spain*
> *Will be repenting.*

In Washington their father left his Navy Department office in a building adjacent to the White House to see McKinley. "I have the Navy in good shape," he reported proudly. Adding that he would be useless to the war effort on a ship, he asked to be allowed to raise a regiment of cavalry. Admitting that he had little experience, he proposed he be appointed second in command, with the rank of lieutenant colonel, and that the unit be led by

Leonard Wood. A physician by training, he had joined the army and become a hero, receiving the Congressional Medal of Honor for valor during the army's recent campaign to capture the Indian renegade Geronimo. Officially named the First United States Volunteer Cavalry, the regiment was organized at a training camp near San Antonio, Texas. Consisting of an unlikely mixture of former college footballers and polo players from the east and scores of rough-and-ready cowboys, the unit was immediately nicknamed "Roosevelt's Rough Riders."

When four-year-old Archie heard that Father would be going off to war, he asked, "Will he bring back a bear?"

One day while taking rifle practice at Sagamore Hill before departing for Texas, Roosevelt was flat on the ground taking aim at a life-size paper image of a man tacked to a tree. Eleven-year-old Ted watched and waited for the bang of the gun. When the bullet punched a hole in the target, he exclaimed, "Excellent shot, Father!"

"Bunnies mustn't talk," TR admonished. "Father needs to concentrate on shooting if he is to kill enough Spaniards to win the war."

Soon after he arrived in Texas, the first of many letters arrived with vivid descriptions of the training camp and about Rough Riders who were exhibiting all the qualities he had taught his bunnies to value and live by. The soldiers he and Wood were training, he wrote, were "obedient and yet thoroughly self-reliant and self-helpful, not afraid of anything and able to take care of themselves under all circumstances."

Along with the letters Ted and his siblings could turn to vivid accounts in newspapers of the adventures of "Teddy Roosevelt's Rough Riders" as they trained in Texas and then as they camped near Tampa Bay, Florida, awaiting orders to embark for Cuba. When Edith showed Ted where Tampa Bay was on a map of Florida, he said proudly, "I suppose Father will get the war wind full in his face."

In relating this in a letter to TR, Edith wrote, "He says he should think every boy should want to go to war and wished you could have taken him just to clean your guns for, of course, he would not expect a shot at the enemy! He subsequently remarked he was sure he would be angry in a battle and ping away at the foe as fast as he could ram in cartridges. Ted hopes there will be one battle so you can be in it, but come out safe. Not every boy has a father who has seen a battle."

On the evening of June 13, 1898, the War Department in Washington, D.C., flashed to the troopships at Tampa to sail. Of this energizing and exhilarating spectacle, the author who had penned *The Naval War of 1812* wrote to Ted in the vivid style of his tales of hunting game in the West:

> Ship after ship weighed anchor and went slowly ahead under half-steam for the distant mouth of the harbor, the bands playing, the flags flying, the rigging black with the clustered soldiers, cheering and shouting to those left behind on the quay and to their fellows on the other ships. The channel was very tortuous; and we anchored before we had gone far down, after coming with an ace of a bad collision with another transport. The next morning we were all again under way, and in the afternoon the great fleet steamed southwest until Tampa Light sank in the distance.

American history had recorded no greater armada. Writing about the soldiers who sailed off to war as members of "Teddy's Rough Riders," newspaperman, and ardent Roosevelt friend, Jacob Riis, found them to be the latest incarnation of western manhood rallying to serve the country. Riis wrote:

> In the War of the Revolution they came out of the West and killed or captured the whole of the British forces at King's Mountain. They furnished the backbone of Andrew Jackson's forces in the War of 1812. As the Texas Rangers they became famous in the troubles with Mexico. They conquered the French towns on the Illinois, and won the West from the Indians in a hundred bloody fights. In the Civil War they lost, to a great extent, their identity, but not their place in the van and the thick of the fight. Theodore Roosevelt as a historian knew their record and their value; as a hunter and plainsman he knew where to find the material to fill up the long-broken ranks. It came at his summons from the plains and cattle-ranges of the great West, from the mines of the Rocky mountains, from the counting-rooms and colleges of the East, and from the hunting-trail of the wilderness, wherever the spirit of adventure had sent the young men out with the rifle to hunt big game or engage in the outdoor sports that train mind and body to endure uncomplaining the hardships of campaigning. The Rough Riders were the most composite lot that ever gathered under a regimental standard, but they were at the same time singularly typical of the spirit that conquered a continent in three generations, eminently American.

Roosevelt would say of the men he led into battle, and into history and glory in a charge up the San Juan Heights, "We had a great time and this is a regiment of crackerjacks—American from start to finish, in the best and fullest sense of the term."

Could he have succeeded as a soldier and leader of men in battle in Cuba without having first been a hunter in the West? Possibly. But time and again after the Spanish-American War, and following his presidency, he credited his achievements to the preparation provided by his time there. "I owe more than I ever can express to the West," he wrote in his autobiography. "Not only did the men and women whom I met in the cow country quite unconsciously help me, by the insight which working with them enabled me to get into the mind and soul of the average American of the right type, but they helped me in another way. I made up my mind that the men were of just the kind whom it would be well to have with me if ever it became necessary to go to war. When the Spanish War came, I gave this thought practical realization."

With the Spaniards at last kicked out of Cuba in the summer of 1898, Roosevelt's friend John Hay, the U.S. ambassador to England, pronounced the shortest armed conflict in American history "a splendid little war." When the Rough Riders arrived at Montauk, New York, to be disbanded, Roosevelt was sun-bronzed and twenty pounds lighter.

Belted to a hip was the pistol he'd used to kill a Spanish soldier in the rush to capture a fortress at the crest of Kettle Hill. As he bounded down the gangplank, he told an inquiring reporter that he was "feeling disgracefully well" and that he'd had "a bully time and a bully fight." He added with a toothy grin, "I feel as big and strong as a bull moose!"

Returning to Sagamore Hill, he noted "all this fuss now about the Rough Riders and me" and said, "I've reached the crest of the wave. Now I'll probably begin to go down."

Leaders of New York's Republican Party and Empire State voters believed otherwise.

What they had in mind was that the war hero—now the most famous man in America—run as a Republican for governor of New York. In a lifelong Theodore Roosevelt habit of seeing gloom ahead, he wrote to a friend, "I haven't bothered myself a particle about the nomination, and have no idea whether it will be made or not. In the first place, I would rather have led this regiment [the Rough Riders] than be Governor of New York three times over. In the next place, while on the whole I should like the office of Governor and would not shirk it, the position will be one of such extreme difficulty and I shall have to offend so many good friends of mine, that I should breathe a sigh of relief were it not offered to me." He won the nomination and the governorship handily. In his inaugural address on January 2, 1899, he did not see himself coming into office as a man expected to play the role of a hero on a white horse. "There is much less need of genius or of any special brilliance in the affairs of our government," he said, "than there is a need of such homely virtues and qualities as common sense, honesty and courage."

Shortly after taking office, speaking to the Hamilton Club in Chicago, he provided a self-portrait and a philosophy of a life shaped by his time in the West. "I wish to preach, not the doctrine of noble ease," he declared, "but the doctrine of the Strenuous Life—the life of toil and effort, of labor and strife; to preach the highest form of success which comes, not to the man who desires more easy peace, but to the man who does not shrink from danger, from hardship, or from bitter toil, and who out of these wins the splendid ultimate triumph."

Although his attempts to reform government were often constrained by opponents in both political parties, especially by the Republican political boss, Senator Thomas E. Platt, the new governor felt free to pursue policies to promote goals that had motivated him to found the Boone & Crockett Club. The actions he took in the cause of the conservation of wildlife and forests, he later wrote, provided a "foreshadowing" of the course he would follow as president. Concerned with the "inefficiency" of game wardens and game protectors in the Adirondacks and Catskill mountains, he told the state legislature that the regions "should be great parks kept in perpetuity for the benefit and enjoyment of our people."

Calling for a "careful study of the resources and conditions of the forests," he expected that woodlands to be "managed as efficiently as the forest on private lands." The sawmills and wood-pulp mills would have to be restrained from dumping waste into streams. If reservoirs were to be created, they must not be made "where they will tend to destroy large sections of the forest, and only after a careful and scientific study of the water resources of the region."

Nearly a century before the emergence of "ecology" as part of public policy, the advent of organizations such "Friends of the Earth" and the save-the-rain-forests movement, and the "environmental impact" survey as a requirement of almost all construction projects in the United States, Governor Roosevelt pointed out that a "primeval forest is a great sponge which absorbs and distills the rain water. And when it is destroyed the result is apt to be an alternation of flood and drought. Every effort should be made to minimize their destructive influence."

On the subject of wildlife, he drew on his experience in observing the depletion of game as the result of over-hunting. "The people of the forest regions," he asserted, "are themselves growing more and more to realize the necessity of preserving both trees and game. A live deer in the woods will attract to the neighborhood ten times the money that could be obtained for the dead deer's carcass." But this did not mean hunting should be banned. Such "hardy outdoor sports" were of no small value to the national character, and therefore should be encouraged in every way. "Men who go into the wilderness, indeed, men who take part in any field sports with horse and rifle," he said, "receive a benefit which can hardly be given by even the most vigorous athletic games."

In a message to the legislature, Governor Roosevelt must have felt a tugging on his sleeve by a boy called Teedie when he wrote, "The State should not permit within its limits factories to make bird skins or bird feathers into articles of ornament or wearing apparel. Ordinary birds, and especially song birds, should be rigidly protected. Game birds should never be shot to a greater extent than will offset the natural rate of increase."

Observation of birds filled Roosevelt's accounts of his hunting trips. Whether after wolf in Texas or bear-hunting in Louisiana and Mississippi, he was not only enthralled by the sport, but also by the strange new birds. The feeling of excitement at encountering a species that he'd not seen before was still there in June 1910 when he visited England. He arrived feeling that he knew a good deal about English birds by having read Shakespeare and Shelley (the lark), Milton and Keats (nightingale), and Wordsworth (cuckoo). What he did not know was their songs. On a hike with a guide through the New Forest he observed forty-one species and heard twenty-three sing. The one that surprised him was the blackbird. "I knew that he was a singer," he wrote, "but I really had no idea how fine a singer he was."

At sundown on his first day back at Sagamore Hill, he sat in his rocking chair on the broad veranda, looking across Long Island Sound, with the grassy hillside sloping away to a belt of forest. From the woods rose "the golden, leisurely chiming of the wood thrushes, chanting their vespers. Through the still air came the warble of vireo and tanager. As night fell he heard the flight song of an ovenbird in the woods. An oriole sang in weeping elm while "now and then breaking his song to scold like an overgrown wren. There were song-sparrows and catbirds in the shrubbery, a robin in a nest over the front door and another over the back entrance.

During the next twenty-four hours, Roosevelt recalled, he saw and heard forty-two birds that he listed in a chapter of his autobiography. Titled "Outdoor and Indoors," it is a thirty-five-page description of his home at Oyster Bay. "At Sagamore Hill," he wrote, we love a great many things—birds and trees and books, and all things beautiful, and horses and trees and children and hard work and the joy of life."

Especially important in Roosevelt's first summer respite from Albany was the family's annual Fourth of July celebration. The father beamed with pride as Ted led seventeen boys as they pretended to be Rough Riders in a parade from Cove Neck to Sagamore Hill. That evening saw a dazzling display of fireworks. A pyrotechnic picture of the hero of San Juan Hill, noted Edith in a letter, was "accompanied by the national salute of twenty-one bombs which quite overcame some of the smaller children." An added thrill for the children was helping TR and other adults in stamping out grass fires kindled by rocket sparks. When the last Roman candle had lit up the sky, the children sat in a circle on the ground to listen to Theodore Roosevelt's adventures in the wild and woolly West, from roping cattle to sitting around a campfire under a sky sparkling with a hundred million stars. An observer said, "He knew how to tell such a story so boys would feel the sting of the smoke in their eyes."

At the start of the Independence Day ceremonies, the Reverend Mr. Henry Washburn, rector of the Episcopal Church attended by the Roosevelts, had electrified the townspeople by declaring that they were welcoming into their midst not only the governor of New York, but a future president of the United States. When the sentiment was echoed by the Reverend John L. Bedford, a Roman Catholic priest, a reporter for the New York Times noted, and wrote for his readers, "The Governor's expression was ludicrously like that of a boy trying to keep an impassive face while something pleases him."

Despite the enthusiasm of the two clerics and the people of Oyster Bay, whatever ideas a governor might have regarding seeking the presidency as a Republican would have to wait. The party's nomination in 1900 would go to President McKinley. But there were indications that his vice-president, Garret A. Hobart, might not run again. When political allies such as Henry Cabot Lodge inquired if Governor Roosevelt might be interested in seeking the nomination, Roosevelt he replied that the office was "about the last thing for which I would care." Even after Hobart died in November, when a reporter asked if Roosevelt would accept his party's vice-presidential nomination, Roosevelt said, "I would rather be in private life than be Vice-President. I believe I can be of more service to my country as Governor of the State of New York."

This adamant position remain unchanged in June 1900 as he traveled to Philadelphia for the Republican National Convention. In seconding the nomination of McKinley, he galvanized the delegates by exhorting America, "glorious in youth and strength," to see the future "with fearless and eager eyes." When he finished speaking, the band struck up the theme song of Roosevelt's Rough Riders, "There'll Be a Hot Time in the Old Town Tonight." Conventioneers reacted with roars and tumults of applause, and in doing so, let it be known that they would not be satisfied until he accepted the vice-presidential nomination. "I am as strong as a bull moose," came the reply, "and you can use me to the limit."

After returning from Philadelphia to Sagamore Hill, the bunnies learned that he would be leaving immediately for Oklahoma City and a Rough Riders reunion, with a stop on the way back to call on President McKinley at his home in Canton, Ohio. When the children learned that the trip would coincide with the traditional Sagamore Hill July 4th celebration, he told them that the festivities would occur as usual, but a few days later. But a week after the delayed fireworks illuminated the skies above Sagamore Hill, he was gone again to campaign through the West.

Everywhere he went on behalf of McKinley and himself he was lauded, with one notable exception. On his arrival in Cripple Creek, Colorado, backers of the Democratic candidate, William Jennings Bryan, greeted him with a hail of rocks. Only a rush by a flying wedge of Rough Riders saved him from injury.

With the campaigning done, Roosevelt awaited election day with assurances from all his friends, as well as party officials, that when all the ballots were tallied, he would be the next vice-president of the United States. Their faith was justified. In their biggest victory since 1872, the Republicans garnered a plurality of nearly a million votes and a 292-to-155 majority in the Electoral College. Because he would not take office until March 4, 1901, he sought refreshment from the campaign on a hunting trip in the wintry wilds of his beloved West.

From Keystone Ranch, Colorado, on January 14, 1901, he wrote a letter to

Ted in which he demonstrated the narrative skill which had made many of his books best-sellers and provided much of the income that supported his family. The letter introduced Ted to "the hunter Goff, a fine, quiet, hardy fellow, who knows his business thoroughly."

Starting soon after sunrise from the town of Meeker, they made their way, "hunting as we went, across the high, exceedingly rugged hills, until sunset."

The letter went on:

The first cat we put up gave the dogs a two hours' chase, and got away among some high cliffs. In the afternoon we put up another, and had a very good hour's run, the dogs baying until that glens rang again to the echoes as they worked hither and thither through the ravines. We walked our ponies up and down steep, rock-strewn, and tree-clad slopes, where it did not seem possible a horse could climb, and on the level places we got one or two smart gallops. At last the lynx went up a tree. Then I saw a really funny sight. Seven hounds had been doing the trailing, while a large brindled bloodhound and two half-breeds between collie and bull stayed behind Goff, running so close to his horse's heels that they continually bumped into them, which he accepted with philosophic composure. Then the dogs proceeded literally to climb the tree, which was a many-forked pinion; one of the half-breeds, named Tony, got up certainly sixteen feet, until the lynx, which looked like a huge and exceedingly malevolent pussy-cat, made vicious dabs at him. I shot the lynx low, so as not to hurt his skin.

Describing hours spent with a friend and a pack of dogs, tracking a cougar that had killed a deer the night before, he continued, "Soon we saw the lion in a treetop, with two of the dogs so high up among the branches that he was striking at them. He was more afraid of us than the dogs, and as soon as he saw us he took a great flying leap and was off, the pack close behind. In a few hundred yards they had him up another tree. They could have killed him by themselves. But he bit and clawed four of them, and for fear that he might kill one I ran in and stabbed him behind the shoulder, thrusting the knife right into his heart. I have always wished to kill a cougar as I did this one, with dogs and the knife."

The tale was even more thrilling for young Theodore Roosevelt Jr., then a student at the Groton School in Massachusetts, because the knife was one that Ted had given him.

A fuller account of the cougar hunt was provided by Roosevelt four years later in the first chapter of *Outdoor Pastimes of an American Hunter.* The book included his experiences in the West before his exploits in Cuba propelled him into the governorship of New York and the vice-presidency, and the shorter-duration, more hurried, and newsworthy adventures as he lived in that "greater kingdom" of the presidency foreseen by Henry Cabot Lodge, and predicted by a pair of clergymen at an Oyster Bay Fourth of July celebration. It was the first book published by a sitting president to that time. Like the previous *Hunting Trips of a Ranchman* (1885), *Ranch Life and the Hunting Trail* (1888), and *The Wilderness Hunter* (1893), the eleven-chapter volume was more a series of anecdote-vignettes than a long, chronological narrative. While recording his own exploits, the stories devoted considerable space to his hunting companions. In the chapter covering the chase that he'd described in Ted's letter, it's obvious that he had been much taken by the performance of four-legged assistants. He called the essay "With the Cougar Hounds."

There were twelve in the pack. Eight hounds and four hunting dogs, they were, he wrote, "of the ordinary Eastern type, used from the Adirondacks to the Mississippi and Gulf in the chase of the deer and the fox." Six hounds were black and tan and two were mottled, differing widely in size and voice. The biggest, and, on the whole, the most useful was Jim, "a vert fast, powerful and true dog with a great voice." Next to Jim in usefulness was Boxer. An older dog, he ran into bad luck. His first cougar bit him through one hind leg, so that for the reminder of the trip he had to run on three legs, or as John Goff put it, "packed one leg."

"In cougar hunting the success of the hunter depends absolutely on his hounds," wrote Roosevelt. "As hounds that are not perfectly trained are worse than useless, this means that success depends absolutely on the man who trains and hunts the hounds. Goff was one of the best hunters with whom I have ever been out, and he had trained his pack to the point of perfection for its special work which I have known another pack to reach."

Other dogs were named Tree'em, Lil and Nel ("Two very stanch and fast bitches"), another female misnamed Pete, Jimmie, Bruno, Tony, Baldy, and Turk, who had lost his lower fangs, but was still "a most formidable dog."

The horses were "stout, hardy, surefooted beasts, not very fast, but able to climb like goats, and to endure an immense amount of work." Roosevelt and Goff each used two. Always the bird-watcher, Roosevelt observed on one of their runs a "party of ravens" fluttering from tree to tree, "making queer gurgling noises and evidently aware that they might expect to reap a reward from our hunting."

While more than half the cougars managed to escape by getting into caves of deep holes in washouts, those that scampered into trees were "easily shot." Roosevelt thought they looked like "large malevolent pussies." Often, before taking aim at a cougar with a rifle, Roosevelt shot it with a camera. Ever the educator on wildlife, he instructed readers of *Outdoor Pastimes of an American Hunter* on the lore and lure of the cougar. "No American beast has been the subject of so much loose writing or of such wild fables," he wrote. "The average writer, and for the matter of that, the average hunter, where cougars are scarce, knows little or nothing of them, and in describing them merely draws upon the stock of well-worn myths which portray them as terrible foes of man, as dropping on their prey from trees where they have been lying in wait, etc., etc."

The reader of "With the Cougar Hounds" came away thoroughly disabused of such fallacies.

Between January 19 and February 14, 1901, Roosevelt and Goff, with the help of their hounds, killed fourteen cougars. They ranged in size from four-feet-eleven inches and 47 pounds to eight feet and 227 pounds. Three were male. When Roosevelt presented their skulls to the Biological Survey, Department of Agriculture in Washington, D.C., its director, Dr. Hart Merriam, wrote a letter that must have made Roosevelt's chest swell with the pride felt by Teedie when he added a prize specimen to his boyish upstairs museum. Roosevelt was so proud of Dr. Merriam's letter that he included it in "With the Cougar Hounds." It said:

> The big [cougar] skull is certainly a giant. I have compared it with the largest in our collection from British Columbia and Wyoming, and find it larger than either. It is in fact the largest skull of any member of the *Felis concolor* group I have seen. A hasty preliminary examination indicates that the animal is quite different from the northwest coast form, but that it is the same as my horse-killer from Wyoming—*felis hippolestes*. In typical *Felis color* from Brazil the skull is lighter, the brain-case thinner and more smoothly rounded, devoid of the strongly developed sagittal crest; the under jaw straighter and lighter.

Your series of skulls from Colorado is incomparably the largest, most complete and most valuable series ever brought together from any single locality, and will be of inestimable value in determining the amount of individual variation.

The last cougar shot by Roosevelt was the biggest (227 pounds), gotten on his last day of hunting. As it lay stretched out, he thought it looked like a small African lioness. "It would be impossible to wish a better ending to a hunt," he wrote.

Wistfully, he added, "My holiday was over."

Eighteen days later, Theodore Roosevelt became the twenty-fifth vice president of the United States. Considering the position "a fifth wheel on a coach," he saw the office as "not a stepping stone to anything but oblivion." With so much time on his hands, and believing that he had gone as far as he ever could in politics, he thought about studying law again, with an eye toward taking up law as a profession after he left office. He toyed with the idea of becoming a history professor, or writing a monumental history of the United States. Yet as a fifth wheel on the wagon, he discovered that he enjoyed the "perfect ease" of his life, "just living out in the country." In a letter to Ted, dated May 31, 1901, he asked, "Have you made up your mind whether you would like to try shooting the third week in August or the last week in July?"

They settled on a week's shooting in Long Island marshlands and fishing off the sloop *Showabase*. For a moment the vacation seemed imperiled when Roosevelt's friend Paul Morton, president of the Santa Fe Railroad, announced that he hoped to visit Roosevelt at Sagamore Hill at the same time as the outing. Roosevelt informed the railway tycoon, "On Monday I start with two of my sons and four of their little cousins for a four days' shooting trip, and it would break their hearts if I abandoned it."

Ted wrote of the adventure, "It was a most courageous undertaking on Father's part, and the fact that we all returned uninjured speaks volumes of his discipline. Kermit was so small that, when he shot, Father had to support the gun. We wandered about the marshes and were bitten by mosquitoes. We sat patiently in eelgrass blinds and felt the thrill that comes when the first birds circle down half-seen in the gray of early dawn."

As Ted returned to Groton, Roosevelt wrote to his friend William Howard Taft, who was serving as governor-general of the Philippines, and confessed that he was rather ashamed to say that he was happy "doing nothing but ride and row with Mrs. Roosevelt, and walk and play with the children; chop trees in the afternoon and read books by the fire in the evening."

At summer's end he went on a speaking tour that included a meeting on September 6 of the Vermont Fish and Game League on Isle La Motte in Lake Champlain. Not many miles away in Buffalo, New York, President McKinley was at the Pan American Exposition. In an appearance at the Temple of Music at the end was the two-day visit, the ever-affable chief executive was to greet anyone from the public who might wish to shake his hand. As he took his place amid a bower of palm trees, his secretary, George B. Courtelyou, pleaded with him to cancel the event.

With a fatherly smile which had helped persuade American voters to grant him a second term, McKinley asked the worried aide, "Why should I? No one would want to hurt me."

Moments later as an organist played a Bach cantata, the president smiled at a young man whose right hand was wrapped in a handkerchief. When the president extended his left hand, the man's seemingly injured hand came up to press a pistol to McKinley's chest and squeeze the trigger twice.

Sometime later, as Roosevelt was about to attend a reception on Isle La Motte, he was informed of the shooting, that the gunman—an anarchist by the name of Leon Czolgosz—was in custody, that McKinley was undergoing exploratory surgery, and that there was a special train waiting to take Vice President Roosevelt to Buffalo. Upon his arrival, he was relieved to learn that the president had come through the surgery and was rallying. Informed on September 10 that McKinley appeared to be out of danger, Roosevelt returned to the Adirondacks to join his family at a camp near Mount Tahawus.

On the thirteenth, he set out with friends to climb Mount Marcy (5,344 feet, the highest point in the state of New York). The day was overcast and rainy, the footing slippery, the climb exhausting. When the men reached the peak and the sun broke through the clouds, Roosevelt exclaimed, "Beautiful country." Enjoyment of the vista was brief. As the leaden clouds closed, obliterating the view, the party began its descent. While they paused in the downward trek for a dinner of sandwiches by a small lake named Tear-of-the-Clouds, Roosevelt felt that they'd had "a bully tramp" and was looking forward to his repast "with the interest only an appetite worked up in the woods gives you." At that moment he saw a man on a trail, running toward them, and "instinctively knew he had bad news—the worst news in the world."

It was a telegram from George Courtelyou that McKinley's condition had taken a turn for the worse. When word came from Buffalo at ten o'clock that he was dying, Roosevelt climbed into a buckboard to begin a forty-mile wild ride on difficult roads to the town of North Creek and a waiting special train. Arriving at the North Creek railroad station at daybreak, he was handed a telegram—his first message as the 26th president of the United States.

Shortly after three in the afternoon on September 14, in Buffalo's Wilcox Library, with members of McKinley's Cabinet, guests, and reporters looking on, the youngest man to become president glanced toward a window and observed a small bird. Perched on the sill, it fluttered its wings and chirped its song.

PART TWO

★ ★ ★

For the Generations to Come

5

★ ★ ★

To Learn to Swim, You Must
Get into the Water

TWO WEEKS before succeeding to the presidency, Theodore Roosevelt had made a speech at the Minnesota State Fair at St. Paul. "Our country has been populated by pioneers," he said, "and therefore has more energy, more enterprise, more expansive power than any other in the wide world."

In an address in Detroit, Michigan, a year and a week after he took the oath of office, he said of the people of America, "Stout of heart, we see, across the dangers, the great future that lies beyond, and we rejoice as a giant refreshed, as a strong man girt for the race; and we go down into the arena where the nations strive for mastery, our hearts lifted with the faith that to us and our children, and our children's children it shall be given to make this Republic the mightiest among the peoples of mankind."

But it had been in his Fourth of July speech at Dickinson in the Dakota Territory in 1886 that the hopeful, adventuring cattleman and hunter of game of prairies and mountains defined America's natural resources and treasures as the foundation on which the future of the United States rested. "It is not what we have that will make us a great nation," he said, "it is the way in which we use it."

Always a believer that actions were more important than words, the new president lost no time in living up to his rhetoric. Placing "the work of reclamation" of the state of the country's national resources at the top of his domestic agenda, he turned his attention to a plan presented by two trusted friends from his time as governor of New York. Gifford Pinchot and F.H. Newell outlined ideas for irrigation projects in the arid lands of the West and consolidation of various offices of the federal Bureau of Forestry. The two men pointed out that through the General Land Office and other bureaus, public resources were being handled and disposed of on the basis of small considerations of petty formalities, instead of for the larger purposes of constructive development. The result was that government policies favored private interests over the public's.

"The idea that our natural resources were inexhaustible still obtained, and there was yet no real knowledge of their extent and condition," Roosevelt wrote. "The relation of the conservation of natural resources to the problem of national welfare and national efficiency had not yet dawned on the public mind. The reclamation of arid public lands in the West was still a matter of private enterprise alone; and our magnificent river system, with its superb possibilities for public usefulness, was dealt by the national government not as a unit, but as a disconnected series of pork barrel problems, whose only real interest was in their effect on the reelection or defeat of a Congressman where and there."

Roosevelt found that the forests which belonged to the United States were administered by one agency of the government, but the foresters who were charged with caring for the forests were employed by another bureau. Realizing that the national forest reserves in the West were inadequate in area to meet the purposes for which they had been created, and having become a "warm believer" in reclamation and in forestry as a rancher and hunter, the new president made these problems a central part of his first message to Congress. Determined to set forth a "new attitude" toward natural resources, he declared, "The forest and water problems are perhaps the most vital internal problems of the United States."

On the day the message was read to Congress (at that time, presidents did not go up to the Capitol to meet their constitutional duty to report on the state of the union), a committee of Western senators and congressmen went to work on writing reclamation legislation. Known as the Newlands Act, the measure was not named for its purpose, as in "new lands," but after the last name of its principal drafter. Formally titled "Reclamation Act of 1902," its objectives were reclaiming waste areas of the arid West through irrigation and encouragement of settlement by creating homes whose occupants would eventually repay the government, thereby providing a revolving fund for continuation of land reclamation.

Roosevelt's first congressional message also called for "laying the foundation of American forestry by scientific study of the forests, and with the promotion of forestry on private lands." Unlike the swift passage of the Reclamation Act, this sweeping forestry plan would take three years to become a reality. In the meantime, Roosevelt launched a study of a pending proposal to create the Appalachian National Forest. Plans were also made for experimental planting in national forests and on Indian reservations. The result of these and other efforts was the transfer in 1905 of national forests from the jurisdiction of the Interior Department to the Department of Agriculture and creation of the United States Forest Service. Under the leadership of Gifford Pinchot, Roosevelt proudly noted, the foresters found themselves handling some sixty million acres. Two years later, by presidential proclamation, he added forty-three million acres.

A direct outgrowth of these efforts on behalf of forestry, Roosevelt believed, was the invigoration of an existing, but largely ineffective, Conservation movement. "Without application to natural resources of principals which had been worked out in connection with the forests that public sentiment had been built up for protection of the forests," he claimed, "the Conservation movement would have been impossible."

In his last year as president, Roosevelt witnessed a unanimous declaration by the U.S. Conference of Governors of States and Territories endorsing conservation during a meeting in the East Room of the White House. This was followed by Roosevelt's appointment of thirty-six state conservation committees, and, on June 8, 1908, a National Conservation Commission. Its task was to prepare an inventory, the first by any nation, of all the natural resources. The survey was authorized by a presidential executive order which placed all federal departments "at the command of the Commission." Headed by Gifford Pinchot, the commission completed its task in six months, and "laid squarely before the American people the essential facts regarding our natural resources, when facts were greatly needed as the basis for constructive action."

The interest of the twenty-sixth president of the United States in conserving and preserving the natural resources of the nation came as no surprise to anyone who knew him, from the maid who had objected to the odors emanating from the specimens in Teedie's museum; parents, brother, and sisters; and his own children and wife; the men who had accompanied him on treks in the forests and mountains of Maine and New York; the members of the Boone & Crockett Club; readers of his books on outdoor life; and leathery-skinned men who hunted with him out West.

Among the first of the hunters who came to visit him at the White House was Sylvane Ferris. But it took two attempts for him to convince a door-keeper that he was indeed a friend of the president. "Next time they don't let you in," said Roosevelt when he learned of Ferris's ordeal, "just shoot through the window."

When another old friend (John Willis) was invited to dine at the White House, he declined, preferring to "get my grub downtown at the hashery where I'm bunking," but if Roosevelt would be "taking any horseback rides out on the trail here tomorrow, I'm your man."

The president's favorite riding trail was in Rock Creek Park. Rarely allowing inclement weather to interfere with his outings, he departed the executive mansion via the south portico with one or two military aides who were expert horsemen. White House visitors who were lucky enough to be invited to go along received a typewritten behavior guide. Titled *Rules of the Road For Those Invited to Accompany the President on Horseback Rides*, it said:

First.   The President will notify whom he wishes to ride with him. The one so notified will take position on the left of the President and keep his right stirrup back of the President's left stirrup.

Second.   Those following will keep no less than yards in the rear of the President.

Third.   When the President asks anyone in the party to ride with him the one at his side should at once retire to the rear. Salutes should be returned only by the President, except by those in the rear. Anyone unable to control his horse should withdraw to the rear.

That these rules convey an expectation of a strict military discipline appear to be a carry-over from Roosevelt's role as Lt. Col. Roosevelt of the First United States Voluntary Cavalry Of the Rough Riders, described romantically in the press as "the cowboy cavalry," he'd said in a letter to

Henry Cabot Lodge, "Three fourths of our men have at one time or another been cowboys or else are small stockmen. . . . They are intelligent as well as game. . . . You would enjoy seeing the mounted drill, for the way these men have gotten their wild half-broken horses into order is something marvelous."

Noting in his autobiography that he had been both astonished and pleased by his ability "in the line of tactics," he explained that as a boy he had been fond of horseback riding, but had taken to it "slowly and with difficulty." It took a long time before he became even a respectable rider, he recalled, and never became a "first-flight man in the hunting field, and never even approached the bucking-bronco class in the West."

The only story of "any interest" from his fox-hunting experiences on Long Island after graduating from Harvard, he wrote, involved riding a former buggy horse that had been retired from that task because the horse "insisted on thoughtfully lying down while in harness." When it was turned out to grass, however, it demonstrated a capacity for hopping over fences. It was a natural jumper, although without any speed. "On the hunt in question," Roosevelt remembered, "I got along very well until the pace winded my ex-buggy horse, and it turned a somersault over a fence. When I got on it after the fall I found I could not use my left arm."

Only after three or four jumps did he realize it was broken. The fracture became obvious after a big drop when the jar made the bones slip past one another so as to throw the hand out of position. "It did not hurt me at all," he remembered, and the horse proved to be "as easy to sit as a rocking-chair." Continuing the hunt, he noted proudly, he "got in at the death."

Fourteen months after settling into the "President's House," which he officially renamed "The White House," Theodore Roosevelt offered the readers of the November 6, 1902, issue of *Youth's Companion* a description of his job. "The President," he wrote, "has always to be ready to devote every waking hour to some anxious, worrying, harassing matter, most difficult to decide, and yet which is imperative to immediately decide."

The history of his handling the job is that of a decisive president who personified the confidence of a people with their sights set on the future. He promised a "square deal" for the workingman, battled against industrial trusts and unrestrained power of corporations, and put the federal government in the business of food and drug regulation. He saw that the Panama Canal was built for the benefit of the United States and an American two-ocean navy, enforced the Monroe Doctrine by thwarting expansion of European colonies in the western hemisphere, and flexed American muscle wherever he deemed necessary in accord with his policy of speaking softly while carrying a big stick.

In the spring of 1903, after fifteen months seated solidly in the saddle of the presidency, and with a tight grip on the reins of the U.S. government, Roosevelt happily cleared his calendar to make room for his first look at the West since his cougar hunt in Colorado.

6

★ ★ ★

Former Stamping Ground

THE PURPOSES of Theodore Roosevelt's journey westward were to preside at a ceremonial laying of the cornerstone at the entrance to Yellowstone Park, to tour the natural wonders of California's Yosemite forest, and break ground for a statue of President McKinley in Golden State Park in San Francisco. While en route he wrote to John Hay, "Wherever I stopped at a small city or country town, I was greeted by the usual shy, self-conscious, awkward body of local committeemen, and spoke to the usual audience of thoroughly good American citizens—a term I can use in a private letter to you without being thought demagogic. That is, the audience consisted partly of the townspeople, but even more largely of rough-coated, hard-headed, gaunt, sinewy farmers and hired hands from all their neighborhood, who had driven in with their wives and daughters and often with their children, from ten or twenty or even thirty miles round about. For all the superficial differences between us, down at the bottom these men and I think a good deal alike, or at least have the same ideals, and I am always sure of reaching them in speeches which many of my Harvard friends would think not only homely, but commonplace."

After receiving an honorary doctor of laws degree from the University of Chicago, he eagerly crossed the Missouri River and came into his "own former stamping ground." At every railway station, he noted, he found "somebody who remembered my riding there when the Little Missouri roundup went down to the Indian reservation and then worked across the Cannon Ball and up Knife and Green Rivers; or who had been an interested and possibly malevolent spectator when I had ridden out with other representatives of the cow men to hold a solemn council with the leading gangsters on the vexed subject of mavericks, or who had been hired as a train hand when I had been taking a load of cattle to Chicago, and remembered well how he and I had at the stoppages had run frantically down the line of cars and with out poles jabbed the unfortunate cattle who had lain down until they again stood up and thereby gave themselves a chance for their lives; and who remembered how when the train started we had to clamber hurriedly aboard and make our way back to the caboose along the tops of the cattle cars."

Arriving at Medora, he found Sylvane and Joe Ferris waiting to welcome him back, along with many old friends and familiar faces. The older men and women he knew well, he wrote, while "the younger ones had been wild tow-headed children" when he lived and worked along the Little Missouri. Overcome with nostalgia, he wrote to John Hay, "I had spent nights in their ranches. I still remembered meals which the women had given me when I had come from some hard expedition, half famished and sharpest as a wolf. I had killed buffalo and elk, deer and antelope with some of the men. With others I had worked on the trail, on the calf roundup, on the beef roundup. We had been together on occasions which we still remembered when some bold rider met his death in trying to stop a stampede, in riding a mean horse, or in the quicksands of some swollen river which he sought to swim."

At the Yellowstone stone-laying ceremony at Gardiner, Montana, on April 24, 1903, he began his remarks by noting, "Nowhere else in any civilized country is there to be found such a tract of veritable wonderland made accessible to all visitors, where at the same time not only the scenery of the wilderness but the wild creatures of the park are scrupulously preserved, the only change being that these same wild creatures have been so carefully protected as to show a literally astounding tameness."

When Roosevelt reached Butte, Montana, the friend who'd preferred to have supper at a Washington hashery rather than a dinner at the White House was there to welcome him. Looking Roosevelt up and down, John Willis exclaimed, "My God, Theodore, where in hell did you get that pot belly? You know I made a man of you, and now you are spoiling all my work."

"Yes, and I made a Christian of you," Roosevelt replied through his famous grin, "and don't spoil my work."

Arriving in California, Roosevelt eagerly anticipated meeting the leading proponent of conservation in the country. Born in Scotland in 1838, John Muir emigrated to the United States with his family in 1849. Gripped with a wanderlust in 1867, he walked a thousand miles from Indiana to the Gulf of Mexico, sailed to Cuba, then traveled to Panama and crossed the Isthmus where, more than thirty years later, President Theodore Roosevelt would advocate building of an ocean-linking canal.

Landing in San Francisco in 1868, Muir walked across the San Joaquin Valley and into "the most beautiful of all the mountain chains I have ever seen." Settled in the region known as Yosemite, he eventually joined with Robert Underwood Johnson, associate editor of *Century* magazine, to advocate creation of Yosemite National Park, and to form the Sierra Club to "do something for wildness and make the mountains glad."

With publication in 1901 of a book, *Our National Parks*, Muir captured the attention and admiration of a new and powerful ally in Theodore Roosevelt. Convinced that Muir "of all people in the world was the one with whom it was best worth while thus to see the Yosemite," he was met by Muir, pack horses and mules to carry tents, food for a three-day trip, and bedding.

"The first night was clear," Roosevelt wrote, "and we lay down in the darkening aisles of the great sequoia grove. The majestic trunks, beautiful in symmetry, rose round us like the pillars of a mightier cathedral than ever was conceived even by the fervor of the Middle Ages."

Delighted by hermit thrushes that "sang beautifully in the evening and again, with a burst of wonderful music, at dawn," Roosevelt was "a little surprised" to find that Muir cared little for birds or bird songs, and knew little about them. "The hermit thrushes meant nothing to him," he recalled, the trees and the flowers and the cliffs everything. The only birds he noticed or cared for were some that were very conspicuous, such as the water-ousels—always particular favorites of mine too."

On the second night they camped in a snowstorm on the edge of the canyon walls. The next day, they went down into "the wonderland of the valley itself."

Still thrilled by the experience, Roosevelt later wrote to Muir, "I shall never forget our three camps; the first in the solemn temple of the giant sequoias; the next in the snowstorm among the silver firs near the brink of the cliff; and the third on the floor of the Yosemite, in the open valley, fronting the stupendous rocky mass of El Capitan, with the falls thundering in the distance on either hand."

Compared to the natural paradise of Yosemite, the national capital to which Roosevelt returned in June 1903 was a man-made place that broiled in a notoriously hellish heat that had sent previous presidents and their families, Cabinet officers, and members of Congress fleeing to cooler places. For Roosevelt it was Sagamore Hill, enjoying "the happiest, healthiest, most old-fashioned kind of summer" with his children and wife, he especially liked spending time with Edith. "We have ridden horseback much together," he wrote to sister Corinne, "and have frequently gone off for a day at a time in a rowboat, not to speak of the picnics upon which everybody went. In the intervals I have chopped industrially."

Among the guests that summer were Owen Wister, known to friends as Dan, and George Grinnell, with whom Roosevelt wanted to talk about Indian reservations and "incidentally some points on big-game zoology."

Ruminating about the bond between the president and himself in *My Friendship with Roosevelt*, Wister disputed a widely held belief that Roosevelt's demeanor was the result of a fondness for strong drink. He wrote, "I do not know how that ridiculous rumor that Roosevelt was intemperate ever gained currency, and was kept alive for so long. I can only surmise that the exuberance of manner, into which he could explode on almost any occasion when he was extremely diverted, or suddenly surprised by enthusiasm, gave it some show of likelihood among people who knew nothing about him, and whose minds were unequal to the effort of thinking."

Published in 1930 (eleven years after Roosevelt's death), Wister's memoir provided a portrait of America's most physically active president, to that time and since. "Any man doing Roosevelt's daily work," he wrote, "besides wrestling for exercise, walking pedestrians weary, riding fat majors and colonels to a bruised pulp (he rode a hundred miles at one stretch with Amos W. Barber, Governor of Wyoming and seasoned to the saddle, finishing fresh himself with Barber exhausted), hitting bear and elk accurately in the Rock Mountains, lions in Africa, able to rough it anywhere, is not the kind of person who habitually drinks too much."

Following Roosevelt's claim on the presidency in his own right in the 1904 election, it was to Wister that he explained his victory came not from "the politicians" and the "financiers," but "to the folk who work hard on the farm, in shop, or on the railroads, or who own little stores, little businesses which they manage themselves." He continued, "I would literally, not figuratively, rather cut off my right hand than forfeit by any improper act of mine the trust and regard of these people. I may have to do something of which they will disapprove, because I deem it absolutely right and necessary; but most assuredly I shall endeavor not to meet their disapproval by any act inconsistent with the ideal they have formed of me."

Analyzing this appeal among "the folk," Roosevelt biographer H.W. Brands saw him, as the title of his book declared, "The Last Romantic." But the ideal that the public had formed, Brands noted, was largely a reflection of Roosevelt's view of himself. Brands wrote:

> Better than any president since Lincoln, Roosevelt embodied a romanticized view of American life. His was no rags-to-riches story, to be sure, but then the rags of that hoary tale had never been as popular as the riches, as long as the rich man didn't put on airs, which Roosevelt conspicuously didn't. Many politicians affected the common touch; some affected it quite persuasively. But for Roosevelt it was no affectation. He really did feel a bond with the "plain people" of America. Not for years had he shared their life, the way he did in Dakota, but his political trips across the country, especially through the West, periodically reconnected him to his adopted roots.

Owen Wister's reference to Roosevelt's "wrestling for exercise" referred to Roosevelt's decision in early 1904 to hire two Japanese wrestlers to give him lessons in the art of jiu-jitsu three times a week. Revealing this astonishing turn of events to sons Ted and Kermit in a letter dated March 5, Roosevelt was reassuring. "I am not the age or the build one would think to be whirled lightly over an opponent's head and batted down on a mattress without damage," he wrote. "But they are so skillful that I have not been hurt at all. My throat is a little sore, because once when one of them had a strangle hold I also got hold of his windpipe and thought I could perhaps choke him off before he could choke me. However, he got ahead."

In a letter to Ted dated April 9 he said that he was "very glad I have been doing this Japanese wrestling, but when I am through with it this time I am not sure I shall ever try it again while I am so busy with other work as I am now. Often by the time I get to five o'clock in the afternoon I will be feeling like a stewed owl, after an eight hours' grapple with Senators, Congressmen, etc."

The tussles with Congress and others which marked the Roosevelt agenda had centered on criticism of the administration's foreign policy, especially U.S. intervention in a rebellion in Colombia by insurgents seeking independence for Panama. Seeing an opportunity for the United States to complete a long-abandoned French project to carve out a canal linking the Atlantic and Pacific Oceans, he told a reluctant Congress, "Under such circumstances the government of the United States would have been guilty of folly and weakness, amounting in their sum to a crime against the nation, had it not acted otherwise than it did in the revolution of November 3 last took place in Panama. This great enterprise of building the inter-oceanic canal cannot be held up to gratify the whims, or out of respect to the governmental impotence, or to the even more sinister and evil peculiarities, of people who, though they dwell afar off, yet against the wish of the actual dwellers on the Isthmus, assert an unreal supremacy over the territory."

At the end of May, following a visit to Washington by Ted and Kermit, he wrote to Ted that despite having "a reasonable amount of work and rather more than a reasonable amount of worry" associated with living and working in the Executive Mansion, "I do not think that any two people ever got more enjoyment out of the White House than Mother and I. We love the house itself, without and within, for its associations, for its stillness and its simplicity. We love the garden. And we like Washington."

When he wrote this letter, he had been president for more than two-and-a-half years, but, in his words, "an accidental" one because he had come into office as the result of the assassination of McKinley. Whether the American people would deem him worthy to continue in office in the November 1904 election remained to be seen. With confidence that the people would do so, he asserted, "I am sure that the policies for which I stand are those in accordance with which this country must be governed, and up to which we must all live in public and private life, under penalty of grave disaster to the nation."

On the campaign trail he coined a motto for his kind of government, declaring, "We must treat each man on his worth and merits as a man. We must see that each is given a square deal, because he is entitled to no more and should receive no less."

When he won 7.6 million votes and his Democratic Party opponent, Alton P. Parker, got 5.1 million, he cabled Senator Henry Cabot Lodge, "Have swept the country by majorities which astound me."

Basking in the confidence of voters and looking ahead to being sworn in as president in his own right, he welcomed reporters to cover the White House Thanksgiving Day celebration. At one point in the festivities the smaller children were seen chasing a turkey around the grounds as their father looked on laughingly. Also watching the spectacle, a correspondent for the Boston *Herald* found nothing funny in it and wrote that he considered it cruelty to an animal. Infuriated by the story, the president accused the reporter of "deliberate fabrication" and ordered agencies of the government to drop the *Herald* from lists of publications which received press releases. On behalf of the children, he also demanded a retraction and a printed apology. After the paper complied, the news embargo was lifted.

While Roosevelt could protest reports of his children harassing a turkey, he found himself unable to prevent press attention to his vivacious first-born. He wrote to Ted about Alice, "Sister continues to lead the life of social excitement, which I think is all right for a girl to lead for a year or two, but I do not regard it as healthy from the standpoint of permanence. I wish she had some pronounced serious taste."

Pretty, teenage Alice Lee Roosevelt had created such a whirl of "social excitement" that reporters named her "Alice in Wonderland." She flaunted propriety by smoking, placing bets at the racetrack, and driving a red run-about through Washington at breakneck speeds. At a White House dinner on January 12, 1905, attended by Henry James, Henry Adams, sculptor Augustus Saint-Gaudens and other luminaries, an eager press was interested in knowing only what Alice did, what Alice said, what Alice wore. With her good looks, stylish dresses and cartwheel hats, she caught every eye and all ears listened for her latest bon mot.

Speculation concerning whom Alice might choose for a husband came to an abrupt and astonishing end when she announced her engagement to Congressman Nicholas Longworth, and that the nuptials would occur on February 16, 1906, in the East Room of the White House.

Alice did not disappoint. She let it be known that there would be no bridesmaids. The spotlight would be on her alone. After the exchange of vows, she surprised her stepmother by kissing Edith on the cheek. At the reception protocol was abandoned. "If the Secretary of State ranked the chambermaid," remarked White House usher Ike Hoover, "no one worried about it this day." When time came to cut the cake, Alice used a sword, grabbed from the hand of a startled military aide.

Three months after Alice's wedding, the presidential father of the bride again gave in to the lure of the West by going to Texas for a Rough Riders reunion and on to Oklahoma "for a few days' coyote coursing in the Comanche Reserve." He teamed with local ranchers, a few army officers, including two who had served in the Rough Riders, and professional wolf hunter Jack "Catch-'em alive" Abernethy. The nickname had been earned by "the really remarkable feat of jumping on to the wolf," Roosevelt explained in a letter to Ted. "He never used a knife or a rope in taking these wolves, seizing them by sheer quickness and address and thrusting his hand into the wolf's mouth in such a way that it lost all power to bite."

The dogs on the hunts were half a dozen "sets" of greyhounds, the only breed able to keep up with the speedy coyote.

"It was a thoroughly congenial company all through," Roosevelt noted. "The weather was good; we were in the saddle from morning until night; and our camp was in all respects all that a camp should be; so how could we help enjoying ourselves?"

The hunters ventured onto flats and great rolling prairies that stretched north of the camp in the direction of the Wichita Mountains and south toward the Red River. With Roosevelt on a "beautiful Kiowa pony, the sky bright and beautiful, and the air just cool enough to be pleasant, the riders shuffled along, strung out in an irregular line that invoked images of Lt. Col. Roosevelt and the cowboy cavalry known as the Rough Riders who had trained near San Antonio seven years earlier. Barely twenty minutes out of camp, they spied a pair of coyotes three or four hundred yards in front. As dogs and horses raced at them, the coyotes edged to the left where a creek's deep banks and narrow fringe of timber promised cover. "The little wolves knew their danger and ran their very fastest," Roosevelt recalled with admiration, "while the long dogs stretched out after them, gaining steadily. It was evident that the chase would be a short one, and there was no need to husband the horses, so every man let his pony go for all there was in him."

At the end of the last day of the hunt, Abernethy "suddenly appeared, his tired hounds trotting behind him, while he carried before him on the saddle a live coyote." It made "curiously little effort to fight with its paws," Roosevelt observed, "seeming to acquiesce in its captivity, and looking around, with its ears thrust forward, as if more influenced by curiosity than by any other feeling."

In five days of hunting the party claimed seventeen coyote, three raccoons, and numerous rattlesnakes. Brimming with enthusiasm, Roosevelt wrote to Kermit, "It was tremendous [fun] galloping over cut banks, prairie dog towns, flats, creek bottoms, everything. One run was nine miles long and I was the only man in at the finish except [Abernethy]. We were in the saddle eight or nine hours every day."

Moving on to Colorado, he joined John Goff, his "old guide on the mountain lion hunt," and another guide, Jake Borah. Once again in "a great, wild country" on a bear hunt for the first time using dogs, he discovered he was the center of attention for "some twenty good-natured, hard riding young fellows from the ranches within a radius of a dozen miles" who couldn't resist the temptation to "see a president kill a bear." Reporting to Ted in a letter dated April 20, 1905, from Glenwood Springs, he wrote, "Up here we have opened well."

On the third day the chase for "a fine black bear, an old male" lasted nearly two hours and ended with "a hard scramble up a canyon side." Before Roosevelt killed it with a shot from a 30-40 Springfield rifle that "worked to perfection" the bear killed one of the pursing dogs and crippled three. Among the pack were dogs Roosevelt remembered fondly from the mountain lion hunt, including Tree 'em, Bruno, Jim, and four terriers. One of the other hounds was "a preposterous animal who looked as if his ancestry had included a toadfish."

The dog that captured Roosevelt's heart was a little black-and-tan terrier. Called Skip, he was a "most friendly little fellow," affectionate and intelligent, and "especially fond of riding in front or behind the saddle of anyone who would take him up, although he was perfectly able to travel forty miles a day on his own sturdy legs if he had to." When there was a bear or lynx at bay, he joined the fight "with all the fury of a bulldog."

On one chase the quarry was pursued across snowy ground and treed "far up in the mountainside in the thick spruce timber. Because the horses could not get through the snow, Roosevelt, Goff, and the fascinated cowboys proceeded on foot. After half an hour of hard-going they sighted a female bear about forty feet up a tall spruce. Admiring the bear's glossy black-brown coat, Roosevelt first feared that she might come down, but reasoned that after running for about four hours, she would not have "the slightest idea of putting herself of her own free will within reach of the pack, which was now baying at the foot of the tree."

Roosevelt aimed for the bear's heart. As the bullet struck, she climbed higher "with great agility." Then her muscles relaxed, and "down she came, nearly burying herself in the snow." One of the first dogs to seize her was Skip, but "in another moment he literally disappeared under the hounds as they piled on the bear."

While zestfully recalling this bear hunt in *Outdoor Pastimes of an American Hunter,* the intrepid amateur ornithologist diligently noted that in bushes by streams "the handsome white-crowned sparrows and green-tailed towhees were in full song, making attractive music; although the song of neither can rightly be compared in point of plaintive beauty with that of the white-throated sparrow, which, except some of the thrushes, and perhaps the winter wren, is the sweetest singer of the Northeastern forests."

With the hunt over and trophies on the backs of the pack horses, Roosevelt, Goff, and the hounds headed for Glenwood Springs, hemmed in by lofty mountain chains. "As we left ever farther behind us the wintry desolation of our high hunting grounds," Roosevelt wrote, "we rode into full spring."

7

★ ★ ★

A Bear Named Teddy

H ERE I AM BACK AGAIN," reported the president of the United
States on May 14, 1905, to his second son, Kermit, who was away at
school. "Of course I was up to my ears in work as soon as I reached
the White House, but in two or three days we shall be through it and can
settle down into our old routine." Noting that Skip had accompanied him,
but that the little dog was not yet entirely at home in the White House, he
wrote, "He can stand any amount of hard work if there is a bear or bobcat
ahead, but now that he is in the White House he thinks he would much
rather do nothing but sit about all day with his friends, and threatens to turn
into a lap dog. But when we get him to Oyster Bay I think we can make him
go out riding with us."

Another place to take Skip for riding and romping that was closer to the
White House at this time was a country retreat in the form of a cottage in
woods near Charlottesville, Virginia, named Pine Knot. "I am immensely
pleased with Mother's Virginia cottage and its name," the president told
Kermit. "It is a perfectly delightful little place; the nicest little place of the
kind you can imagine." Most pleasing was the piazza. Broad and running
along the whole length of the cottage, it was ideal for sitting in a rocking
chair and hearing "all the birds by daytime and at night the whippoorwills
and owls and little forest folk."

When Kermit and Ted came home from Harvard to spend summer vacation at Sagamore Hill, they discovered that the parent who called himself "Big Bear" was not as quick to join in the usual athletic pastimes. Admitting to being out of condition as a result of too much eating, not exercising enough and working in a "sedentary fashion," Roosevelt felt that he had become "both old and fat." He told Henry Cabot Lodge that he had "reached that time of life when too violent exercise does not rest a man when he has had an exhausting mental career."

What had not changed was the liveliness and quality of conversation at the dinner table. On the agenda through 1905 and 1906 were efforts to negotiate an end to a war between Russia and Japan, seemingly incessant squabbles of European Powers, anti-Asianism among citizens on the West Coast who demanded restrictions on Japanese immigration, and a movement that favored U. S. intervention in Cuba against insurgents who threatened the interests of the American sugar trust.

"If I am forced to intervene," asserted the hero of San Juan Hill and famous fighter for *Cuba Libre,* "it will be not until it is evident that no other course is left me. Just at the moment I am so angry with the infernal little Cuban republic that I would like to wipe its people off the face of the earth."

Domestic issues included a perennial issue of tariff rates, regulations regarding railroads, and a Roosevelt plan to impose federal food and drug inspections. When Congress passed a pure food and drug law, he claimed that the measure, along with passage of a railroad rate bill, "mark a noteworthy advance in the policy of securing Federal supervision and control of corporations."

Then Theodore Roosevelt surprised everyone by announcing his intention to become the first sitting president to leave the country, to see how the work was progressing on the Panama Canal. Accordingly, he and Edith boarded the U.S.S. *Louisiana* on November 8, 1905.

The former assistant secretary of the navy who had once labored to create a world-class American fleet toured the ship and declared, "It gives me great pride in America to be aboard this great battleship and to see not only the material perfection of the ship herself in engines, guns and all arrangements, but the fine quality of the officers and crew."

After surveying the progress of "the big ditch" being gouged across the isthmus, he took great delight in operating one of the huge earth moving shovels. He found the work on the canal "being done with a very high degree of efficiency and honesty."

Sailing toward home on November 20, 1905, he wrote so vividly to Ted at Harvard that Ted felt as if he were also on the *Louisiana:*

> This is the third day out from Panama. We have been steaming steadily in the teeth of the trade wind. It has blown pretty hard, and the ship has pitched a little, but not enough to make either Mother or me uncomfortable.
>
> Panama was a great sight. In the first place it was strange and beautiful with its mass of luxuriant tropic jungle, with the treacherous tropic rivers trailing here and there through it; and it was lovely to see the orchids and brilliant butterflies and the strange birds and snakes and lizards, and finally the strange old Spanish towns and the queer thatch and bamboo huts of the ordinary natives. In the next place it is a tremendous sight to see the work of the canal going on.

On March 3, 1907, the eve of the second anniversary of being sworn in as president in his own right, with Ted and Kermit at school, third-son Archibald (called Archie) stricken with diphtheria, daughter Ethel "away at Philadelphia," and the youngest child, Quentin, "not allowed to see other little boys [because of Archie's illness] and leading a career of splendid isolation among the [White House] ushers and policemen," Roosevelt wrote to Kermit that since he'd returned from Panama, "I have not done a thing except work as the President must during the closing days of a session of Congress."

In mid-May, after hosting a Japanese general at a formal dinner, the president who had been instrumental in settling the Russo-Japanese War noted that Japan's army and navy were "a formidable outfit," that he wanted to try to keep on "best possible terms with Japan and never do her any wrong, but "I want still more to see our navy maintained at the highest point of efficiency, for it is the real keeper of the peace."

The next day, May 12, 1907, the First Family discovered that Skip had disappeared, but at two in the morning on the 13th the president heard "a sharp little bark" downstairs and knew it was Skip. "So down I went and opened the door on the portico," he related to Kermit, "and Skip simply scuttled in and up to Archie's room."

Six months later, the entire family was plunged into mourning when the beloved little dog died at Sagamore Hill. "We mourn little Skip," Roosevelt

noted, "although perhaps it was as well the little doggie should pass pain-
lessly away, after his happy little life." But on September 28, it was a trio of
snakes that momentarily occupied his mind. Brought home by Quentin
from an animal store, they were "eagerly deposited" in his lap while the president was discussing several matters with the Attorney General. Roosevelt
suggested that Quentin take the reptiles into the adjoining room where four
congressmen were "drearily waiting until I should be at leisure."

At first the congressmen thought the snakes were wooden ones. Only
when they saw one of them recoil did they realize they were alive. When one
of them, three or four feet long, went up Quentin's sleeve, President Roosevelt watched with glee as one of the congressmen "gingerly helped him
[Quentin] off with his jacket, so as to let the snake crawl out of the upper end
of the sleeve."

A few days later, Roosevelt again welcomed an opportunity to leave the
White House, this time for a trip through the West and South, ending with a
hunting excursion in Louisiana. On October 1, 1907, he wrote to Kermit from
his cabin on the U.S.S. *Mississippi*, "It was my first trip of the Mississippi
River, and I am greatly interested in it. How wonderful in its rapidity movement has been the history of our country, compared with the history of the
old world. For untold ages this river had been flowing through the lonely
continent, not very greatly changed since the close of the Pleistocene Age.
During all those myriads the prairie and the forest came down to its banks.
The immense herds of the buffalo and the elk wandered along them season
after season, and the Indian hunters or in canoes trudged along the banks or
skimmed the water."

On October 6, he was camped on Tennessee Bayou. The big picturesque
camp had a fly tent for the horses and hunting hounds. There was a white
hunter, Ben Lily. A "really remarkable character," he had tramped, with one
dog, for twenty-four hours through the woods, without food or water, and
had slept a couple of hours in a crooked tree, like a wild turkey." He had a
mild, gentle face, blue eyes, and full beard, was a religious fanatic, and was as
"hardy as a bear or elk, literally caring nothing for fatigue and exposure."

Writing to Archie on October 16, he reported, "We have had no luck with
the bear; but we have killed as many deer as we needed for meat, and the
hounds caught a wildcat." But in a P.S. he joyfully noted, "I have just killed a
bear." Telling Ted of the success, he admitted that he'd shot it "more by luck
than anything, as it was a difficult shot."

*   *   *

In taking the Louisiana hunting trip, Roosevelt understood that his activities would be of interest to editors of newspapers across the country whose readers never seemed to grow tired of stories about their colorful president. Since his first appearance on the floor of the New York State Assembly, Theodore Roosevelt had been portrayed as a rising political star. That he was a man with the right stuff in him had been shown in the figure of the dashing war hero leading the cowboy cavalry up Kettle Hill in the San Juan Heights. As president, he had been depicted as the doting father of boisterous children that reporters affectionately termed "the White House gang." But none of this coverage had endeared him quite so much as a story about a bear-hunt in 1902 in Mississippi. Like the 1907 Louisiana outing, the hunt had proved disappointing because of the scarcity of bears. When, at last, a large bear was run down by hounds and roped, Roosevelt was invited to shoot it. Declaring the prospect unsportsmanlike, he'd refused to kill it. When word of this reached Clifford K. Berryman, a cartoonist for the *Washington Post,* he drew the drama with the caption "Drawing the line in Mississippi" that touched the hearts of the paper's readers. The cartoon also inspired Brooklyn, New York, toy shop owner Morris Beacham to make a stuffed bear for children that he wanted to call a "Teddy bear." But before daring to do so, he wrote to Roosevelt for permission to use his nickname. In one of the great presidential misjudgments of all time Roosevelt answered, "I don't think my name will mean much to the bear business, but you're welcome to use it."

Another toy maker who followed Beacham's lead produced a mechanical "Teddy" bank showing Roosevelt aiming a rifle at a tree. When a coin was placed atop the barrel and a spring was released, the coin catapulted into a slot in the tree trunk, causing the top of the trunk to pop open and a bear to emerge. (Such banks were all the rage at the time and have become desirable, and expensive, collectors' items, even as latter-day reproductions.)

While preceding and successive presidents attracted news coverage for their acumen as fishermen, including Cleveland, Coolidge, Hoover, Truman, Eisenhower, and George H. W. and George W. Bush; and Ronald Reagan was often pictured emulating Theodore Roosevelt by chopping down trees and clearing brush, only "Teddy" is indelibly remembered in presidential history as being comfortable with gun in hand, trekking through forests, riding across plains, and trudging through Southern cane breaks and bayous with his heart set on shooting a bear.

Certainly, no president knew as much about American bears as Theodore

Roosevelt, and he was eager to share what he knew with others by writing about them. Holding forth on the topic in *The Wilderness Hunter*, he provided the following primer on the many species and varieties of bear found in the United States:

> One is the small black bear, a bear which will average about two hundred pounds weight, with fine, glossy, black fur, and the fore-claws but little longer than the hinder ones; in fact the hairs of the fore-paw often reach to their tips. This bear is a tree climber. It is the only kind found east of the great plains, and it is also plentiful in the forest-clad portions of the Rockies, being common in most heavily timbered tracts throughout the United States. The other is the grisly [TR's spelling], which weighs three or four times as much as the black, and has a pelt of coarse hair which is in color gray, grissled, or brown of various shades. It is not a tree climber, and the fore-claws are very long, much longer than the hinder ones. It is found from the great plains west of the Mississippi to the Pacific coast. This bear inhabits indifferently lowland and mountain; the deep woods, and the barren plains where the only cover is the stunted growth fringing the streams . . . The grisly is now chiefly a beast of the high hills and heavy timber; but this is merely because he has learned that he must rely on cover to guard him from man, and has forsaken the open ground accordingly.

Roosevelt's quarry on the Louisiana hunt was the black bear. Finding the original camp at Tensas Bayou unrewarding, the party shifted about twenty miles to the encouragingly named Bear Lake. A tranquil stretch of water that was part of an ancient river bed, it was a few hundred yards wide and several miles long. Giant cypress trees grew at the edge, their "knees" rising in every direction, while their bottoms were marked by cavernous openings beneath the surface of the water, and, as Roosevelt observed, serving as dens for alligators.

"From our new camp we hunted as steadily as from the old," the eager bear-hunter from the White House wrote. "We saw bear sign, but not much of it, and only one or two fresh tracks. One day the hounds jumped a bear, probably a yearling from the way it ran. After a three hours' run it managed to get clear without one of the hunters ever seeing it, and it ran until the dogs were tired out."

Disappointed but undaunted, Roosevelt and a professional hunter, Clive

Metcalf, along with others, set out the next morning to follow tracks of a female that they'd spotted the day before. After an hour or two of waiting in the shelter of a canebreak, they heard, "very far off, the notes of the loudest-mouthed hounds," and instantly rode toward them. Some hard galloping brought them to the probable line of a bear's flight, and the spots at which it could be expected to break cover. But on this occasion the bear failed to do so, requiring another gallop through bushes and dodging in and out among the tree trunks.

"We had all we could do to prevent the vines from lifting us out of the saddle, while the thorns tore at our hands and faces," wrote Roosevelt of the chase. "Hither and thither we went, now at a trot, now at a run, now stopping to listen for the pack. Occasionally we could hear the hounds, and then we would go racing through the forest toward the point for which we thought they were heading."

Hearing the baying of the dogs, the hunters galloped as near the spot as they could, got off their horses, and plunged into the cane, trying to cause as little disturbance as possible. But before they came within gunshot, the bear was again on the move in what was called a "walking bay." Well-acquainted with ways of bears, Metcalf led Roosevelt to a spot where he expected the quarry to pass. Crouching with rifle at the ready, Roosevelt didn't have long to wait. Peering through the thick-growing cane stalks, he suddenly made out the dim outline of the bear coming straight toward him. Noiselessly cocking and half-raising the rifle, he waited for a clearer chance to shoot.

When the bear appeared, it turned almost broadside to Roosevelt, then walked forward with a stiff-legged gait, "almost as if on tiptoe," now and then looking back at the nearest dogs. With the bear partially blocked by cane about twenty yards away, Roosevelt aimed at the bear's outline, pointing at the shoulder. When the shot hit, the bear stumbled and fell forward with a bullet passing through both lungs and coming out the opposite side. It was a female, very lean, and weighing 202 pounds.

After the death of what he called "my bear," with only a couple of days left of the hunt, the party moved again, having to cross two bayous before reaching the next shooting ground. A shot at a deer missed, leaving Roosevelt to describe, as only he could, "the flicker of its white tail through the dense bushes." At the end of the hunt, he noted for the record, "we killed and brought into camp three bears, six deer, a wildcat, a turkey, a possum, and a dozen squirrels, and we ate everything except the wildcat."

In the evenings they sat around the blazing campfires as each hunter "told tales of his adventures and of the strange feats and habits of the beasts of the wilderness."

While Roosevelt could always spin a good yarn, he was content on such occasions to let the others talk. As historian Stephen E. Ambrose wrote in his introduction to a paperback reprint of *Hunting Trips of a Ranchman* and *The Wilderness Hunter,* "He was a great listener. Many of the hunting stories he tells he heard around the campfire. He seldom identifies a specific source, [but this] gives the stories a timeless quality."

When Roosevelt returned to the capital, he found little time to bask in the remembered delights and rewards of bear hunting as some of the nation's vital financial institutions failed and others appeared to be on the brink of collapse. After negotiations with financier J.P. Morgan and other Wall Street moguls, the crisis eased in the form of a statement issued by Morgan. In the president's name, it confidently asserted that "underlying conditions which make up our financial and industrial well being are essentially sound and honest."

Wall Street reacted with a vigorous rally, triggering an end to what became known as the Panic of 1907. But when details of the deal which had been struck between the White House and the House of Morgan became known, Roosevelt was excoriated for agreeing to "a scheme" in which Mr. Morgan's U.S. Steel corporation was able to reap a financial windfall. Explaining the deal in his *Autobiography,* published in 1913, Roosevelt said, "It was necessary for me to decide on the instant." To stop the panic it was necessary to restore confidence. The only way to do so, he asserted, was to turn to Morgan. "The result justified my judgment," Roosevelt wrote. "The panic was stopped, public confidence in the solvency of the threatened institution being at once restored."

With the turning of the calendar from 1907 to 1908, the nation's politicians wondered if Roosevelt would stand by his pledge, made after his 1904 victory, not to seek re-election. With pressures increasing on him for a decision, Republican leaders urged him to make up his mind soon, so that if he chose not run, the party would have time to organize the nomination of a standard-bearer. As he weighed the pros and cons of running again, he electrified the country with a show of American power in the world by announcing that a "great white fleet" of warships would unfurl the Stars and Stripes in the major ports of the world in a globe-circling cruise. As the sixteen white-painted battleships got under way from Hampton Roads, Virginia, they passed in review for the former assistant secretary of the navy who was now a commander-in-chief whose declared foreign policy was "Speak softly, but carry a big stick." Beaming with pride, Roosevelt gazed at the gleaming armada and asked, "Did you ever see such a fleet? Isn't it magnificent? Oughtn't we all feel proud?"

The fleet's odyssey would prove a resounding success, and as the ships steamed into port again at Hampton Roads on February 22, 1909, the president would be there to greet them. "Not until some American fleet returns victorious from a great sea battle," he declared solemnly, "will there be another such homecoming."

Early in May 1908 President and Mrs. Roosevelt sought the peace and quiet of Pine Knot in the company of Roosevelt's naturalist-friend John Burroughs.

The woodsy respite was "great fun," Roosevelt reported in a letter to Ted, now a senior at Harvard, but there had been an event one night in which Burroughs "fell into great disgrace" because of a nest of flying squirrels. In residence at Pine Knot since the previous Christmas in the room Ted slept in, and which had been assigned to Burroughs, they had "raised a brood" that at night "held high carnival."

"Mother and I do not mind them at all," Roosevelt wrote, "and indeed rather like to hear them scrambling about, and then as a sequel to a sudden frantic fight between two of them, hearing or seeing one little fellow come plum down to the floor and scuffle off again to the wall. But one night they waked up John Burroughs and he spent a misguided hour hunting for the nest, and when he found it took it down and caught two of the squirrels and put them in a basket. The next day under Mother's direction I took them out, getting my fingers somewhat bitten in the process, and loosed them in our room, where we had previously put back the nest. I do not think John Burroughs profited by his misconduct, because the squirrels were more active than ever that night in his room and ours, the disturbance in their family affairs having evidently made them restless!"

During the presidential campaign, the nation's most famous hunter and a president who would be a lame duck predicted victory for the Republican candidate, William Howard Taft. In the expectation that because Taft would carry on Roosevelt policies, he ventured the opinion that Taft would rank with any other man [excluding Washington and Lincoln] who has ever been in the White House."

Taft's opponent, third-time presidential aspirant and long-time Roosevelt nemesis, William Jennings Bryan, was "the cheapest faker we have ever had proposed for president."

Raging at criticism leveled by the opposition press at the record of the past seven years, Roosevelt declared, "I don't think the worst politicians or the worst businessmen reach the level of infamy attained by so many newspapermen. I happen to have seen recently editorials from all these papers which for malignant mendacity, whether purchased or unpurchased, come well up to anything I have known. I do not think there is any form of lying slander at which these men would stop."

Roosevelt the naturalist considered replying to the critics the same as the task of skinning skunks. It was not a pleasant occupation, he said, and while he was "glad to get rid of the skunks, it is at least an open question whether the game is worth the candle."

By mid-October he was feeling so optimistic about a Taft victory that he expected to see "substantially the electoral vote of four years ago." He was right. Taft garnered a large majority, although a smaller one than Roosevelt's in 1904. Expressing confidence that his successor's "policies, principles, purposes and ideals are the same as mine," he had "profound satisfaction" in "knowing that he will do all in his power to further every one of the great causes for which I have fought and that he will preserve in every one of the great governmental policies in which I most firmly believe."

With the campaign over and his man elected, Roosevelt spent a day "taking a scramble walk over Rock Creek." Recounting the outing to Archie in a letter dated November 8, he told of coming to "that smooth-face of rock which we got round by holding on to the little butt of a knob that we call the Button." But when he gripped the knob, its top broke off between forefinger and thumb. "I hadn't supposed that I was putting much weight on," he continued, "but evidently I was, for I promptly lost my balance, and finding I was falling, I sprang into the creek. There were big rocks in it, and the water was rather shallow, but I landed all right and didn't hurt myself the least bit in the world."

The youngest man to be elected president, a record held until John F. Kennedy took office in 1961, he was, therefore, the youngest president to ponder the question of what to do after leaving office. "Every now and then," he'd written to Ted, "solemn jacks come to me to tell me that our country must face the problem of 'what it will do with its ex-presidents.' I always answer them that there will be one ex-president about whom they need not give themselves the slightest concern, for he will do for himself without any outside assistance; and I add that they need waste no sympathy on me—that I have had the best time of any man of my age in all the world, that I have enjoyed myself in the White House more than I have ever known any President to enjoy himself, and that I am going to enjoy myself thoroly [Roosevelt had adopted a controversial system of phonetic spelling] when I leave the White House, and what is more, continue just as long as I possibly can to do some kind of work that will count."

As ex-president, "instead of leading a perfectly silly and vacuous life around the clubs or in sporting fields," he intended to enjoy himself. Consequently, he listened intently to a guest at a White House dinner expound on the natural glories and animal life of the Alaska Territory. As everyone entered the State Dining Room, Roosevelt turned to another adventurer, Carl Akeley, who claimed Africa as his "back yard," and exclaimed, "When I am through with this job, I am going to Alaska for a good hunt."

Seated beside Roosevelt in anticipation of having "an excellent dinner," Akeley found himself peppered with questions from Roosevelt that came so rapidly that Akeley had little time to eat. Among the stories that the hunter-president devoured with gusto involved sixteen lions that were seen emerging from a cave. As Akeley described them, he found himself competing with several congressmen who were eager to claim Roosevelt's attention. Finally, with great irritation, Roosevelt said to one of them, "Congressman, I wish I had those sixteen lions to turn loose on Congress."

"But, Mr. President," said the congressman with a smile, "aren't you afraid that they might make a mistake?"

Roosevelt replied, "Not if they stayed long enough."

When the last course of the meal was finished, Akeley hoped to continue his regaling of Roosevelt with stories of hunting in Africa, but Roosevelt had evidently heard enough. Rising from his chair, he announced, "When I am through with this job, I am going to Africa."

With an astonished look, the man from the far north blurted, "But what about Alaska?"

Eyes already alight with anticipation of hunting lions and other exotic game of the "Dark Continent," Roosevelt replied, "Alaska will have to wait."

PART THREE

★ ★ ★

Hurrah for Africa

★ ★ ★

"Health to the Lions!"

WITHIN THREE WEEKS after observing William Howard Taft take the oath of office as the twenty-seventh president of the United States, the twenty-sixth, along with his second son, Kermit, and a small group of professional naturalists, boarded an eastbound ship at Hoboken, New Jersey. Observing the departure from the dock, Henry Cabot Lodge gazed at his happy friend waving from the ship's bridge. "In all the striking incidents of your career," he later wrote to Roosevelt, "I never saw one which impressed me more. It was not merely the crowd but the feeling which was manifested which was so striking."

Enthusiasm at seeing Roosevelt embark was of a different stripe among Wall Street tycoons who had felt the bite of Theodore Roosevelt's trust-busting policies. Some lifted glasses of champagne in the macabre toast, "Health to the lions." The nation's most powerful financier, J.P. Morgan, expressed the hope that the lions would "do their duty."

Conspicuously absent at the send-off was President Taft, but he had sent as farewell gifts a gold ruler and an autographed photograph of himself. The accompanying letter said in part, "When I am addressed as Mr. President, I turn to see whether you are not at my elbow."

Keenly aware of speculation in political circles and the press that although Taft was the president Roosevelt would lurk nearby to manipulate Taft like a puppeteer pulling the strings, and this on his mind, Roosevelt had confided to newspaperman William Allen White, "My main reason for wishing to go to Africa for a year is so that I can get where no one can accuse me of running [the U.S. government] nor do Taft the injustice of accusing him of permitting me to run the job." This explanation for the African odyssey only served to underscore the widely held conviction that Roosevelt considered himself the indispensable man who fully expected Taft's presidency to be a continuation of Roosevelt policies. Had Roosevelt chosen to be truthful with William Allen White, rather than a politician, regarding the reason for going to Africa, he would have given White the reply he'd made to another questioner about the purpose of the journey. "I feel that this is my last chance," he said, "for something in the nature of a great adventure."

If his desire had been to yield the limelight to Taft, that intent was not reflected in the itinerary that he planned to follow after concluding the proposed African safari. His first stop was to be England on the invitation of the chancellor of Oxford University to add his name to a roster of distinguished historical, political, and literary personalities who had delivered the Romanes Lectures. He would also go across the Channel to the continent and make his way to Oslo, Norway, for a formal acceptance of the Nobel Peace Prize for his arbitration that ended the Russo-Japanese War. Upon returning to the United States, he planned to become a contributing editor of the magazine *Outlook* (at a salary of $12,000 a year).

To assure that he would not fade from the thoughts and hearts of the American people during his one-year hiatus in the African wilds, he would depart the United States with a contract from *Scribner's Magazine* for $50,000 to write twelve articles to be published monthly while he was on safari, then brought out in book form for which he would receive author royalties.

He anticipated that his every move would be pounced on by an ever-avaricious press that never got its fill of stories about Teddy Roosevelt with a gun in his hand and wild beasts as his quarry. About having been hounded by reporters in the West, he told his friend Archie Butt, "I feel absolutely ferocious at times when I am not allowed to have a moment to myself."

As to that, he expressed confidence that English newspapermen would not attempt to follow him, "for the English are rather decent in such matters." Should he feel harried by "our own people," he hoped that he would be able to get the authorities in Africa "to intervene until I elude them [reporters] in the wilds." Finding amusement in the prospect of dodging the press, he vowed to Archie Butt, "They will never catch up with me if I get ahead of them once, and if they do in the jungle you may see my expense report to the National Museum [a financial underwriter of the safari] read something after this order: 'One hundred dollars for buying the means to rid myself of one *World* reporter; three hundred dollars expended in dispatching a reporter of the *American;* five hundred dollars for furnishing wine to the tribal chiefs with which to wash down a reporter of the New York *Evening Post.*"

Concerning feeding himself and his safari companions, aside from dining on the flesh of African wildlife, a veteran African hunter/explorer, Frederick Selous, advised taking along "a certain number of delicacies and traveling in comfort." Excited by visions of himself going after Africa's exotic animal inhabitants, he told Selous, "I have never shot dangerous game, unless you can call the very few grizzly bears I have shot dangerous."

Writing to Selous in the summer of 1908, he peppered the expert for recommendations on the ideal weaponry for going after lions, hippos, elephants, and every other species. He also sought to elicit advice in a letter to an outfitter of safaris in Nairobi on the best time of year to go. "People have told me that I can not start with a caravan in the rainy season," he wrote, while other people had told him that it was not only "entirely possible" to venture forth in the rainy season, but that "is a good season."

To conservationists and other animal lovers who voiced alarm of witnessing a Teddy Roosevelt onslaught against unwitting, innocent animals for the sheer sport of it, Roosevelt was quick to assure them that his expedition was a scientific one on behalf of collecting specimens for the Smithsonian museum.

Sounding the same note to a British official in Kenya, he explained, "Except for actual food—and these only to the extent that I am permitted under your general regulations—I shall merely desire to get one specimen, or perhaps one specimen of the male and one of the female of each of the different kinds of game, for the National Museum at Washington."

To pay for the journey he dipped into his bank account for $20,000 to augment funds from the Smithsonian, then beseeched philanthropist–steel tycoon Andrew Carnegie to render "a great service to science" by providing additional money. Before the year in Africa was over the man who had been born in Scotland, arrived in the United States as a penniless youth, and then used a small part of one of the greatest personal fortunes in American history to finance the building of libraries across the country found himself being asked for an additional $30,000 because Roosevelt's expedition had run out of funds.

While the safari would be taken in the company of professional experts of the game of Africa, along with native guides and a small army of bearers, Roosevelt wanted to share the experience with at least one of his two adult sons. His first choice was his namesake. But Ted begged off going. A senior at Harvard, he had fallen in love with beautiful, brainy, and vivacious Eleanor Alexander, and planned to marry her when Father returned from Africa.

Roosevelt then turned to his second-born son, Kermit, a second-year student at Harvard.

Born prematurely on October 10, 1889, while Roosevelt was serving on the Civil Service Commission, Kermit was, his mother wrote to a sister, a yellow-haired child with "big dark eyes, full of poetry." While Ted was a rambunctious boy, Kermit proved so quiet that Edith described him "as a good deal of a hermit" who "never need retire to a cloister for a life of abstraction."

When Kermit was a year old, his adoring father wrote to his own mother, "Kermit crawls with the utmost rapidity; and when he is getting towards some forbidden spot we call to him to stop. Ted always joins in officiously and overtaking the small yellow-haired wanderer seizes him with his chubby hands round the neck and trys (sic) to drag him back—while the enraged Kermit endeavors to retaliate. Kermie is a darling little fellow, so soft and sweet."

Always more intellectually inclined than his older brother, Kermit received letters from his father with accounts of exciting hunting adventures, but he was just as likely to open a letter to find a discussion of characters in books. Writing from the White House on February 12, 1908, Roosevelt said, "I quite agree with you about Tom Pinch. He is a despicable kind of character; just the kind of character Dickens liked, because he had himself a thick streak of maudlin sentimentality of the kind that, as somebody phrased it, 'made him wallow naked in the pathetic.' It always interests me about Dickens to think how much first-class work he did and how almost all of it was mixed up with every kind of cheap, second-rate matter."

The most bookish of the Roosevelt children, Kermit was one of his father's closest confidants, receiving almost daily letters in which Roosevelt shared his views on almost every subject. Like his robust parent, Kermit delighted in hunting, exploring, and history. He was also a linguist (Spanish and French) who had taught himself Greek and the gypsy language Romany. As avid a book-lover as Roosevelt, he read at least a book a day. But father and son differed in their mood. Roosevelt's was generally rosily spirited, optimistic, and embracing. Kermit was noted for long periods of brooding pessimism that once prompted his mother to describe her only fair-haired child as the one with the white head "and the black heart."

In a book about the Roosevelt sons, *The Lion's Pride*, Edward J. Renehan Jr. observed of Kermit, "His participation in family games and activities was always good-natured, but never joyous. As boys, while his brothers would happily trudge behind Roosevelt on his famous point-to-point hikes (in the course of which one might go over, under, through but never around obstacles), Kermit would follow doggedly and somberly while the others shouted and laughed. What was a game to the others was a gauntlet to Kermit. The boy was just as capable as any of his brothers, Roosevelt told one of his teachers. Where they succeeded, he likewise succeeded. But it was a question of attitude and motivation; that was where the 'fatal' difference lay, said Roosevelt."

Although Kermit had a sometimes difficult youth, and had been an indifferent student at the Groton School, the preparatory-school alma mater of both father and older brother, and with a year at Harvard behind him, at the age of nineteen, wrote Roosevelt biographer H.W. Brands, Kermit "seemed to be finding himself." In the summer of 1907, at seventeen, he had warmed the heart of the old colonel of the Rough Riders by going West to "rough it" with the Thirteenth Cavalry in Dakota.

More than his "big brother" Ted, Brands explained, Kermit had always been admired by their father as possessing an adventurous and romantic spirit that Roosevelt valued in himself and in others. Kermit doubtless saw, Brands surmised, what constant laboring in the shadow of a famous father— and having the same name—had cost Ted in his peace of mind because of relentless attention from the press and high expectations from everyone else.

Although Kermit was often more excited than his father about adventuring in Africa, Roosevelt occasionally had second thoughts about taking him on what would certainly be a very arduous odyssey on a continent that was plagued by mysterious diseases that were simply termed "fever." Roosevelt confided to an expert of the subject, "I have been a little worried about him [Kermit] in connection with the fever." But he held out hope that in British East Africa, where most of the hunting would be done, that "the fever was not as bad" as in other regions on their itinerary, such as Uganda and the Upper Nile.

Realizing that it would "absolutely break Kermit's heart" if he decided to leave him behind, Roosevelt also had moments of wondering if he himself was up to making the safari. After "ten years of close office work," he had worried aloud to Frederick Selous early in the planning stage, he expected to be "soft and out of condition."

In looking forward to her husbands' life after he'd shed the trappings of the presidency, Edith had wanted him to be "the simplest American alive." But the problem in that dream, she felt, was that "he has really forgotten how to be."

Although experiencing misgivings about him going to Africa, Edith understood that his heart was set on it and go he would. Plans called for her to pass the year in residence with a sister in Italy, then reunite with him for a grand tour of European cities. She confided that in whiling away the time in a cottage on the Mediterranean the effect on her would be the same "as the forty years of wandering had for the Jews." When the adventure was over, she saw them returning to their home at Oyster Bay "as gladly and meekly as ever the Children of Israel entered the Promised Land."

Rather than bid husband son bon voyage from the Hoboken pier, she waved goodbye from the piazza of Sagamore Hill. Kermit reported to Archie Butt that "she appeared perfectly calm and self-possessed," but that he knew "her heart was almost broken."

Roosevelt and Kermit went on board the German steamer *Hamburg* on March 23, 1909.

The scene that Archie Butt witnessed reminded him of the quality of an election night. But in this scene the "frenzied" people on the dock were literally fighting their way to the ship's side in hopes of seeing the president they'd all called "Teddy," as though they actually knew him.

Sailing "thither from New York," Roosevelt wrote, he looked forward to collecting birds, mammals, reptiles, and plants, "but especially specimens of big game."

9

★ ★ ★

The Man on the Cowcatcher

S AILING WITH Roosevelt and Kermit were three professional natu-
ralists: Retired army Surgeon-Lieut. Col. Edgar A. Means, Edmund
Heller of California, and J. Alden Loring of Oswego, New York.
Arrangements for the trip had been made by two valued English friends,
Edward North Buxton, a "mighty hunter," and Frederick Courteney Selous,
"the greatest of the world's big-game hunters." Upon landing in Naples,
Italy, the party was joined by two more famed hunters, R.J. Cuninghame, a
Scot and longtime resident of Africa and professional elephant hunter, and
Leslie Tarlton, an Australian who had hunted whales in the Arctic and had
been a transport rider in South Africa, as well as a collector for the British
museum "in various odd corners of the earth."

During the Atlantic crossing, the *Hamburg* made a port call in the Azores
where the trio of naturalists collected scores of birds that were skinned and
prepared in Roosevelt's cabin, the largest and best suited for that purpose.
Transferring to another German ship, the *Admiral*, at Naples, Italy, Roosevelt
greeted Selous, who was bound for a hunting trip to East Africa. "No other
hunter alive," Roosevelt noted admiringly, had more experience than Selous,
nor had anything like his gift of penetrating observation joined to his power
of vivid and accurate narration. "To hear him tell of what he has seen and
done," Roosevelt said, "is no less interesting to a naturalist than to a hunter.
There were on the ship men who loved wild nature, and we who were keen
hunters of big game; and almost every day, as we steamed over the hot,

smooth waters of the Red Sea and the Indian Ocean, we would gather on deck around Selous to listen to the tales of those strange adventures that only come to the man who has lived long the lonely life of the wilderness."

After the ship reached Suez, the "ordinary tourist type of passenger ceased to be predominant," replaced by Italian officers going out to a desolate coast town on the edge of Somalia; German, English, and American missionaries; English planters, magistrates, forest officials, and army officers on leave from India, and other officers of Great Britain's army going out to take command "of black native levies in out-of-the-way regions where the English flag stands for all that makes life worth living."

Observing these emissaries of the Union Jack, Roosevelt was reminded of Americans who had reflected such honor "on the American name," whether fighting to free Cuba in 1898, serving in civil and military positions in the newly acquired U.S. colonies in Puerto Rico and the Philippines, and building the Canal Zone in Panama. "I felt as if I knew most of them already," he wrote, "for they might have walked out of the pages of Kipling."

Sailing into the harbor of Mombasa and watching an armada of small boats called "dhows," the former assistant secretary of the navy, expert rowboater on the waters of Oyster Bay, and writer of history mused that many centuries before the Christian era, such boats had carried seafarers of Semitic races whose very names had perished rounded the Lion's Head at Guardafui and crept slowly southward along the barren African coast. "Bold indeed" were those men "of iron heart and supple conscience" who had first steered their dhows across unknown oceans, fronted inconceivable danger and hardship, established trading stations for gold and ivory and slaves, then turned the trading stations into little cities and sultanates.

If ever the spirit of Roosevelt's friend Kipling ever blazed in the heart of another man, it did so in Roosevelt's on April 21, 1909. As he dined that night at the Mombasa Club among the planters, merchants, and government officials, he might have recited from Kipling's *The Ballad of East and West*, written in 1889 while Roosevelt was a civil service commissioner:

> *Oh, East is East, and West is West, and never the twain shall meet,*
> *Till Earth and Sky stand presently at God's great Judgment Seat;*
> *But there is neither East nor West, border, no breed, nor birth,*
> *When two strong men stand face to face, though they come from the*
> *ends of the earth!*

Certainly, Roosevelt embraced a line written by Kipling when Roosevelt was governor of New York: "Take up the White Man's Burden." All around him were men who had done just that. They included not only Englishmen, but Germans and Italians who had labored to make Africa one kind of "white man's country." They had worked "heartily together, doing scrupulous justice to the natives, but remembering that progress and development in this particular kind of new land depended exclusively upon the masterful leadership of the whites, and that therefore it is both a calamity and a crime to permit the whites to be riven in sunder by hatreds and jealousies."

The next day, Roosevelt and Selous boarded a special train with the English governor of the region and his party to travel "with the utmost comfort through a naturalist's wonderland" in the form of a large game reserve on the way to Nairobi, "stretching far to the south, and one mile to the north, of the track." Not content to observe "swarms of game" from inside a railway car, he seated himself, along with Selous and the governor, on the locomotive's cow catcher. Fitted with a comfortable seat, it afforded unobstructed views.

Although the first afternoon produced few wild animals to observe, birds abounded, including a black-and-white hornbill. Feeding on the tracks, it took flight so late that Roosevelt nearly caught it. There were guinea-fowl and francolin, and the occasional bustard, brilliant rollers, sun-birds, bee-eaters, and waver birds, either flying past or sitting among the trees. In the dusk the train nearly ran over a hyena.

When the train stopped at stations, Roosevelt observed natives of the neighborhood and found them "still wild pagans," many of whom appeared "unchanged from what their forefathers were during the countless ages when they alone were the heirs of the land—a land which they were utterly powerless to improve." Some of them wore red blankets, and "in deference to white prejudice draped them so as to hide their nakedness." Others appeared, men and women, with literally not a stitch of clothing, although they might have rather elaborate hair-dresses, and masses of metal ornaments on their arms and legs. One group of women, nearly nude, had their upper arms so tightly bound with masses of bronze or copper wire that their muscles were completely malformed. Some men, armed with primitive bows and arrows, were stark naked with oddly shaved heads and front teeth ground down to sharp points.

Passing through game country while seated on the British-made Baldwin locomotive's cow-catcher, Roosevelt felt that he was riding through a vast zoological garden. From his perch he joyfully observed a herd of a dozen or so giraffes, cows and calves, cantering along through the open woods a couple of hundred yards to the right of the train. Even closer were four waterbuck cows, their big ears thrown forward, eyes staring back at the men on the train. Hartebeests were everywhere, including on the tracks, until the engine's whistle sent them all bucking and springing with ungainly ability to gallop clear of the danger.

With the delight of the boy called Teedie, Roosevelt recorded a long-tailed straw-colored monkey dashing from one tree to another. Huge black ostriches appeared from time to time. One troop of impala, close by the track, took fright, and "as the beautiful creatures fled we saw now one and now another bound clear over the bushes." A herd of zebra clattered across a cutting of the railway not a hundred yards ahead of the train. After the whistle "hurried their progress, but for 'only for a moment,' they continued to graze." Roosevelt wrote, "The wild creatures were in their sanctuary and they knew it."

Citing the reserve as "one of the most valuable possessions the country could have" and "the home of all homes for the creatures," he appreciated that the protection given to them was "genuine, not nominal," and that they were preserved "not for the pleasure of the few, but for the good of all who choose to see this strange and attractive spectacle; and from this nursery and breeding-ground the overflow keeps up the stock of the game in the adjacent land, to the benefit of the settler to whom the game gives fresh meat, and to the benefit of the whole country because of the attraction it furnishes to all who desire to visit a veritable happy hunting ground."

While observing African animals in their reserve was a treat for Roosevelt's eyes, he had come for a different purpose. The aim of his expedition was to kill, "cure and send home" all the specimens of "the common big game" he could find, in addition to "as large a series as possible of the small animals and birds."

To mount such a safari ("being the term employed throughout East Africa to denote both the caravan with which one makes an expedition and the expedition itself," Roosevelt explained in his account of the adventure), it was necessary to carry an elaborate apparatus of naturalist supplies. One of the biggest such outfittings, if not *the* largest, the Roosevelt safari was loaded with four tons of fine salt for curing skins, hundreds of traps for small creatures, many boxes of shotgun cartridges and other ammunition, tents, bedding, cooking and eating utensils, and every other type of equipment for a year-long trek.

As Roosevelt's train arrived at the Kapiti Plains railway station, the safari that was ready and waiting appeared to the legendary leader of the Rough Riders "as if some small military expedition was about to start." He was especially thrilled to see a large American flag floating over his tent. Flanking it were large tents for the members of the party, along with a dining tent and skinning tent. Smaller tents were for 200 porters, gun bearers, boys who put up and took down the tents, and horse boys (saises). Each native soldier (askari) wore a red fez, blue blouse, and white knickerbocker trousers. Each carried a rifle and ammunition belt.

The porters were "the backbone" of the safari and were generally composed of Swahili, whom Roosevelt defined as "the coast men who have acquired the Moslem religion, together with a partially Arabicized tongue and a strain of Arab blood from the Arab warriors and traders who have been so dominant in the coast towns for so many centuries."

Finding the living quarters for himself and Kermit, plus a host of servants, "almost too comfortable" for someone who knew the camp life of the North Woods of Maine, the Great Plains, and the Rockies, he wrote, "Quite a contrast to life on the round-up!"

Remembering so many hunts in the American West, he had arranged a few of the little pleasures that Selous had advised by bringing cans of Boston baked beans, California peaches, and tomatoes. His own experiences had dictated what personal gear to bring. It consisted of lots of warm bedding for the cold nights he was warned to expect "even under the equator," and his standard hunting kit: heavy shoes with hobnails or rubber soles; khaki trousers, the knees faced with leather, and the legs buttoning tight from the knee to below the ankle; khaki-colored army shirt; a slicker for wet weather, an army overcoat and a mackinaw for cold; and a sun helmet, worn in deference to local advice, instead of his far more convenient slouch hat. His saddle was an army tree-type. He also had a pocket compass and a waterproof matchbox. For bird-sighting he preferred army field glasses. A telescope had been a gift from an Irish hussar captain and game hunter whom he'd met on the boat. A friend had also presented him a "very ingenious" beam scale for weighing game. From the boxing champion John L. Sullivan had come "for good luck" a gold-mounted rabbit's foot.

The rifles were an army Springfield, 30-calibre, stocked and sighted to suit himself; a Winchester 405; a Fox No. 12 shotgun; and a double-barreled 500-405 Holland elephant rifle that had been a gift from a group of English admirers. Kermit's weaponry was of the same type, but rather than a Springfield, he carried a Winchester rifle that fired army ammunition, and his double-barreled shotgun was a Rigby.

Another "bit of impedimenta" that was "less usual for African travel, but perhaps almost as essential for real enjoyment of a hunting trip, if it is to be of any length," was a set of books bound in pigskin, and therefore named the "Pigskin Library." The volumes were carried in a light aluminum and oil-cloth case. Weighing a combined sixty pounds, "making a load" for the porter assigned to carry them, the library consisted of:

> Holy Bible
> Apocrypha
> Murray's translations of Euripides' *Hippolytus* and *Baccahe*
> The works of Shakespeare
> Marlowe
> Carlyle's *Frederick the Great*
> Shelley
> Keats
> Percy's *Reliques*
> Milton's *Paradise Lost* (Books I and II)
> Bacon
> Spenser's *Faerie Queene*
> Homer's *Iliad* and *Odyssey*
> Sir Walter Scott's *Legend of Montrose, Guy Mannering, Waverley,*
>   *Rob Roy,* and *Antiquary*
> Longfellow
> Tennyson
> Browning selections
> Poems of Edgar Allen Poe
> Chanson de Roland
> Nibelungenlied
> Lowell, Literary Essays and Bigelow Papers
> Emerson's poems
> Oliver Wendell Holmes's *Autocrat of the Breakfast Table* and
>   *Over the Tea Cups*

Bret Harte poems, *Tales of the Argonauts* and *Luck of Roaring Camp*

Mark Twain's *Huckleberry Finn* and *Tom Sawyer*

Crothers' *Gentle Reader* and *Pardoner's Wallet*

Bunyan's "Pilgrim's Progress"

Macaulay's History, Essays, and Poems

The Federalist

Gregorovius's *Rome*

Cooper's *Pilot*

Thackeray, *Vanity Fair* and *Pendennis*

Dickens, *Mutual Friend* and *Pickwick Papers*

Alfred Thayer Mahan, *The Influence of Seapower Upon History 1660–1783*, a book that was of great influence in Roosevelt's vision of an American two-ocean navy built on the role of the battleship.

These books were for use, not ornament, Roosevelt pointed out, and one or more of them would be "either in my saddle pocket or in the cartridge-bag." Reading would be done "while resting under a tree at noon, perhaps beside the carcass of a beast I had killed, or else while waiting for camp to be pitched." As a result, "the books were stained with blood, sweat, gun oil, dust, and ashes." He chose pigskin bindings because ordinary coverings "either vanished or became loathsome, whereas pigskin merely grew to look as a well-used saddle looks."

With the camp well established, Roosevelt and Kermit rode out on the afternoon of the third day on their first African hunt, guided by their host, Sir Alfred Pease and a friend, Clifford Hill. Along with gun bearers and porters to carry in the game they ventured across desolate flats or short grass until the ground began to rise at places into low hills (called koppies) with rock-strewn tops. Soon they began to see game, but the flatness of the country and the absence of cover made stalking difficult.

Among sparsely scattered, stunted, scantily leaved mimosas were herds of hartebeests, wildebeests, and small parties of two kinds of gazelles (Thompson and Grant, named for the discoverers of the species). Peering across the bare plain through a rain squall, Roosevelt saw a fine Grant and began stalking it. When he fired his Springfield, he underestimated the range. His bullets fell short and the gazelle raced away. Aiming for a smaller gazelle buck and shooting "for the table," he felled it at 225 yards. But what the specimen collector really desired were a wildebeest bull and cow. The powerful, ungainly variety of the brindled gnu or blue Wildebeest of South Africa, with shaggy manes, heavy forequarters and generally bovine look were "interesting creatures of queer, eccentric habits" that at a distance reminded him of the bison of the Great Plains.

In an account of the quest for the benefit of Americans who eagerly awaited the reports he'd agreed to provide *Scribner's Magazine* he wrote:

> I first tried to get up to a solitary old bull, and after a good deal of maneuvering, and by taking advantage of a second rain squall, I got a standing shot at him at four hundred yards, and hit him, but too far back. Although keeping a good distance away, he tacked and veered so, as he ran, that by much running myself I got various other shots at him, at very long range, but missed them all, and he finally galloped over a distant ridge, his long tail twitching, seemingly not much the worse. We followed on horseback, for I hate to let any wounded thing escape to suffer. But meanwhile he had run into view of Kermit, and Kermit, who is of an age and build which better fit him for successful breakneck galloping over unknown country dotted with holes and bits of rotten ground, took up the chase with enthusiasm. Yet it was sunset, after a run of six or eight miles, when he finally ran into and killed the tough old bull, which had turned to bay, snorting and tossing its horns.

A wildebeest cow that Roosevelt shot at and missed was killed by Sir Alfred Pease just before sundown. Both it and the bull were fat and in fine condition, providing meat for dinner and their skins for the National Museum.

By the law of the veldt, Roosevelt noted, because his shot had been the first to hit the bull, he was entitled to claim the kill. Yet in reality, he wrote, "the credit was communistic, so to speak, and my share was properly less than that of the others" on the hunt.

The next day the hunting party rode about sixteen miles to Pease's farm (to Roosevelt it was a ranch, "as we should call it in the West") in the hills of Kitanga. Always careful to set the scene, Roosevelt dutifully recorded, "The house was one story high, clean and comfortable, with a veranda running round three sides; and on the veranda were lion skins and the skull of a rhinoceros. From the house we looked over hills and wide lonely plains, the green valley below, with its flat-topped acacias, was very lovely; and in the evening we could see, scores of miles away, the snowy summit of mighty Kilimanjaro turn crimson in the setting sun. The twilights were not long; and when night fell, stars new to northern eyes flashed glorious in the sky."

The veranda also provided Roosevelt a sight that he could never have while seated in a rocking chair at Sagamore Hill. One morning he watched hartebeests came "right up to the wire fence, two-score yards from the house itself." On long afternoons "in plain view, on the hillsides opposite" the "black-and-white-striped zebra, and ruddy hartebeest, grazed or rested."

Unless there was a lion or rhinoceros hunt involving all the hunters, Roosevelt went out accompanied only by a few native gun bearers and porters. He felt that riding through teeming herds of game was like retracing the steps of time for sixty or seventy years, and being back in the days when white men first came to Africa. He enjoyed "a peculiar charm" on these rides in "the wild, lonely country," with only his "silent black followers." Always alert to everything, he provided this vividly poetic description of such an outing, from the climate to the kill:

When the sky was overcast it was cool and pleasant, for it is high country; as soon as the sun appeared the vertical tropic rays made the air quiver above the scorched land. As we passed down a hillside we brushed through aromatic shrubs and the hot, pleasant fragrance enveloped us. When we came to a nearly dry watercourse, there would be beds of rushes, beautiful lilies and lush green plants with staring flowers; and great deep-green fig trees, or flat-topped mimosas. In many of these trees there were sure to be native beehives; these were sections of hollow logs hung from the branches; they formed striking and characteristic features of the landscape. Whenever there was moisture there were flowers, brilliant of hue and many of them sweet to smell; and birds of numerous kinds abounded. When we left the hills and the wooded watercourses we might ride hour after hour across the barren desolation of the flats, while herds of zebra and hartebeest stared at us through the heat haze. Then the zebra, with shrill, barking neighs, would file off across the horizon, or the high-withered hartebeests, snorting and bucking, would rush off in a confused mass, as unreasoning panic succeeded foolish confidence. If I shot anything, vultures of several kinds, and the tall, hideous marabou storks, gathered before the skinners were through with their work; they usually stayed at a wary distance, but the handsome ravens, glossy-hued with white napes. long-billed, long-winged, and short-tailed, came round more familiarly.

With so much game available he found that he rarely had to stalk. Shooting was from a long range, but by maneuvering, and never walking straight toward the quarry, he was usually able to collect whatever specimen the naturalist desired. Sometimes he shot well, sometimes he did not. Failures were confessed in his diary. One entry noted, "Missed steinbuck [an antelope], pig, impala and Grant: awful."

Kills were noted in terms of the game, distances, his position when shooting, and where the bullet struck. On one very successful day the diary entry read: "Hartebeest, 250 yards, facing me; shot through face, broke neck. Zebra, very large, quartering, 160 yards, between neck and shoulder. Buck Grant, 220 yards, walking, behind shoulder. Steinbuck, 180 yards, standing, behind shoulder."

Generally, each head of game that he collected cost him "a goodly number of bullets." But the expenditure of a few cartridges was "of no consequence whatever compared to the escape of a single head of game which should have been bagged." Because shooting at a long range required running, his proportion of misses was sizeable, and there were "altogether too many even at short ranges."

As in his ventures in the West, he would have preferred to go out by himself, but he was not in the Dakotas or the Rockies. He was in Kitanga, and that meant being accompanied by natives who knew the land and the ways of the East African hunt that began before the tropic sun rose to flame over the brink of the world as strange creatures rustled through the brush or fled dimly in the long grass before the light grew bright and revealing.

Here, in the still heat of noon when he sat beneath a tree, with his water canteen, lunch, and a volume from the Pigskin Library at hand, he could peer through his pocket telescope to watch the herds of game that hardly any Americans had ever heard about, and very few had seen for themselves, lying down or standing drowsily in the distance. Then, as the afternoon waned and a red sunset paled to amber and opal, he returned to Sir Alfred's home with whatever the vast, mysterious African landscape had provided in trophies.

10

★ ★ ★

The Lions of the Kapiti

FTER NIGHT FELL, Theodore Roosevelt heard hyenas. Although he had yet to see one, he'd listened to hair-raising tales about their savagery. The wild creatures were always lurking on the threshold of Nairobi, and often crossed it. Just a few months before his arrival, one had crept into a hut on the outskirts of the town and seized and killed a man. When one of Sir Alfred's native hunters was attacked as he slept beside a campfire, part of his face was torn off. In 1908 and throughout the early part of 1909, as sleeping-sickness ravaged the region, hyenas had grown constantly bolder. They haunted camps where the stricken lay, burst into huts, and carried off their helpless prey.

It was with great pleasure and parental pride, therefore, that Roosevelt looked on as Kermit killed one. Coming across the hyena in a dry creek bed, known as a donga, he galloped after it. The chase was a long one. Twice the hyena got onto such rocky ground that he almost outran his determined pursuer. At last, after covering nearly ten miles, Kermit ran into it in the open, shooting from the saddle as it shambled along at a canter, growling with rage and terror.

Regarding hyenas with contempt, Roosevelt described them as hideous spotted beasts that were a dreadful curse to the weak and helpless, but "too cowardly ever to be a source of danger to a hunter." When he inquired of veteran hunters as to which African animals they knew to be the most dangerous to men, he found a wide difference of opinion. The territorial governor placed the buffalo first, then the elephant, lion, and rhinoceros. Another professional hunter and writer on the topic of African game put the rhino first. But for the hunter whom Roosevelt most admired, Frederick Selous, it was the lion. Allowing that opinions on the relative prowess and ferocity of the various animals were based on personal experience, Roosevelt wrote that what must be kept in mind was that "surrounding conditions, the geographical locality, and the wide individual variation of temper within the ranks of each species must all be taken into account."

Consequently, he concluded that "the weight of opinion among those best fitted to judge is that the lion is the most formidable opponent of the hunter, under ordinary conditions."

As evidence, he noted that during the last three or four years, in German and British East Africa and Uganda, more than fifty men had been killed or mauled by lions, buffaloes, rhinos, and elephants, but that "the lions have much the largest list of victims to their credit."

Everywhere he went he'd found signs that the lion was lord and that his reign was cruel. Lions took livestock of settlers, ravaged the herds and flocks of natives, and preyed at will on swarming zebras and kongoni. Observing the remains of a zebra that had been killed not more than eighteen hours earlier, he found the stripped bones all in place and the skin still on the lower legs and head. The zebra was lying on its belly, the legs spread out, the neck vertebra crushed. From this Roosevelt deduced that the lion had "sprung clean on it, bearing it down by his weight while he bit through the back of the neck, and the zebra's legs had spread out as the body yielded under the lion."

Brimming with excited anticipation of a lion hunt, he told a companion, "If only I can get *my* lion I shall be happy—even if he is a small one—but I hope he will have a mane."

Initial hunting sojourns proved disappointing. The ravines they beat either had no lions, or efforts to make them leave a particularly difficult hill or swamp failed. But if anybody knew just the right place to seek them, Roosevelt believed, it was Sir Alfred Pease. Confident that he would get his lion, he and Kermit set out again with Sir Alfred in charge of an all-day hunt. In the party were Lady Pease, their daughter, a fellow-guest named Medlicott, another amateur hunter named Percival, and several Masai beaters, gun bearers, porters, and dogs.

After pausing for lunch under a great fig tree at the foot of a high, rocky hill, the party followed a long dry donga with low, steep banks and here and there patches of brush that might hold hyena, cheetah, wild dog, or lion. Soon, in the sandy bed, Sir Alfred discerned lion spoor, then the footprints of a big male and those of a lioness. As the hunters walked cautiously along each side of the donga, with their horses following close behind, the dogs began to show signs of scenting the lions.

As beaters thrashed away at each patch of brush, shouted, and threw stones, Roosevelt and the others stood watching any probable exit with rifles at the ready. After a couple of false alarms the dogs drew toward one patch, their hair bristling, and showing such eager excitement that Roosevelt knew "something big was inside."

"Simba!" shouted a beater, pointing to the patch of bushes just across a small ravine.

Shifting position, Roosevelt peered eagerly at the spot for several moments before he caught a glimpse of tawny hide.

As the lion moved, someone yelled, "Shoot!"

Roosevelt fired. So did Kermit.

Out of the brush came not the hoped-for big lion, but two large cubs. Each was so badly wounded, Roosevelt recorded, that they had to be "finished off." But even if they'd not been shot, he added, the mastiff-sized cubs "were too big to take alive."

With remarkable understatement, Roosevelt wrote, "This was a great disappointment."

Because it was well on in the afternoon, and the country most apt to harbor lions had proved unrewarding, it seemed to Roosevelt that he would not have another chance that day. But Sir Alfred was not so easily discouraged. Although he said nothing, he intended to have another try. As he rode toward another donga, Roosevelt and the others followed at a canter. When they reached the shallow donga, Pease found the spoor of two large lions. With "every sense acock," Roosevelt recalled, the hunters dismounted and approached the first patch of tall bushes. But shouts and thrown stones produced no result.

Again disappointed, Roosevelt got back on his horse, a stout and quiet sorrel named Tranquility. About a quarter-mile farther along the donga, out of a patch of tall, thick brush, he heard loud gruntings and crashings. Off Tranquility in an instant, he waited, uncertain whether he would see the lions charging out ten yards distant or running away.

"Fortunately, they adopted the latter course," he wrote in an account of the encounter. As only the accomplished author of three books on big-game hunting could, he captured the thrill of the moment:

> Right in front of me, thirty yards off, there appeared, from behind the bushes which had first screened him from my eyes, the tawny, galloping form of a big maneless lion. Crack! the Winchester spoke; and as the soft-nosed bullet ploughed forward through his flank the lion swerved so that I missed him with the second shot; but my third bullet went through the spine and forward into his chest. Down he came, sixty yards off, his hind quarters dragging, his head up, his ears back, his jaws open and lips drawn up in a prodigious snarl, as he endeavored to turn his face to us. His back was broken; but of this we could not at the moment be sure, and if it had been merely grazed, he might have recovered, and then, even though dying, his charge might have done mischief. So Kermit, Sir Alfred, and I fired almost together, into his chest. His head sank, and he died.

Unhit, the second lion to emerge from the brush galloped across the plain. When a few shots missed, Roosevelt and the others leapt onto their horses to try to ride him down over a plain that sloped gently upward for three-quarters of a mile to a low crest. Topping the hill, both Kermit and Pease fired again and missed. With Miss Pease riding close behind Tranquility, and Medlicott keeping up, Roosevelt saw the lion loping along close behind a few kongoni. In hot pursuit of the speeding lion in a downhill race, he gained rapidly until the lion suddenly halted in long grass in a slight shallow.

Dismounted, Roosevelt found him difficult to discern. Concerned that the lion might charge, and certainly outrun him, he decided to stay put and rely on his marksmanship, rather than try to vault back onto Tranquility. He would write of this decision, "Now, an elderly man with a varied past which includes rheumatism does not vault lightly into the saddle; as his sons, for instance can; and I had already made up my mind that in the event of the lion's charging it would be wise for me to trust to straight powder rather than to try to scramble into the saddle and get under way in time."

Kneeling, Roosevelt was still unable to see the lion. But it suddenly stood, looking first at one group of horses and then at the other. His tail was flashing to and fro, his head held low, while his harsh and savage growling rolled thunderously over the plain. When he turned toward Roosevelt and Roosevelt's sais (horse-watcher), ironically named Simba, his tail was lashing quicker and quicker, a sign that he was preparing to charge. Resting an elbow upon Simba's bent shoulder, Roosevelt took steady aim and fired. The bullet struck between neck and shoulder. The lion fell over on his side, one foreleg in the air, but recovered enough to stand facing the man who'd shot him and growl hoarsely. Expecting a charge, Roosevelt fired again, breaking the lion's back just behind the shoulders. Standing over the body, he gave the lion a coup de grace.

"These were two good-sized maneless lions," Roosevelt wrote of the kills, "and very proud of them I was."

With two porters carrying each lion, and two others bearing the skins of the two cubs, the party started back to camp at dusk on a trail that was soon illuminated by a brilliant tropic moon. It was a scene that stirred both Roosevelt's sense of place and his unflagging romanticism. He noted that the "stalwart savages who carried the bloody lion skins swung along at a faster walk as the sun went down and the moon rose, chanting in unison, one uttering a single word or sentence and the others joining in a deep-toned, musical chorus."

Nor did Roosevelt-the-historian and self-appointed instructor of his readers pass up an opportunity to teach. "The men on a safari, and indeed African natives generally," he wrote, "are always excited over the death of a lion, and the hunting tribes then chant their rough hunting songs, or victory songs, until the monotonous, rhythmical repetitions make them grow almost frenzied."

Ever the naturalist, he continued, "The ride home in the moonlight, the vast barren landscape shining like silver on either hand, was one to be remembered; and above all, the sight of our trophies and of their wild bearers."

Three days later, Roosevelt, Sir Alfred Pease, Medlicott, Edmund Heller, Clifford and Harold Hill, and a small army of porters, beaters, and bearers established a fresh camp at a water hole in a little stream called Potha by a hill of the same name. Teamed in riding out with Kermit and Medlicott, Roosevelt dismounted at a likely place for lions and soon heard the distant shouts of beaters coming toward him. But the only game he saw were mountain reedbuck does that he chose not to shoot. But Kermit, with keen eyes following a male cheetah, "bowled it over in good style as it ran, then, moments later, killed a reedbuck and a steinbuck."

At that moment, a 150 yards away on the opposite side of the hill, Harold Hill shouted, "Lion!"

Unable to see it at first, Roosevelt thought he'd sighted the lion and fired, but the bullet was aimed too high. When the startled quarry moved, the next shot hit behind his shoulders. Assessing the trophy, Roosevelt was disappointed to find that it was a half-grown male, which Roosevelt deemed "not much of a trophy."

After lunch under a tree overlooking a long, wide valley, Roosevelt and Harold Hill stationed themselves on one side of the valley, while Kermit and Sir Alfred took positions on the opposite side, and waited for the beaters to do their work, starting at the lower end of the valley and slowly and noisily beating toward them in tall grass. Presently, Hill directed Roosevelt's attention to two lions, but it took Roosevelt a few seconds to realize that a dim yellow smear in the yellow-brown grass was a lion. Having difficulty getting a bead on it, he overshot. When the lion jumped up and faced in the direction of the rifle's crack, it growled, lowered its head with its tail straight up, and charged at a trot. Before it could reach galloping speed, Roosevelt took aim with his Winchester and fired a soft-nosed bullet between neck and shoulder. The lion went down with a roar, but Roosevelt was taking no chances. He shot twice more. But before he was able to approach the dead lion, Hill shouted another alert. This time it was a lioness.

Walking toward Hill, Roosevelt discerned the lion clearly. Facing him, the lion snarled as Roosevelt aimed at her chest. What followed was, in Roosevelt's astonished description, "a series of extraordinary antics, tumbling about on her head, just as if she were throwing somersaults, first to one side and then to the other." He fired again, but managed to shoot between the somersaults and miss. As the shot seemed to bring her to herself, she charged toward the line of beaters, then suddenly sank down in the high grass. Approaching warily, Roosevelt and the others found her alive, half crouched, half sitting, head down. Recognizing that the lioness still had strength "to do mischief," he sent a fatal bullet through her shoulders.

Weighed in camp, the full-grown lioness was 283 pounds. The male that Roosevelt had difficulty in seeing at first, although only half-grown, tipped the scale at nearly 400 pounds. In the light of the full moon and the glow of the campfire, Roosevelt again observed the victory dance of the natives as the firelight "gleamed and flickered across the grim dead beasts and the shining eyes and black features of the excited savages."

Next morning, the hunters started for another water hole about eight miles away at a rocky hill called Bondoni. The move afforded Roosevelt-the-intrepid-diarist an opportunity to record the formidable task of uprooting a safari camp. He wrote, "When we were to march, the camp was broken as early in the day as possible. Each man had his allotted task, and the tents, bedding, provisions, and all else were expeditiously made into suitable packages. Each porter is supposed to carry from fifty-five to sixty pounds, which may all be in one bundle or in two or three."

From the start of the journey into the heart of Africa, Roosevelt had placed above his tent an American flag. But he found that his pride in the Stars and Stripes was equaled by porters who carried it at the head or near the head of the line of march. After it in single file came a long line of bearers, some blowing horns or whistles and others beating small tomtoms. At intervals during the trek some suddenly began to chant. Headmen carried no bundles, tent boys little if anything, and the horse-tending saises concerned themselves only with tending them.

Roosevelt found the outfits of the natives so fascinating that in an article for *Scribner's Magazine* (and the subsequent book, *African Game Trails*) he described the clothing at some length. Expressing amazement that a porter "thought nothing whatever of walking for hours at mid-day under the equatorial sun with his head bare," or trudging solemnly and proudly along either with an umbrella open or furled as if it were "a wand of dignity," Roosevelt expounded on the head gear of other natives that "varied according to the fancy of the individual." He wrote with amusement:

Normally it was a red fez, a kind of cap only used in hot climates, and exquisitely designed to be useless therein because it gives absolutely no protection from the sun. But one [man] would wear a skin cap; another would suddenly put one or more feathers in his fez; and another, discarding the fez, would revert to some purely savage headdress which he would wear with equal gravity whether it were, in our eyes, really decorative or merely comic. One such headdress, for instance, consisted of the skin of the top of a zebra's head, with the two ears. Another was made of the skins of squirrels, with the tails both sticking up and hanging down. Another consisted of a bunch of feathers woven into the hair, which itself was pulled out into strings that were stiffened with clay. Another was really too intricate for description because it included the man's natural hair, some strips of skin, and an empty tin can.

Many years before Americans could subscribe to *National Geographic* magazine to read about the mysterious African continent, its animals, its people, and their ways, Roosevelt gave them a keen sense of being with him on his historic safari. From its start as an idea, throughout his planning, on the day of his departure, and as he proceeded, the thrilling odyssey of their beloved "Teddy" was eagerly followed in press reports. As the fifty-year-old ex-president and his energetic second son plunged into an adventure that was excitedly shared, if vicariously, by countless countrymen, Henry Cabot Lodge wrote to Roosevelt that Americans "follow it all with the absorbed interest of a boy who reads 'Robinson Crusoe' for the first time."

Theodore Roosevelt Jr., who had passed up the chance to go to Africa because he had fallen in love, was greatly amused to learn that the father he knew as "Big Bear" had gotten a new name from the Africans, "Bwana Makuba," meaning "Great Master." Ted also learned that Big Bear was having "a bully time," and that Kermit was "as hardy as a bullmoose" and the admiration of everyone on the safari. The favorite of the gun bearers, twenty-year-old Kermit was, Big Bear reported, "cool and daring." His African given-name was "Bwana Medogo," or "the young master." Later, Kermit was called "Bwana Morodadi," meaning "the Dandy." But on occasion his father found him "a little too reckless and keeps my heart in my throat," but he was able to "outrun, when after a wounded beast, or outlast, in a day's or week's tramp, any man, black or white, in the outfit."

And what an outfit the Roosevelt safari was! With the American flag aloft at the head of the march, it could easily have been mistaken by the native population for yet another colonial army set on the total conquest and subjugation of their continent. It was an image that certainly fit into Theodore Roosevelt's view of the world and its peoples.

As he had embraced the policy of "Manifest Destiny" in which white Americans believed they were entitled to fill up the lands from the Atlantic to the Pacific, from Canada to Mexico, even if that meant the eradication of the Indians and their culture if it came to that (as it very nearly did), Roosevelt looked upon East Africa as ripe for civilization. With no apologies, he declared, "It is a white man's country." His vision encompassed imposition of the better life for the original inhabitants as could be found in Africa wherever the English flag flew.

But it was not the Union Jack that preceded "Bwana Makuba" Roosevelt as the biggest safari ever mounted in East Africa wended its way from the hospitality of Sir Alfred Pease's comfortable ranch toward the foot of Kilimakiu Mountain. The route took him across bare plains thickly covered with short grass. All around the long safari he observed herds of hartebeests, zebras, gazelles, and wildebeests. Occasionally they crossed the trails of natives, "worn deep in the hard soil by the countless thousands of bare or sandaled feet that had trodden them." Africa, he lectured his readers, "is a country of trails." Across the high veldt, in every direction, ran the "tangled trails of multitudes of game that have lived thereon from time immemorial."

Through all the epochs of Africa, neither natives nor animals had witnessed such a panoply of grandeur as that of Theodore Roosevelt's safari. When it made camp at Kilimaiku, it was in a grove of shady trees. From it at sunset, Roosevelt looked across the vast plain and marveled as the far-off mountains grew umber and purple as the light waned. Established near an ostrich farm belonging to Captain Arthur Slatter, Roosevelt's new host, the camp was also close to a tribe of the Wakamba. When its chief paid a call, he presented Roosevelt with a traditional welcoming gift, "a fat hairy sheep, of the ordinary kind" in that part of Africa where, Roosevelt noted, "the sheep very wisely do not grow wool."

The headman, wearing khaki clothing, proudly showed the honored guest an official document which confirmed him in his position by the direction of the government, and required him "to perform various acts, chiefly in the way of preventing his tribespeople from committing robbery or murder, and of helping to stamp out cattle disease."

The natives were to Roosevelt's eyes "wild savages with filed teeth, many of them stark naked, though some of them carried a blanket," whose heads were "curiously shaved so that the hair tufts stood out in odd patterns." They carried small bows and arrows with poisoned heads.

What the headman and his entourage thought of Roosevelt in his hunting garb, toothy grin, mustache, eyeglasses, and bubbling personality was not recorded.

The following morning, accompanied by Captain Slatter and the requisite retinue of bearers and porters, Roosevelt rode out to hunt.

11

★ ★ ★

I Am Not a Rhinoceros Mind-Reader

O N DROUGHT-STRICKEN GROUND that was largely open, but thinly covered in part by bush, meager forest, and scattered mimosa trees, Roosevelt and the others were guided by Captain Slatter among herds of zebras and hartebeests. But it was a small herd of the type of antelope called the eland that triggered Roosevelt's interest. There were about a dozen cows with reddish-looking coats. The pelts of two huge bulls were salty blue with great dewlaps hanging down and legs that seemed too small for their massive bodies.

As Roosevelt crept toward them he was struck by their likeness to great, clean, handsome American cattle of the Great Plains and thought the eland ought to be domesticated. Grazing or resting, they switched their long tails at swarms of pestering flies. Firing at them, he misjudged the distance. The shot sent the eland running, with a few of the cows bolting in such a hurry that as they skipped over those that were in their way, Roosevelt was surprised by the agility of such large animals. A few hundred yards distant, they settled into the slashing trot that was their usual gait, then disappeared over the brow of a hill.

That morning, Roosevelt noted, was "a blank," with no game killed, but early in the afternoon, they found the elusive herd around a tree in an open space that prevented Roosevelt and his companions from getting close.

Undaunted by the distance, Roosevelt felt "warranted" in shooting. Although he wanted a bull, he had to settle for a "fine cow" that stood about a quarter of a mile away.

A moment later, a Wakamba man rushed forward to excitedly report that on a hillside three-quarters of a mile away he'd seen a rhinoceros. Racing to the spot with Captain Slatter and a couple of gun bearers, Roosevelt soon saw his first rhino in the wild. The hulking animal was standing in open country a short distance away, with the wind blowing from him to the hunters.

To Roosevelt the big beast stood like "an uncouth statue, his hide black in the sunlight, looking like a monster surviving over from the world's past, from the days when the beasts of the prime ran riot in their strength, before man grew so cunning of brain and hand as to master them." So little did the rhino dream of the hunters' presence, Roosevelt noted, "that when we were a hundred yards off he actually lay down."

Walking lightly, and with every sense keyed up, the human stalkers at last reached a patch of brush. Releasing the safety lock on a double-barreled Holland rifle, the first time he'd used the gun, Roosevelt stepped to one side of the brush to get a clear aim. Suddenly, the rhino jumped to his feet with "the agility of a pony." Roosevelt fired the right-hand barrel and sent the shot into the rhino's lungs. Wheeling round with blood spurting from its nostrils, the rhinoceros galloped forward. Firing the left-hand barrel, Roosevelt hit it between neck and shoulder, a shot that tore into the rhino's heart.

Looking back on the "wicked charge," Roosevelt said, "I am not a rhinoceros mind-reader, and its actions were such as to warrant my regarding it as a suspicious character." The rhinos, he decided, "are truculent, lumbering beasts, much the most stupid of all the dangerous game I know." If it had been a lion the first bullet would have knocked all the charge out of it, but the vitality of the rhino was so great that one shot from the hard-hitting Holland rifle could not stop it outright.

When a group of Wakamba skinners returned to camp, the rhino's meat was divided among them and the white hunters, with the Makamba feasting on their portions in their camp. As Roosevelt went to bed, he could still hear the drumming and chanting.

The next afternoon found him looking down the barrel of his rifle at giraffes, but they were "such enormous beasts" that he thought they were closer than they were. When his shot missed, they broke into their "leisurely looking gallop" and disappeared among the mimosas.

"Of all the beasts in an African landscape," Roosevelt wrote, "none is more striking than the giraffe." Because of its height and keen vision, no animal was harder to approach unseen. Observing them through army field glasses, he saw "a striking-looking animal and handsome in its way." But its length of leg and neck and sloping back made it appear awkward even at rest. Yet when alarmed and stirred to action, it could take off, not in its long swinging pace or walk, but in a peculiar gallop or canter.

"The tail is cocked and twisted," Roosevelt noted, "and the huge hind legs are thrown forward well to the outside of the forelegs. The movements seem deliberate and the giraffe does not appear to be going at a fast pace, but if it has any start a horse must gallop to overtake it. When it starts on this gait, the neck may be dropped forward at a sharp angle with the straight line of the deep chest, and the big head is thrust in advance."

Disappointed that he'd missed his chance, he was out the next day with Captain Slatter. While eating lunch under a huge fig tree on a hill about three miles from camp, he scanned the country with field glasses and spotted a herd of eland and three giraffes about a mile and a half away. He wanted to kill a bull eland, but he wanted a giraffe even more. His goal was to collect a bull and cow for the museum in whose name he'd ventured into Africa. With the Winchester loaded with full metal-jacketed bullets, he approached the stately trio, moving in a straight line with Captain Slatter and natives. As they neared their quarry, the giraffes "showed symptoms of uneasiness." As a smaller one bolted, the others shifted positions slightly. Dropping to a knee, Roosevelt took a bead on the large bull's shoulder with the rifle's 300-yard sight and got off one shot. It struck where he'd aimed, but all three giraffes ran in their rocking-horse canter. Chasing them, Roosevelt chambered a soft-nosed bullet and fired at one of the smaller giraffes. It was a long shot, between 400 and 500 yards, but the bullet brought it down. As the others fled, he jumped on Tranquility and rode full speed after them.

The pursuit proved harder than expected. Although the bull was wounded and lagging in its desperate flight, it put on a spurt. Believing he was close enough to get off a telling shot, Roosevelt leapt from Tranquility and opened fire. The bull dropped, but as Roosevelt remounted the horse, the giraffe struggled to his feet and bounded off and disappeared with the second in a thicket of trees at the bottom of a valley. Tearing after them, Roosevelt spurred Tranquility and scrambled through a dry donga, then up the other side, determined to get close enough to the bull to finish him off.

But the usually reliable sorrel horse, as Roosevelt colorfully described what happened, "did not quite like the look of the thing ahead of him." The horse did not refuse to come up to the giraffe, but he evidently felt that, with such an object close by, it behooved him to be careful as to what might be lurking in the brush and trees. When Tranquility shied away at every bush or clump of trees, Roosevelt jumped off with rifle in hand and fired one at the bull giraffe. This time it went down for good.

At the very same time, Roosevelt learned, another giraffe hunt was going on, involving Kermit and their intrepid companions on this part of the safari, Sir Alfred Pease and Medlicott. They'd come across a dozen giraffes on the open plains. As the hunt began, Kermit had found himself alone, galloping after a giraffe and firing again and again with his Winchester. When his horse gave out, he jumped off, and as Roosevelt proudly noted, "being an excellent long distance runner," chased the giraffe on foot for more than a mile. The race ended with wounded giraffe slowing down, stopping, and falling dead.

The bullets retrieved from Kermit's and Roosevelt's giraffes were saved, in keeping with Roosevelt's decision, made before he'd left for Africa, to preserve as many as possible of the bullets that brought down quarry in order to assess what could be done by the different types of rifles used on the expedition.

It was on this portion of the year-long odyssey that the natives honored the white hunters with Swahili names, and became so impressed with Kermit's prowess that thereafter he was, to them, Bwana Medogo, the young master.

While Kermit and the party moved on to the next destination, Roosevelt took time off from hunting to visit the American Mission Station at Machakos. Accompanied by Sir Alfred, he found the little town "both interesting and attractive." He also admired the manner in which the ancient native village on the old route taken by Arab caravans engaged in the slave trade was being run by the British. It was here that Roosevelt found evidence justifying the tenets of a philosophical view of the world known as Social Darwinism. In applying the evolutionary theories that Charles Darwin had advanced in *Origin of Species* and *The Descent of Man,* the Social Darwinists of the years of Theodore Roosevelt's youth had argued that various peoples were at different stages in the evolutionary process. Because some were far more advanced than others, it went without saying that white Europeans, and their American cousins, stood at the top of the evolutionary ladder.

They therefore had the moral duty to protect their interests and lead inferiors toward higher civilization, as English colonialists and Christian missionaries were doing in Machakos.

Writing about his visit, Roosevelt was a Social Darwinist in full bloom, but not without handing out some advice to His Majesty Edward VII's government. He wrote:

> The English rule in Africa has been of incalculable benefits to the Africans themselves, and indeed this is true of most European nations. Mistakes have been made, of course, but they have proceeded at least as often from an unwise effort to accomplish too much in the way of beneficence, as from a desire to exploit the natives. Each of the civilized nations that has taken possession of any part of Africa has had its own peculiar defects. Some of them have done too much supervising and ordering the lives of the natives, and in interfering with their practices and customs, even when of an immoral and repulsive character, and to do no more than what is obviously necessary, such as insistence upon keeping the peace and preventing the spread of cattle disease. Excellent reasons can be advanced in favor of this policy, and it must always be remembered that a fussy and ill-considered benevolence is more sure to awaken resentment than cruelty itself; while the natives are apt to resent deeply even things that are obviously for their ultimate welfare. Yet I cannot help thinking that with caution and wisdom it would be possible to proceed somewhat farther than has yet been the case in the direction of pushing some of the least of the East African tribes; and this though I recognize fully that many of these tribes are of a low and brutalized type. Having said this much in the way of criticism, I wish to add my tribute of unstinted admiration for the disinterested work being done, alike in the interest of the white man and the black, by the government officials whom I met in east Africa. They are men in whom their country [England] had every reason to feel a just pride.

Constantly describing Africans as "wild" and "savages" in his writings about the safari, Roosevelt was, of course, a man in step with his times and, therefore, a man who by standards of enlightened people of a century later would be called a racist, just as today's environmentalists and wildlife preservationists deem Roosevelt's hunting an outrageous slaughter of animals for the pleasure of showing his trophies and bragging about his manliness. Yet, is it fair to fault Theodore Roosevelt for holding the prevailing beliefs, and prejudices, of his times from the vantage point of one whose present existence lay in a future that Roosevelt couldn't envision? It seems especially egregious to look back on his safari as a year-long bloody campaign against innocent animals when at that time he was engaged in what he and his sponsors believed was an educational enterprise. Had television been available, he certainly would have ventured into Africa, and on his later expedition in the uncharted jungles of Brazil, with video equipment and come back to produce documentaries for Public Television, had it been around then. He should be credited for taking with him not only guns, but photographic equipment. Nearly ten years before his African adventure, he'd declared from Sagamore Hill, "More and more, as it becomes necessary to preserve the game, let us hope that the camera will largely supplant the rifle."

As Theodore Roosevelt found much to praise, and to criticize, in the colonialism that was represented by the English rule in East Africa on his visit to the village of Machakos, he met in American missionaries a group of white men whose "work among the savages" offered many difficulties that often met with "dishearteningly little reward." Again a man of his time, and as a Christian, he saw nothing wrong with efforts to convert the people of Africa to the Cross. While he endorsed proselytizing, he cautioned against "zealous missionaries, fervent in their faith," who did not always find it easy to remember "that savages can only be raised by slow steps" and that "empty adherence to forms and ceremonies" amounted to nothing, and that the "gradual elevation of mind and character is a prerequisite to the achievement of any kind of Christianity which is worth calling such." Nevertheless, he wrote, "after all this has been said, it remains true that the good done by missionary effort in Africa has been incalculable."

After returning from Machakos, and spending the night at Sir Alfred Pease's home, he set out with Kermit across the Athi Plains in a grand procession of horses, porters, bearers, and equipment, with the U.S. flag unfurled at the head of the impressive retinue, for a place owned by Mr. and Mrs. W.N. McMillan in the beautiful Mua Hills, known as Juja Farm.

12

★ ★ ★

Land of the Masai

LYING ON THE EDGE of the Athi Plains near the junction of the Nairobi and Reworo Rivers, the home of Roosevelt's welcoming countrymen, the McMillans, Juja Farm was typical of those of the white settlers. The one-story house with a broad, vine-shaded veranda was surrounded by numerous out-buildings, cornfields, flocks and herds of animals, and a vegetable garden tended by "unsmiling Kikuyu savages." One that especially fascinated Roosevelt evidently had been so attracted by the shiny surface of a tobacco can that he wore it on one ear as a complement to a curiously carved wooden drum on the other. Another native, whose arms and legs were "massive with copper and iron bracelets," was naked except for a blanket that he wore except when he used a lawn mower. For this task he wrapped the blanket around his neck and the handle of the lawn mower, in Roosevelt's words, "with the evident feeling that he had done all that the most exacting conventionalism could require."

House boys and gun-bearers, and most of the boys caring for the horses, were Somalis. Men and women field workers were Kikuyus. Herders were Masai. The former Little Missouri cattle rancher found them to be "wild heathen of the most martial type." Observing that they looked carefully after the cattle, and were delighted to join the chase of dangerous game, but thoroughly despised regular work, Roosevelt wrote, "Sometimes when we had gathered a mass of Kikuyus or of our own porters to do some job, two or three Masai would stroll up to look on with curiosity, sword in belt and great spear in hand." In their erect carriage they had a fearless bearing in which the hero of the San Juan Heights discerned "a soldierly race."

In temporary residence at Juja Farm when Roosevelt arrived in mid-May was his friend Frederick Selous. His purpose was to join McMillan on a safari in company with one of the most notable professional hunters of East Africa, H. Judd. Eager to learn from him, Roosevelt and Kermit went hunting with him almost every day. Rising before dawn, they took an eastward course toward the mountain mass called Donyo Sabuk in search of waterbuck and impala, in Roosevelt's view the most beautiful of all the antelope. About the size of the American white-tailed deer that was so familiar to Roosevelt, they had annulated horns that formed a single spiral. Their coat was as shiny as satin with contrasting shades of red and white.

What surprised Roosevelt about the impala and other African antelope was that they succumbed to wounds quicker than similar American game. In citing the shooting of an impala buck as evidence of this unexpected behavior, he described creeping up an anthill to get a shot at the animal from about 250 yards. The buck dropped, and while putting in another cartridge he said to Judd that he didn't like to see an animal drop like that, so instantaneously, as there was always the possibility that it might only be creased, and that if an animal so hurt got up, it always went off exactly as if unhurt. Roosevelt wrote:

> When we raised our eyes again to look for the impala, it had vanished. I was sure that we would never see it again, and Judd felt much the same way, but we walked in the direction toward which its head had been pointed, and Judd ascended an ant hill to scan the surrounding country with his glasses. He did so, and after a minute remarked that he could not see the wounded impala; when a sudden movement caused us to look down, and there it was, lying at our very feet, on the side of the ant hill, unable to rise. I had been using a sharp-pointed bullet in the Springfield, and this makes a big hole. The bullet had gone too far back, in front of the hips. I should not have wondered at all if the animal had failed to get up after falling, but I did not understand why, as it recovered enough from the shock to be able to get up, it had continued to travel, instead of falling after going one hundred yards.

Another impala buck that Roosevelt shot also showed an "unexpected softness" as it succumbed to a wound which Roosevelt believed would not have felled either a white-tailed or black-tailed deer at home.

Having claimed two impala, Roosevelt returned to the place where he and Judd had left their horses. They discovered the boys who tended the horses exclaiming that they had seen a large snake nearby. When Roosevelt looked for it, he found a python coiled up in long grass under a small tree. Perhaps recalling his encounters with Dakota rattlesnakes, he chambered his gun with a solid bullet and fired into the middle of its body. To his surprise, the snake lashed at him with open jaws, and then, recoiling, glided forward.

"I did not think it was charging," Roosevelt wrote. "I thought it was merely trying to escape. But Judd, who was utterly unmoved by lion, leopard, or rhino, evidently held this snake in respect, and yelled at me to get out of the way. Accordingly, I jumped back a few feet, and the snake came over ground where I had stood; its evil genius then made it halt for a moment and raise its head to a height of perhaps three feet, and I killed it by a shot through the neck."

When Roosevelt picked it up, first by the tail and then by the head, the porters were aghast that he would touch it. "It was," Roosevelt noted calmly, "only twelve feet long."

A close call for Kermit was with a leopard. Hunting in a ravine with McMillan and a few natives, Kermit observed the leopard slinking through bushes, then lost sight of it. Supposing that the leopard had sought cover in a large thicket, the beaters went to work in hopes of driving it out. But without a warning snarl, the leopard lunged into the open and charged at Kermit. With an icy calm as the leopard came within six yards, Kermit shot it in the chest. Seemingly unfazed, it continued its forward rush. Unmoving, Kermit fired a crippling shot into its hips.

Excited by the sight of the charge and the way in which it was stopped, the beaters rushed jubilantly forward, only to discover that the leopard wasn't finished. Though crippled, it lunged at one of the beaters. Although shot again by McMillan, the thrice-wounded leopard managed to run down the beater and sink fangs and claws into the man's leg. Wrenching free, the beater heard the bang of McMillan's rifle, but rather than dropping, the leopard retreated into the thicket. As the wounded beater was taken away and dogs were sent to sniff out what all in the party expected to be a carcass, the leopard darted from the brush and again raced toward Kermit. With a single shot, Kermit killed it. A female, it weighed just under sixty pounds, but although it was small, Theodore Roosevelt was so impressed by the tale of the struggle that he admiringly wrote that Kermit's first bullet "would have knocked the fight out of any animal less plucky and savage than the leopard." There was, he said, "not even in Africa, a beast of more unflinching courage than this spotted cat."

With a far larger trophy in mind, Roosevelt rode off one day with Judd, the famed hunter's Masai gun-bearer, and two of Roosevelt's bearers in search of the animal that ancient Greeks found living in streams and had named "hip- popotaus," the Greek for "riverhorse." The species abounded in the rivers of Juja farm, along with the scaled, gaping-mouthed, river-god of the old king- doms of Egypt, the fearsome crocodile.

Noiselessly approaching a great pool in which they expected to find hip- popotami, the party advanced with utmost caution to a steep bank of the pool and a sight that was, Roosevelt thought, "typically African." The scene he described was both primeval and could have been a descriptive passage for scenarists of yet long-in-the-future African adventure *Tarzan* movies:

> On the still water floated a crocodile, nothing but his eyes and nostrils visible. The bank was covered with a dense growth of trees, festooned with vines; among the branches sat herons; a little cormorant dived into the water; and a very small brilliantly colored kingfisher, with a red beak and large turquoise crest, perched unheedingly within a few feet of us. Here and there a dense growth of tall and singularly graceful papyrus rose out of the water, the feathery heads, which crowned the long smooth green stems, waving gently to and fro.
>
> We scanned the waters carefully, and could see no sign of hippos, and, still proceeding with utmost caution, we moved a hundred yards farther down to another lookout. Here the Masai detected a hippo head a long way off on the other side of the pool; and we again drew back and started cautiously forward to reach the point opposite which he had seen the head.

Just as they reached the point where they'd intended to turn toward the pool, they heard a succession of snorts and the sound of trampling of heavy feet and of a big body being shoved through dense tropical brush.

"Shoot, shoot," shouted Judd.

Suddenly, it was not a hippo that appeared, but a rhinoceros, twitching its tail and twisting its head from side to side. As it crashed toward Roosevelt and the others, Roosevelt thought it did not have very good horns, and would rather not have killed it. But faced with no alternative, "for it showed very symptom of being bent on mischief," and with the hulking animal less than forty yards away, he fired with his Winchester. Two full-jacketed bullets struck between the neck and shoulder, bringing the lumbering rhino to a halt. A third and fourth bullet hit its flank. The rhino then disappeared with a crash of branches into a dense thicket of thorn-bushes, reeds, and small, low-branching trees.

Examining the grass at the far end of the thicket, Roosevelt and Judd found so much blood that it was clear the rhino had been badly hit. With his heavy double-barreled Holland at the ready, Roosevelt moved gingerly through the grass, peering into the thicket and "expectant of developments." He wasn't disappointed. Hearing furious snorting and crashing directly opposite him in the thicket, he brought up his rifle. But the rhinoceros broke out of the cover, some thirty yards away. Firing both barrels, Roosevelt hit it behind the shoulder. Wheeling round, the rhino struggled back into the thicket. A crashing of brush signaled that it had fallen. When Roosevelt crept under the branches and saw the rhino on the ground, he thought it was dead. Taking no chances, he loaded the gun and fired a heavy bullet into it. An old female that was smaller than the rhino bull he'd already claimed, it had a front horn that measured fourteen inches (the bull's horn was nineteen inches) and weighed almost a ton.

"Now I did not want to kill this rhinoceros," Roosevelt wrote, "and I am not certain that it really intended to charge us. It may very well be that if we had stood firm it would, after much threatening and snorting, have turned and made off; veteran hunters like Selous could, I doubt not, have afforded to wait and see what happened. But I let it get within forty yards, and it still showed every symptom of meaning mischief, and at a shorter range I could not have been sure of stopping it in time."

To kill the rhino he'd needed eight bullets, five from the Winchester and three from the Holland. In keeping with his policy of comparing the effects of various bullets, he concluded that with the full-jacketed Winchester bullets he had inflicted wounds from which the rhino would have died in a short time. But it was the Holland that provided an immediate kill. From this study he recognized that the Winchester and Springfield did admirably against giraffes, elands, and lions, but for heavy game, rhinos and hippos, his rifle of choice ought to be the Holland. Ultimately, he noted, the determining factor would always be the quality of the man behind the gun.

That afternoon Roosevelt and Judd were out again, looking for hippos in the Rowero River. With light failing, and no hippos encountered, Judd announced that he was going home, but as he took a last look around, he dropped to his knees and beckoned to Roosevelt. Creeping forward on all fours, Roosevelt peered toward an object in the stream. About fifty yards off, he saw a hippo looking toward him, ears up and nostrils, eyes, and forehead above the surface. He aimed at the center of the head. The hippo sank without a splash. Informed by Judd that when a hippo was killed, it sank and that the body would not surface for several hours, Roosevelt went back to the McMillan house with the intention of returning to the spot in the morning.

Accompanied by Judd and a group of porters, and joined by R.J. Cuninghame, in a very leaky boat, they soon found the dead hippopotamus. A cow, it weighed almost 3000 pounds. A full-jacketed Winchester bullet had gone into the brain, where the jacket remained lodged as the remainder of the bullet plowed into the neck to break the atlas vertebra.

Having claimed a hippo and rhinoceros, Roosevelt departed Juja Farm and moved to the neighboring estate of Hugh H. Heately, a Roosevelt admirer who'd invited him to hunt African buffalo. Comprising 20,000 acres between the Rewero and Kamiti Rivers, and stretching seventeen miles, Heatley's property was a thriving farm with large herds of cattle, a dairy, hundreds of cultivated acres, and an impressive game preserve. With the party's tents pitched by the Kamiti, Roosevelt could not ride out in any direction without seeing swarms of hartebeest and zebra.

But he was after buffalo. Esteemed by many professional hunters as the most dangerous game, the species was nothing like the bison of the American West. With a coat of black hair, it had massive horns. Seeking them on the morning after making camp, Roosevelt, Kermit, their host (Heately), Cuninghame, and a neighbor of Heatley (identified by Roosevelt only as a Boer farmer), proceeded to a swamp that promised buffalo. The Roosevelts carried double-barrel Hollands, with Winchesters as backups. Grazing close to the edge of the swamp were four bulls, staring sullenly at the intruders. Instead of fleeing into cover of papyrus reeds, the herd moved to open country. Grateful for their luck, Roosevelt and Kermit opened fire. The result was three "fine trophies," one old bull and two young.

Three days later, Roosevelt sought a buffalo cow. What the party encountered was a herd lying in a curving, dry watercourse flanked by high banks and dotted with patches of high grass and papyrus. As the hunters crept toward the buffalo, one of the huge animals saw the crouching figures and reacted in a way that caused the herds to rise from their beds. They were at a long range for heavy rifles, but Roosevelt and the others had no choice but to fire. Two bulls were hit, but as they stumbled Roosevelt was startled to see not half a dozen buffalo rising from the grass, but scores of them bolting to their feet. He aimed at a cow and wounded it, but now his attention was distracted from his expected prize by the sight of the wounded bulls turning in a quarter-circle and drawing into a phalanx facing him and his companions with outstretched heads, a sure sign of defiance.

With teasing understatement, Roosevelt would write of that moment, "It was not a nice country on which to be charged by the herd, and for a moment things trembled in the balance."

In describing the thrill of going into battle in Cuba, Roosevelt would say in the autobiography that he would publish in 1913 that all men who feel any power of joy in battle know what it is like when the wolf rises in the heart. He called it three-o'clock-in-the-morning courage, and it was to him the most desirable kind. He'd shown it by leading the Rough Riders up Kettle Hill in the San Juan Heights. Now, discerning "a perceptible motion of uneasiness" in men, white and black, who stood in the path of menacing African buffalo, he called out, "Stand steady! Don't run!"

Knowing that any kind of movement would invite a charge, Cuninghame shouted, "And don't shoot."

After a few tense, expectant seconds, it was the buffalo herd that moved; first those that had not been wounded, then the two injured bulls. With the peril passed, Roosevelt turned his attention to finishing off the cow. Later that day, after collecting several different animals that he wanted, he returned to the place of the stand-off with the herd. Having "a vaguely uncomfortable feeling that as it grew dusk the buffalo might possibly make their appearance again," he found a number of them. "It seemed very strange that after the experience in the morning any of the herd should be willing to come out in the open so soon," he wrote. "But there they were. They were grazing to the number of about a dozen." Looking at them through field glasses, he could see them looking at him. For a moment he wondered if they might charge. "But it was only curiosity on their part," he recorded, "and after having grazed their fill, they sauntered back to the swamp and disappeared."

Camp was broken the next morning, providing Roosevelt another opportunity to watch the porters at work. Through the eyes of the man of his times that he was, they were "strapping grown-up children" who "felt as much pleasure and excitement over breaking camp after a few days' rest as over reaching camp after a fifteen-mile march." On this occasion, after they had made up their loads, "they danced in a ring for half an hour, two tin cans being beaten into tomtoms." As they strode off in a long line with a white man's burdens, each greeted Roosevelt with a smile as they said, "Yambo, Bwana!"

So far the Roosevelt safari had collected hundreds of specimens that had to be recorded and shipped from Nairobi. It was, Roosevelt noted, a task of "herculean proportions." He found the city of Nairobi so "very attractive" and "most interesting" that he believed the city and all of East Africa were ideal for settlement as a white man's country, and that the region was an ideal "playground alike for sportsmen, and for travelers who wish to live in health and comfort, and yet see what is beautiful and unusual."

With the classifying and packing of specimens completed, and on the move again on June 5, 1909, the Roosevelt expedition began a trek across sixty miles of waterless country called "the thirst."

13

★ ★ ★

Crossing the Thirst

H AD THEODORE ROOSEVELT been able to travel in the manner he preferred when on a hunt in the Dakotas—alone—the sixty-mile trek across the arid wasteland would have been made in one night. Instead, he set off in the company of stalwart son Kermit; intrepid R.J. Cuninghame; and the leathery veteran of hunts in the Australian outback and East Africa, Leslie Tarlton. With them were a "fine young colonial Englishman" named Ulyate; seasoned hunters Alden Loring and Edmund Heller; three other white wagon drivers, two of them English and the third a Boer; a boy from the Cape of Africa; a Kaffir wagon-driver; 196 porters; numerous askaris, tent boys, gun bearers, and saises; and various natives described in the usual Roosevelt way as "primitive savages in dress and habit, but coming from the cattle-owning tribes." Huge wagons, with white tops or "sails," were drawn by teams of oxen.

Because of the heat and blazing sun, they moved mostly at night. Horses were loaded lightly. Each man took only what he could carry. Roosevelt and Kermit each had an army overcoat, rifle, and cartridges. As they pushed steadily across the plain, the dust rose in clouds under a spectral moon and the stars of the Southern Cross.

This was not the first time Theodore Roosevelt had gazed in wonder at the constellation. Eleven years earlier, aboard the troopship *Yucatan,* bound for Cuba, with the wolf rising in his warrior's heart, he'd written to his sister Corinne, "All day we have steamed close to the Cuban coast, high barren looking mountains rising abruptly from shore, and at a distance looking much like those on Montana. We are well within the tropics, and at night the Southern Cross shows low above the horizon." The evening before, he'd gazed from the ship "through a sapphire sea, wind-rippled under an almost cloudless sky." There were some forty-eight craft in all, in three columns, the black hulls of the transports setting off the gray hulls of men-of-war. He watched "the red sun sink and the lights blaze up on the ships, for miles ahead and astern," while the band played piece after piece, from the "Star Spangled Banner" at which everyone rose and stood uncovered. It was a great historical expedition, Roosevelt wrote, "and I thrill to feel that I am part of it."

People might perceive in Theodore Roosevelt a blood-thirsty slaughterer of animals, but he knew how to set a scene.

Now, at intervals he heard the barking call of hyenas and shrieks of jackals. Overhead, plains plover circled. When the sun came up, the porters received rations of water and food, then lay down to sleep. Horses were fed and got half a pail of water.

Three-quarters of the way into the journey, black clouds gathered and thickened in the west, promising rain. Making good time, riding in advance of the lumbering wagons, Roosevelt and Kermit reached a fording place on the Suavi River and made camp. Seven and a half hours later, the porters arrived in excellent spirits, the Stars and Stripes waving, to an accompaniment of chanting and horn-blowing. The wagon train appeared in mid-morning. After a day's rest, the safari pushed on with the expectation of two days of easier travel to the Guaso Nyero, a rapid little river edged by yew trees and wooded cliffs.

"It was cool, rainy weather, with overcast skies and misty mornings, so that it seemed strangely unlike the tropics," Roosevelt noted. "The country was alive with herds of Masai cattle, sheep, and donkeys. The Masai, herdsmen by profession and warriors by preference, were stalwart savages, and showed the mixture of types common to this part of Africa, which is the edge of an ethnic whirlpool."

The safari was in "high feather." After nightfall the camp fires blazed in the cool air as the white hunters stood or sat around the blazes to do what Roosevelt liked most about being among such men—listening to and joining in the swapping of hunting tales. Cuninghame and Tarlton spun accounts of hunting elephants in the Congo. Loring and Heller spoke of Rocky Mountain hunts, the deserts of the Mexican border which were familiar to Kermit, and Alaska, where Roosevelt might have gone had he not become enthralled with Africa.

All these naturalists exhibited interest not only in big game, but many small mammals. Their catches ranged from big-eared mice and those with spiny fur, rats striped like chipmunks, and large cane rats to meercats, akin to the mongoose. Large game was not plentiful, but on one outing Kermit killed the party's first topi. The bull was, Roosevelt recorded, "a beautiful animal the size of a hartebeest, with satin-sheened coat."

Desiring a topi himself, Roosevelt soon encountered a herd of the shy, agile creatures in an open area that afforded him no cover. Aware of him as he maneuvered their way, the topi let him get within 600 yards. They stood motionless, as if tempting him to shoot. Uncertain of the range, Roosevelt fired more times than he cared to remember before getting a "handsome cow." Feeling delighted, he returned to camp and sat at the mouth of his tent to enjoy himself, not only with thoughts of his prize, but in taking a book from the Pigskin Library. The selection had been added to during the journey, including a copy of *Alice's Adventures in Wonderland* and *Louves de Macnecoul*, by Alexander Dumas, presented to Roosevelt at Port Said by the brother of an old and valued friend who had been the French ambassador to the United States, and vice-president of President Theodore Roosevelt's group of friends and tennis players, known then as Roosevelt's "Tennis Cabinet."

If members of the Roosevelt safari had inquired of Kermit about his father's game of tennis, they might have been told that the children of a father who advocated "the strenuous life" were expected to take part in all kinds of sports, both individual and team. For Sagamore Hill tennis, there was a makeshift dirt court. Kermit's older brother Ted remembered it as a place where moles traversed regularly, giving the court an uneven surface. In addition, it was so well shaded that moss grew over it. The branches of the trees were so low that there was a special rule that when a ball hit a branch and might have gone in it was a 'let.' The children batted the ball in whatever fashion seemed best. "While Father played with us whenever he had the time, and was always welcome," Ted wrote in a family memoir. "His method of playing was original, to say the least. He gripped the racquet halfway up the handle with his index finger pointed back. When he served he did not throw the ball into the air, but held it in his left hand and hit it from between his fingers. In spite of this, and in spite of his great weight, he played a surprisingly good game. We used him as a sort of milestone of progress. When we were able to beat him in singles it was equivalent to having passed the entrance examinations to college."

In winter the children's strenuous life included hikes through the snow, sledding, and snowball fights. When their father came home one day with "snowshoes" which had been given to him by a Norwegian diplomat, they were introduced to a new sport that would be known in the future as skiing. When old enough to hold a rifle, the Roosevelt boys were introduced to the adventures of hunting and exploration, so that when Ted and Kermit were adults, following their valiant service in the army during World War I, they teamed for big-game hunts and exploring in the Himalaya mountains of Central Asia. But because falling in love had stood in the way of Roosevelt's namesake joining his father in Africa in 1909, it was the second son about whom Roosevelt joyfully wrote after his account of getting a prize topi, "The next day was Kermit's red-letter day."

Riding with Leslie Tarlton, Kermit killed two cheetahs and "a fine maned lion" that was better than any that the safari had so far collected. Roosevelt recorded that on the same day "I merely got some ordinary game," then proudly described Kermit having seen the lion feeding, then galloping a mile in pursuit of the big male. When it suddenly turned to charge, Kermit got off a crippling shot, then a fatal one. Although nearly a foot longer than any lion Roosevelt had claimed, Kermit's prize was so thin as to be called gaunt and weighed only 412 pounds. Still, in a photograph taken by Kermit, the lushly maned lion appeared formidable, even though dead.

After five days camped by the Guaso Nyero the hunt had resulted in the collection of heads and pelts of fourteen animals of ten different species. With the meticulousness of little Teedie Roosevelt's entries into his note-books, Theodore Roosevelt's journal recorded not only the safari's trophies, but details of how they were gotten. In the register were: "one lioness, one hyena, one wart-hog boar, two zebra, two eland, one wildebeest, two topi, two impala, one Roberts' gazelle, one Thompson's gazelle."

Making it clear that he had killed "nothing that was not absolutely needed, both for scientific purposes and for food," and that skin of every animal was preserved for the museum, he recorded how each prize had been obtained. He wrote:

> Except the lioness and one impala (both of which I shot running), all were shot at rather long ranges; seven were shot standing, two walking, five running. The average distance at which they were shot was a little

over two hundred and twenty yards. I used sixty-five cartridges, an amount which will seem excessive chiefly to those who are not accustomed actually to count the cartridges they expend, to measure the distances at which they fire, and to estimate for themselves the range, on animals in the field when they are standing or running a good way off. Only one wounded animal got away; and eight of the animals I shot had to be finished with one bullet—two in the case of the lioness—as they lay in the ground. Many of the cartridges expended really represented range-finding.

Perhaps because Roosevelt told his stories of hunting in Africa in the articles he sent back for publication at the time in *Scribner's Magazine,* and their later compilation in the book *African Game Trails* in 1910, he devoted less than two pages of his 1913 autobiography to his year in Africa. But the stories he chose to relate in it were about the charges by the elephant that "came through the thick brush to my left like a steam plow through a light snow-drift," and the rhinoceros that "charged with the utmost determination." In comparing these harrowing close calls with his confrontation more than twenty years earlier with a charging grizzly bear, he still considered the grizzly's attack his "only narrow escape."

As to the debate among hunters regarding which African animal was the most dangerous, he came down on the side of those who cited the lion, even though, he pointed out, "I personally had no difficulties with lions."

For readers who might shiver in revulsion at the thought of killing wild animals, except in self-defense, of course, Roosevelt revealed empathy for the creatures he killed, and found in their violent deaths, whether at the hands of man or as a part of nature, a lesson for humans, snug in their homes in modern cities. "Watching the game," he wrote, "one was struck by the intensity and the evanescence of their emotions. Civilized man now usually passes his life under conditions which eliminate the intensity of terror felt by his ancestors when death by violence was their normal end, and threatened them every hour of the day and night. It is only in nightmares that the average dweller in civilized countries now undergoes the hideous horror which was the regular and frequent portion of the ages-vanished forefathers, and which is still the everyday incident in the lives of most wild creatures. But the dread is short-lived, and its horror vanishes with instantaneous rapidity."

14

★ ★ ★

With Rifle and Camera

THE ROOSEVELTS' NEXT CAMP was in the middle of a vast plain by limestone springs at one end of a line of dark acacia trees. The day after setting up the camp he rode out, hoping to get either a rhino or a cow giraffe. The day was cloudy and cool and the game shy. Although the safari needed meat, Roosevelt was unable to get within fair range of wildebeest, hartebeest, topi, or large gazelle. He succeeded in claiming only two tommy gazelles, one with a good shot as the animal ran, but he got it, he confessed, after his first shot had missed in a "rather scandalous fashion" while the quarry was standing.

In maneuvering toward a herd of giraffes he found himself being "played around" with by a wildebeest bull. Within two hundred yards of Roosevelt's little Springfield rifle, it pranced, flourishing its tail, tossing its head, and uttering its grunting bellow as if it knew Roosevelt would not shoot at him. The wildebeest was right. Roosevelt was more interested in the giraffes. There were seven, a medium-size bull, four cows, and two calves. Roosevelt's intent was to collect two cows and a young one for the museum. After he shot the three he wanted, he marveled that the remaining four did not run.

Because they stayed, exhibiting what Roosevelt called "tameness bordering on stupidity," Kermit was able to shoot them with a camera. After the exercise of much patience, he managed to get within fifty yards of the bull and take several pictures. Never without a camera, carried by one of the porters, Kermit proved to be a talented photographer whose photos were not limited to showing the animals that were killed. His pictures recorded all kinds of wildlife and birds in their habitats, as well as vistas of the African landscapes and action shots of the safari on the move across plains, fording streams, and encamped. Many of the pictures, of course, captured Roosevelt striking a victorious pose with particularly prized specimens at his feet.

One day when Roosevelt was preparing to shoot at a bull rhino with a stubby horn, and Kermit readied his camera to capture the rhino with a camera, Kermit exclaimed, "Look at him, standing there in the middle of the African plain, deep in prehistoric thought." The photo he got was of the rhino's left profile, the short grass of the plain beneath him and against a cloudless sky. Another photo taken at the same time caught the bull, a cow, and a calf, widely separated in a scene that appeared to Roosevelt to not have changed since the pliocene age, while "the rest of the world, for good or evil," had gone forward.

Kermit's lens also caught giraffes and wildebeest herds for photos that in Roosevelt's book were captioned "at home." Other pictures immortalized a wounded lioness in deep grass as she prepared to charge, and a head-on, angry rhino that was captioned "coming on."

Had audiotape recorders been available, Roosevelt certainly would have preferred to use such a machine to capture the sounds made by the animals, rather than to attempt to describe them in prose. He noted that zebras were the noisiest game. After them came the wildebeest's "queer grunt." The topi uttered only a kind of sneeze, as did the hartebeest. But no sound was as thrilling as the roar of a lion.

A perpetual source of wonder was the difference in the behavior of individuals within the same species, and in behavior of the same individual at different times, such as wariness when going for water, when they rested, and when they showed their ferocity. He also observed how their appearance seemed to change, depending on the light. "At one moment the sun would turn the zebras of a mixed herd white," he noted, "and the hartebeest straw-colored, so that the former could been seen much farther than the latter; and again the conditions would be reversed when under the light the zebras would show up gray, and the hartebeest as red as foxes."

Having collected almost all the specimens of the common type desired by the sponsoring museum, Roosevelt and his safari marched north from the Sotik plain toward Lake Naivasha.

★   ★   ★

"Two or three times we crossed singularly beautiful ravines, the trail winding through narrow cliffs that were almost tunnels, and along the brinks of sheer cliffs, while the green mat of trees and vines was spangled with many colored flowers," Roosevelt wrote of the trek. "Then we came to barren ridges and bare, dusty plains; and at nightfall pitched camp near the shores of Lake Naivasha." He found it "a lovely sheet of water surrounded by hills and mountains, its shores broken by rocky promontories, and indented by papyrus-fringed bays."

To reward the porters for their hard work and good conduct he gave them twenty-five sheep. The men improvised long chants in his honor, then "feasted royally."

For a day of hippo hunting, Roosevelt, Kermit, Cuninghame, and the usual number of natives set out in a steam launch. The boat was provided by a pair of English brothers named Attenborough. To start a farm in Africa one had given up mining in the California Sierras after twenty years and the other had retired from His Majesty's Navy in the rank of commander. Roosevelt saw in them "just the men for work in a new country—for a new country is a poor place for the weak and incompetent, whether of body or mind." As the steam launch plied the waters of a lagoon, Roosevelt was surprised and delighted to see a big hippo walking entirely out of the water on the edge of the papyrus at the far end of a little bay that was filled with waterlilies. Until that moment all the hippos he'd encountered had been submerged with only their eyes and nostrils in view. When the launch was maneuvered to within a few rods of the hippo, Roosevelt switched to the launch's rowboat. As he steadied himself in the bow with the small Springfield rifle in hand, Cuninghame steered. Kermit readied his camera.

To Roosevelt the hippopotamus was a "self confident, truculent beast" that went under water once or twice, only to pop out of the papyrus and wade along the water, its massive body in full view. Cuninghame rowed closer into shallower water, but still more than a hundred yards from the hippo. As it turned as if to break into the papyrus, Roosevelt fired into its shoulder. A truculent beast indeed, it plunged into the water, and with its huge jaws agape, surged straight at the boat, floundering and splashing through the water lilies, bent on mischief. Instead of trying to reach deeper water, and despite being shot again, the hippo continued on. Aimed at its open mouth, Roosevelt fired one more. The jaws closed, Roosevelt noted, "with the clash of a sprung bear trap." The next bullets slammed at the base of an ear, dropping the hippo in its tracks.

While this drama unfolded, Kermit was so busy snapping pictures that he saw the hippo only through his viewfinder. Putting down the camera, he joined in the hard work of dragging the hippo from among the water lilies and tethering it to the back of the launch. Back at camp, the natives welcomed Roosevelt and his prize with a half-hour chant, praising Bwana Makuba for his feat. But Roosevelt did not think much of hippo-hunting. He regarded it as not a very attractive sport, primarily because he usually had to wait an hour or more before finding out if he'd been successful because, as noted earlier, a hippo killed in water sank immediately, only to bob to surface a day later. He also didn't like not knowing if he'd shot a bull or cow because all he could see of the hippo when he shot was a portion of the head sticking above the water. As the time he had to get off a shot was brief, any hesitation ensured that the hippo escaped. This meant that two or three hippo might be killed before the right specimen was secured. This was, the conservationist felt, a waste of wildlife.

But there were times when going after a hippo could afford, as he wrote, "interesting and exciting incidents." The one he had in mind involved him, Cuninghame, and the two Attenborough brothers. They'd started out early in the launch, towing the big, clumsy rowboat manned by a trio of strong porters who knew how to row. Steaming down the lake about fifteen miles, they entered a wide bay that was indented by smaller bays, lagoons, and inlets, all fringed by the ever-present papyrus. Leaving the launch for the rowboat, they immediately heard a hippo, hidden in the green vastness on their right. There were eight hippos, floating with heads above the water. Roosevelt shot one, hoping that it was a bull and disappointed that it was a cow.

Later, in the rowboat with two rowers who did not speak English, he made out about a dozen hippo, two or three of them very big. When he shot the largest, it disappeared in the water. As the rowers brought the boat to the spot, Roosevelt directed one of the rowers to probe the water with a pole. The porter did as told and poked the submerged body, then with a look of alarm on his face, found enough English vocabulary to shout that the hippo was alive.

"Sure enough," Roosevelt recorded for his eventual readership, "bump went the hippo against the bottom of the boat, the jar causing all to sit suddenly down."

Another bump shook the boat, followed by the shallow, muddy water boiling as hippos on all sides, above and below the surface, scattered. As the two horrified rowers struggled to take the boat "out of the dangerous neighborhood," Roosevelt shot at the head of a hippo that appeared to his left. As the hippo made off in frantic haste, Roosevelt had no idea whether he'd hit it. What happened next was described as only Roosevelt could:

I had small opportunity to ponder the subject, for twenty feet away the water bubbled and a huge head shot out facing me, the jaws wide open. There was no time to guess at its intentions, and I fired on the instant. Down went the head, and I felt the boat quiver as the hippo passed underneath. Just here the lily pads were thick; so I marked its course, fired as it rose, and down it went. But on the other quarter of the boat a beast, evidently of great size—it proved to be a bull—now appeared, well above the water; and I put a bullet into its brain.

I did not wish to shoot again unless I had to, and stood motionless, with the little Springfield at the ready. A head burst up twenty yards off, with a lily pad plastered over one eye, giving the hippo an absurd resemblance to a discomfited prize-fighter, and then disappeared with great agitation. Two half-grown beasts stupid from fright appeared, and stayed up for a minute or two at a time, not knowing what to do. Other heads popped up, getting farther and farther away. By degrees everything vanished, the water grew calm, and we rowed over to the papyrus, moored ourselves by catching a hold of a couple of stems, and awaited events. Within an hour four dead hippos appeared: a very big bull and three big cows. Of course, I would not have shot the latter if it could have been avoided; but under the circumstances I do not see how it was possible to help it. The meat was not wasted; on the contrary it was a godsend, not only to our own porters, but to the natives round about, many of whom were short on commons on account of the drought.

Bringing over the launch we worked until after dark to get the bull out of the difficult position in which he lay. It was nearly seven o'clock before we had him fixed for towing on one quarter, the rowboat towing the other, by which time two hippos were snorting and blowing within a few yards of us, their curiosity as much excited as to what was going on. The night was overcast; there were drenching rain squalls, and a rather heavy sea was running, and I did not get back to camp until after three. Next day the launch fetched the rest of the hippo meat.

From Lake Naivasha, the safari proceeded to the railroad town of the same name. There they read news of the outside world from the only news-paper they ever saw, the New York *Oswego Gazette,* that was mailed on a reg-ular basis to Alden Loring. It was now late July 1909 and three months since Roosevelt had debarked the German steamer *Admiral* at Mombasa.

On July 24, in order to ship fresh specimens and trophies to the United States, Roosevelt was again in Nairobi and reunited with Frederick Selous, the McMillans, and Judd. It was race week in the colorful city. White army officers, government officials, and farmers and wives went to the races on ponies, and a few on camels, or drove there in rickshaws, a cart called a gharry, in bullock-towed two-wheel carriages known as tongas, and occa-sionally in automobiles. The races were carried out in the most sporting spirit. Kermit demonstrated the horsemanship his father had seen that all his children develop, and deported himself admirably in what Roosevelt termed the "capital fun."

On the fourth of August Roosevelt was back at Lake Naivasha after stop-ping on the way to lay a cornerstone of a new mission building. While waiting for the safari to get ready for its next leg, and as Kermit went off on a camping trip, Roosevelt spent a couple of days trying for singsing waterbuck. He missed a bull and wounded another that he did not get, but he succeeded in shooting a fine waterbuck cow at a hundred yards, and a buck tommy, both for food.

A four-day march from Naivasha brought the safari to Neri, in the high plateaus and mountain chains of the Aberdare range. Their last camp at that spot was at an altitude of about ten thousand feet. The air was so cold that water froze in wash basins. Fog and rain shrouded the landscape. There was not much game. The land was Kikuyu country. The natives welcomed the Bwana Makuba with one of their dances at a ceremony arranged by the dis-trict commissioner. Two thousand warriors, naked or half so, with faces and legs painted red and yellow, chanted in unison, danced rhythmically in rings while drums throbbed and horns blared. Women shrilled approval and also danced, while Masai tribesmen circled and swung in a pantherlike dance of their own. The dancing continued in their camps, late into the night, long after Bwana Makuba had gone to bed.

Two days later, the clouds lifted. The safari rose from camp in bright sun-light, ahead of them in the distance the high rocky peaks of Mount Kenya.

15

★ ★ ★

Most Interesting of
All the Animals

WITH KERMIT AND LESLIE TARLTON heading north on a safari of their own, Roosevelt, Cuninghame, and Heller traveled for two days through well-peopled farm country in which Kikuyu women worked the fields with hoes, because, Roosevelt observed, "among the Kikuyus, as among other savages, the woman is the drudge and beast of burden." The trail led by clear, rushing streams that formed the headwaters of the Tana River. On the afternoon of the second day the party struck upward among the steep foothills of Mount Kenya and pitched camp by the green wall of tangled forest.

Elephants on his mind, Roosevelt had observed along the route the devastation they had wreaked in farm fields in nighttime rampages, known as "shambas," in which the elephants had pillaged the crops. In his travels Roosevelt found that no other animal, including the lion, was so constant a theme for talk around campfires of African hunters and in the native villages as the elephant. "It is, not only to hunters, but to naturalists, and to all people who possess any curiosity about wild creatures and the wild life of nature," he wrote, "the most interesting of all animals."

After two days of rain that followed the setting up of the camp in an open glade on the mountainside, Cuninghame and a native guide called an 'Ndorobo, set off to look for signs that elephants were nearby. Rain was still falling when Roosevelt, Heller, and Cuninghame tramped in single file through forest that was too thick for horses. Clad in a khaki-colored shirt and khaki trousers that buttoned down the legs, wearing hobnailed shoes and a thick slouch hat, with a book from the Pigskin Library in his kit, Roosevelt climbed in and out of the deep ravines and waded through swift streams for three hours on a route along the edge of the woods. When the sun came out, they plunged into a forest that was a riot of twisted vines and interlacing trees and bushes.

On finding elephant spoor, Cuninghame and the 'Ndorobo minutely examined the dung, then tested the wind by lighting matches to see which way the smoke blew. The frustration of the trek was noted in Roosevelt's account. He wrote, "Each time after an hour's stealthy stepping and crawling along the twisted trail a slight shift of wind in the almost still air gave our scent to the game, and away it went before we could catch a glimpse of it; and we resumed our walk."

As evening fell, they pitched camp beside a little brook at the bottom of a ravine. They dined "ravenously" on bread, mutton, and tea. Two hours after leaving camp in the morning, all the frustration and impatience of yesterday vanished with today's discovery of the fresh signs of between ten and fifteen elephants. Around noon they were heard thrashing around in the woods. They were moving slowly. Roosevelt listened to the crack of tree branches and the elephants' "curious internal rumblings." Carefully, with every sense alert, Roosevelt and his two knowing companions kept pace with the yet unseen quarry. With double-barreled rifle in hand, Roosevelt stepped in the huge footprints left by the elephants, confident that where such a great weight had pressed there were not sticks left to crack under his feet to alert the quarry.

He wrote, "It made our veins thrill thus for half an hour to creep stealthily along, but a few rods from the herd, never able to see it, because of the extreme denseness of the cover, but always hearing first one and then another of its members, and always trying to guess what each one might do, and keeping ceaselessly ready for whatever might befall."

Where the trail took a twist to one side, suddenly there was before Roosevelt, about thirty yards in front, part of the massive gray head of an elephant resting its tusks on the branches of a young tree. A bull with good ivory, it turned in Roosevelt's direction. Roosevelt raised his gun and aimed for an eye, but a little to the side, hoping to send the bullet into the brain. He struck where he'd aimed, but he merely stunned the elephant. As it stumbled forward, half falling, a second bullet "sped true," as the rifleman described the shot, and as Roosevelt lowered the gun from his shoulder, he "saw the great lord of the forest come crashing to the ground."

With both barrels of the rifle emptied, Roosevelt watched as the thick bushes parted to his left, revealing the vast bulk of a charging bull elephant that was so close to Roosevelt that it could have knocked him down with a swipe of his thick trunk. Leaping aside, Roosevelt dodged behind a tree, frantically ejected the two shells from the rifle's barrels, and reloaded. But it was Cuninghame, firing twice, who stopped the charge. The wounded elephant wheeled and ran for thick cover. Unable to follow him, Roosevelt heard him trumpet shrilly. Then all sounds ceased.

Having wisely run for safety when the elephant first crashed from the trees, the 'Ndorobo reappeared to go forward in search of the elephant's trail. He soon returned to report evidence that the elephant had fled fast, but that great amounts of blood marked the route. Rather than go after the wounded giant, Roosevelt decided to tackle the formidable job of collecting the skin of the dead bull for mounting in the museum. Of killing his first elephant, Roosevelt chose an odd noun for a man who professed great respect for "the great lord of the forest." He wrote "I felt proud indeed as I stood by the immense bulk of the slain *monster* [emphasis added] and put my hand on the ivory. The tusks weighed a hundred and thirty pounds. There was the usual scene of joyful excitement among the gun bearers—who had behaved excellently—and among the wild bush people who had done the tracking for us."

When some of the 'Ndorobo looked for the bull that Cuninghame had shot to see if it had fallen, they found that it had traveled steadily, even though its wounds were probably fatal, but the searchers found no carcass. Leaving Cuninghame and Heller to skin the bull and to do the time-consuming curing of the hide, and then transport it to Neri, Roosevelt took one porter and a guide and returned to the base camp. Reaching it in early afternoon, he sent natives back to the scene of the elephant skinning to deliver a week's supply of provisions, tents, and fresh clothing for Cuninghame, Heller, and their workers. He then enjoyed the luxuries of a shave and a warm bath. The next day was devoted to writing, accepting the accolades of a visiting Kikuyu chief, and preparing for the next adventure, a fortnight-long safari that he would lead himself.

* ⋆ *

The immediate destination was Neri. There he added to his entourage a pair of young Scotsmen who spoke the local language. He also assembled fifty Kikuyus to supplement his Swahili porters, and a "head tent boy," an Arab named Ali. The only significant event on the first afternoon was finding "safari" ants, so-called because they moved on foraging expeditions in immense numbers. Roosevelt observed with amused fascination as one of the porters of the human safari laid two twigs on the ground as a peace-offering to the ants, stating that since the ants were on safari, too, it was wise to propitiate them, although it's highly unlikely that the man actually said "propitiate."

After camping for an evening in a forest glade, the Roosevelt safari came out onto plains on which there were no human inhabitants, hardly any game, and no lions. Camp was pitched by a cold stream that was one of the headwaters of the Guaso Nyero. To the east rose the crags and snowfields of Mount Kenya. Roosevelt had been told to expect to hunt in a dry season, but found rains that often turned torrential. During one especially heavy storm, Ali rushed into Roosevelt's tent exclaiming about "a big snake up high." Deciding this was definitely worth investigating, Bwana Makuba exited the tent, looked up, and saw a huge, funnel-shaped, whirling, dark cloud careering across the sky. Fortunately, it passed to one side of the camp harm-lessly.

On another occasion there was such a violent thunderstorm that the natives cowered in fear. "In this desolate and lonely land the majesty of the storms impressed on the beholder a sense of awe and solemn exaltation," Roosevelt-the-naturalist recorded in an almost biblical prose. "Tossing their crests, and riven by lightning, they gathered in their wrath from every quarter of the heavens, and darkness was before and under them; then, in the lull of a moment, they might break apart, while the sun turned the rain to silver and the rainbows were set in the sky; but always they gathered again, menacing and mighty—for the promise of the [rain]bow was never kept, and ever the clouds returned after the rain."

Once as he rode alone facing Mount Kenya "the clouds tore asunder, to right and left, and the mountain towered between, while across its base was flung a radiant arch. But almost at once the many-colored glory was dimmed; for in splendor and tenor the storm that rode in front shrouded all things from sight in thunder-shattered sheets of rain."

On these days alone in the wilderness, happy and content as he had been on his solitary hunts in his beloved, but now lost, American West, he enjoyed being "entirely by myself," except for his native followers. But as he ventured out with them, the gunbearers, sais, and the skinners walked silently, on the lookout for game, until he called a halt and returned to camp. On the front peak of his little triangular tent, called a "thorn boma," flew the American flag.

Late in the afternoon of September 3, 1909, Cuninghame and Heller caught up with the safari to be greeted "joyfully." Next morning, they started toward Mera, a small settlement in the Kenya foothills. Awaiting them were Kermit and Tarleton, eager to relate their own hunts. With Kermit and Tarleton striking out again on their own hunts, Roosevelt and the others spent two weeks hunting elephants and rhinos. Riding through tall grass, which often rattled in the wind, Roosevelt thought about rattlesnakes in the West. Although he knew that no African snakes had rattles, his "subconscious senses" always put him at attention if he heard anything resembling the threatening noise of a rattler.

While at Mera he received a cable informing him that Admiral Peary had reached the North Pole. Perhaps wishing he could have joined that expedition, he recalled that a year before, as President of the United States, he'd said good-bye to Peary at Oyster Bay as Peary started on his Arctic quest on a ship named *Roosevelt*.

On a hunt from Mera, Roosevelt claimed two ostriches and on the same day took a giraffe. A different species than the giraffe he'd hunted south of Kenya, it was a "reticulated" species, so-called because its coloring consisted of a network of reticulation of white lines. It was a type of giraffe that naturalists were eager to obtain and study.

When this phase of Roosevelt's safari ended at Neri on October 20, 1909, after a march through mist and rain across the cold Aberdare tablelands, Roosevelt again admired the blue waters of Lake Naivasha. After a brief pause at Neri, he headed for Nairobi and a reunion with Kermit. Exhilarated by a month-long hunt with Leslie Tarleton, son told father about killing the "great koodoo." With spiral horns and striped coat, the animal was, in Theodore Roosevelt's opinion, "the stateliest and handsomest antelope in the world."

Kermit had turned twenty on October 10. Sixteen days later he was again with father for the next adventure in the company of Tarlton and Edmund Heller. The following day was his father's fifty-first birthday, but because they spent it marching hard toward the Uasin Gishu plateau and the 'Nzoi

River Roosevelt was disappointed that he had no chance to celebrate the occasion by taking a hunt. He'd marked his fiftieth as president by riding his jumping horse, Roswell, over all the hurdles in Rock Creek Park in Washington. Now he was pushing on among rolling hills and along valleys and ravines on a route that crossed and re-crossed the Equator.

As on the Aberdares and the slopes of Mount Kenya, the nights were sometimes so cold that he was glad to have brought a mackinaw and a lumberman's jacket that had been a gift from a dear friend, Jack Greenway, who'd ridden with Roosevelt's Rough Riders. When Roosevelt opened his diary to note the events of the first day of November 1909, his African safari was in a landscape that reminded him of northern California. Some of the hills were bald. Others were wooded at the top. There were wet meadows, hillsides covered with rank, thick-growing grass that alternated with stretches of forest of stately cedars, yews, and tall laurel-leaved olive trees.

It was a land rich in game, including a large party of the despised hyena in a lair laid in the wet seclusion of some reed beds. As natives beat the brush, the hyenas bolted into the clear, allowing both Roosevelts to claim one. The next day, Roosevelt decided, "it was Kermit's turn for a giraffe." After a spirited chase, during which Roosevelt's horse, Tranquility, put both his front feet into a hole and dumped Roosevelt to the ground, Kermit and Tarlton were in a race with a wounded bull giraffe. When it suddenly came to a standstill, looking as if it had had enough and decided to charge, Kermit leaped from his horse and felled it. The kill of the "fine specimen" meant that the safari had to stop so that the giraffe hide could be preserved. The pause allowed Roosevelt to switch from big-game hunter to quiet observer of the region's lush flora, and to write about it at length and in meticulous detail. He noted that some of the acacias "had put forth their small, globular, yellow blossoms, just as the acacias of the Athi Plains were doing in the previous May," and blue lupins were flowering, "for it is cool, pleasant country."

But hunting was not completely forgotten. To "fill out the series of specimens of the big hartebeest and the oribi" needed by the National Museum, Roosevelt and son took advantage of the leisure time to hunt them. The meat of the oribis were reserved for the white men's table, set up in Roosevelt's tent in a way that Colonel Roosevelt of the now-legendary Rough Riders saw as the "officers' mess." His faithful tent boy, "Good Ali," saw to it that the table was adorned by bowls of sweet-scented jessamine.

Kermit's two gun-bearers were Juma Tohari, a "coal-black Swahili Moslem," and "a Christian negro" named Kassitura from Uganda. Roosevelt was pleased that both men were as eager to serve Kermit as those who looked after Bwana Makuba. From time to time Roosevelt gave them chocolate in colorful wrappers, then delighted in watching them puzzling over their pictures of ladies, gentlemen, little girls, and wild beasts.

From the giraffe camp the safari traveled two days to the 'Nzoi River. Until now they'd been on waters that either vanished in the desert or flowed into the Indian Ocean. The 'Nzoi, a rapid, muddy river that passed south of Mount Eglon and emptied into the Victoria Nyanza lake, was part of the watershed of the Nile River. The territory was rife with game, from lions that Roosevelt heard roaring at night, to troops of elephants who marked their passage by tearing off the tops of small thorn trees. Seeing the evidence, Roosevelt marveled over how the elephants could swallow such prickly "dainties" armored with needle-like spikes. Hartebeests were many in number, along with topi, oribi, and herds of zebras.

Nor were the area's birds overlooked, especially honey birds. Before starting for Africa, Roosevelt had been encouraged by naturalist John Burroughs to look into the bird's habits. One whose existence Burroughs had doubted, the species got its name from its facility in finding honey. Camped by the 'Nzoi, Roosevelt found the noisy birds almost a nuisance because they continually accompanied him as he hunted. They flew from tree to tree, never ceasing their harsh chatter.

One day as the honey birds vexed him, and a line of a hundred porters fanned out across a large swamp, Roosevelt shot a couple of bushbuck. After the drive was over Kermit shot a female leopard as she stood on the side of an anthill. Then he had a close call when a wounded singsing buck charged him. But the day turned out to be one on which Roosevelt found himself benefitting from honey birds. They led Kermit and some porters to a bee hive. After the porters smoked out the inhabitants, the hive provided enough honey to be a welcome accompaniment to Roosevelt's lunch.

A few miles beyond the swamp they encountered a small herd of elephants in the open. Roosevelt counted eight cows and two calves, moving slowly and feeding on the thorny tops of mimosa trees. Desiring to photograph them, Kermit wanted to move closer. Having obtained all the elephants he needed for the museum, Roosevelt was content to observe them as their great ears flapped and trunks lifted and curled.

On the way back to camp he saw a white man on the trail ahead and was surprised that he was Carl Akeley, out from New York City on a mission on behalf of the American Museum of Natural History. His goal was elephants, he explained, as Roosevelt remembered that it had been a year ago that Akeley's vivid descriptions of the glories of Africa had persuaded Roosevelt to abandon plans to hunt in Alaska. Now, when Akeley asked Roosevelt to join him in a hunt for elephants, Roosevelt happily agreed. The hunt began the next morning. In addition to Akeley and Roosevelt were Kermit and Tarlton, traveling light. They found elephants around noon, standing in a clump, each occasionally shifting its position or lazily flapping an ear in a grassy area dotted by mimosas. Akeley wanted two cows and a calf. The hunters advanced to within twenty-five yards of them. Standing on an anthill, Roosevelt prepared to shoot.

Tarlton shouted, "Look out! They are coming for us."

Regarding an elephant charge at such close range "a serious thing," Roosevelt stood his ground and shot a menacing cow in the forehead. The elephant lurched heavily forward to her knees. A volley from everyone finished it, while sending the other elephants scurrying as fast as possible for safety. As they turned to run, Roosevelt felled a second cow. Meanwhile, Kermit used a Winchester to kill a bull calf. With a camp set up a hundred yards from the carcasses, Tarlton and Akeley, "working like a demon," had them skinned by nightfall. Before long a pack of hyenas gathered in the dark to quarrel among themselves as they gorged on the remains.

Pleased to have assisted Akeley, Roosevelt left him by the 'Nzoi to go to Lake Sergoi on a two-day march. Not a true lake, but a reed-filled pond, it was the limit at which Englishmen and Boers had settled. But there was a store kept by a South African of Scottish lineage who met Roosevelt with "a kind courtesy." Anticipating Roosevelt's arrival, the English commissioner of the district had arranged for a group of warriors of the Nandi tribe to show Roosevelt how they hunted lions with spears.

The next day, November 20, 1909, Roosevelt and several other white settlers set out on horseback to catch up with Nandi hunters already in the field. The action began around noon when a maned lion rose a quarter of a mile ahead of the line of Nandi and galloped off through high grass. Roosevelt and the others tore after him on horseback. He was, observed Roosevelt, "a magnificent beast, with a black and tawny mane; in his prime, teeth and claws perfect, with mighty thews, and a savage heart."

He was lying near a hartebeest on which he had been feasting. Until this very moment, Roosevelt mused, "his life had been one of unbroken career of rapine and violence; and now the maned master of the wilderness, the terror that stalked by night, the grim lord of slaughter, was to meet his doom at the hands of the only foes who dared molest him."

But not without a tremendous fight. As the Nandi encircled him, the lion rose to his feet. The lush mane bristled. His tail lashed. The great head hung low, fangs revealed. Facing first one way and then another, he grunted and roared. With an eye as true as the lens of Kermit's camera, and invoking the experience of years of hunting dangerous game and then writing about them in articles and books, Roosevelt recorded the drama this way:

> It was a wild sight; the ring of spearmen, intent, silent, bent on blood, and in the center the great man-killing beast, his thunderous wrath growing ever more dangerous.
>
> At last the ring was complete, and the spearmen rose and closed in. The lion looked quickly from side to side, saw where the line was thinnest, and charged at his topmost speed. The crowded moment began.

In writing about a moment twelve years and five months earlier when he had raced on horseback and then afoot in the lead of Rough Riders and other soldiers of the U.S. Army to the top of Kettle Hill in the San Juan Heights of Cuba, Roosevelt had called it "my crowded hour." For the remainder of his life he would try to recapture the thrill of it, to feel once more the wolf rising in his heart. In pursuit of that need he'd come to Africa. In the first line of the foreword to the book he would title *African Game Trails,* he exclaims, "I speak of Africa and golden joys; the joy of wandering through lonely lands; the joy of hunting the mighty and terrible lords of the wilderness, the cunning, the wary, and the grim."

He'd come to Africa with an arsenal of guns and fitted out the grandest safari ever seen to that time, and possibly of all time, to discover "these greatest of the world's great hunting grounds." But he closed the foreword to the book by confessing, "There are no words that can tell the hidden spirit of the wilderness, that can reveal its mystery, its melancholy, its charm."

The hunter who wandered through the lands of Africa, he said, would see sights which ever afterward remain fixed in his mind. On November 20, 1909, he witnessed just such a scene as Nandi warriors, with only their shield and spears held steady, ringed a lion and then braced themselves for its maddened attack. Merely an observer at this point, Roosevelt saw, then wrote:

Bounding ahead of his fellows, the leader reached toward throwing distance; the long spear flickered and plunged; as the lion felt the wound he half turned, and then flung himself on the man in front. The warrior threw his spear; it drove deep into the lion, for entering at one shoulder it came out of the opposite flank, near the thigh, a yard of steel through the great body. Rearing, the lion struck the man, bearing down the shield, his back arched; and for a moment he slaked his fury with fang and talon. But on the instant I saw another spear driven clear through his body from side to side; and as the lion turned again the bright spear blades darting toward him were flashes of white flame. The end had come. He seized another man, who stabbed him and wrenched loose. As [the lion] fell he gripped a spearhead in his jaws with such tremendous force that he bent it double. Then the warriors were round and over him, stabbing and shouting, wild with furious exaltation.

From the moment when he charged until his death I doubt whether ten seconds had elapsed, perhaps less; but what a ten seconds!

The wounded Nandi were treated. Roosevelt promised to reward their bravery with a heifer. Noting that the men prized their cattle more than their wives, Roosevelt was greeted with broad smiles. Then the warriors raised their shields above their heads and chanted a victory song while they danced around the dead lion. It was a celebration of triumph, Roosevelt wrote, that ended "a scene of as fierce interest and excitement as I ever hope to see."

The Nandi marched back to the camp by themselves, carrying the two wounded men on their shields. When Roosevelt tried to get them to remain for a few days to serve as beaters, they declined, unless they would be allowed to kill whatever lions they encountered. Roosevelt was not interested in being a "mere spectator at any more hunts, no matter how exciting—though to do so once was well worthwhile."

The only lion Roosevelt found appeared for an instant at a swamp. He got off one shot that ought to have hit him, but didn't. Efforts to drive the lion in the open by setting fire to the grass failed. The lion was not seen again.

On the last day of November, with genuine regret, Roosevelt said goodbye to his East African safari because on the next phase of the odyssey he could take only a few of his personal attendants. The porters, beaters, and saises had been with him more than seven months. Not one had been killed, either by accident or in an attack by an animal.

Ahead of Roosevelt lay Uganda and the Nile Valley.

16

★ ★ ★

Tales by Poe on the Upper Nile

THE FIRST TEN DAYS of December were spent in beautiful farm country at Njoro on the edge of the Mau escarpment. Roosevelt's host was Lord Delamere. A renowned big-game hunter, he'd bagged fifty-two lions before turning his attention to wheat-growing and was a leader in the work of "taming the wilderness" and "conquering for civilization the world's worst spaces." To Roosevelt he was "a most useful settler, from the standpoint of the all-round interests" of East Africa. To Roosevelt's delight, Lady Delamere had a large library.

Four days passed hunting bongo in the dense forest to avail. But on this fruitless outing Roosevelt observed the resting stance of a dozen 'Ndorobo men as they stood on one leg "like storks." He was also fascinated by squat, woolly, funny animals called tree hyaxes that the natives called "Teddy bears." But it was the bongo, along with the giant hog, that Roosevelt saw as the region's "big game." Again, his efforts at hunting ended in disappointment. This was not the case with Kermit. On a hunt with Lord Delamere he succeeded in collecting one bongo, a fine cow. Following this success, Kermit hunted at the coast near Mombasa, the city where the Roosevelt expedition had begun.

Kermit's objective was sable. He traveled on his own with two gun bearers and a few Swahili porters. After marching from Mombasa and crossing a harbor in a dhow, they arrived in a village in time to observe, and for Kermit to photograph, a ritual dance at the funeral of a chief's dead son.

Kermit reported that the dance "had more life and go to it" than any he'd seen in the ballrooms of New York and Harvard student soirees at Cambridge. The dirge music, he told his father, "had such swing and vivacity" that it was almost as lively as a comic opera.

Arriving in Nairobi, Roosevelt had a reunion with Cuninghame and Tarlton. With three other naturalists they were engaged in sending specimens to America and in preparations for the next trek, into Uganda, by way of Lake Victoria Nyanza. The safari departed on December 18. Sailing on "a smart little steamer" for twenty-four hours, they landed at Entebbe, the seat of the British governor of Uganda. The next morning they crossed the Equator for the last time. They headed north to the native town of Kampalla. The ruler of Uganda, Roosevelt learned, was a boy king. He also found that Ugandans had proved so accessible to Christianity that Kampalla was the headquarters of missions of the Church of England and the Vatican. "For their good fortune." he wrote of the native population, "England has established a protectorate over them."

Well aware of the distinguished stature of their visitor, the missionaries of both faiths received Roosevelt by waving American and British flags. Native children who attended the mission schools sang "The Star Spangled Banner." Also greeting Roosevelt at the Church of England Mission was "Mother Paul." Having met her in New York before leaving for Africa, he'd promised to call on her in Kampalla to "look into the work she, and the sisters associated with her, were doing." Mother Paul had a surprise for Roosevelt. She had received, she said, a "goodwill letter" from two of "the Finest" (the nickname, and the boast, of the New York Police Department). The writers had been members on the force when Roosevelt was the president of a four-commissioner governing Police Board (1895–1897).

When the British commissioner, a man named Knowles, arranged a hunt for sitununga, a bigger relative of the bushbuck, Roosevelt and Kermit eagerly accepted the invitation, and the help of a hundred natives. Only Kermit managed to shoot one of the elusive animals. The next day, the safari left Kampalla for Lake Albert Nyanza. The journey encompassed a holiday that was Theodore Roosevelt's favorite: Christmas. But with a pang of nostalgia he wrote, "There is not much use in trying to celebrate Christmas unless there are small folks to hang their stockings on Christmas Eve, to rush gleefully in at dawn the next morning to open the stockings, and after breakfast to wait in hopping expectancy until their elders throw open the doors of the room in which the big presents are arranged, those for each child on a separate table."

Even though his second son and now grown-up "bunnie" Kermit was with him this may have been the only time in Africa that Theodore Roosevelt felt seriously homesick. Offsetting the longing for Sagamore Hill was his recognition that Kermit had proven himself to be a boon companion and an excellent hunter.

Pressing northward about forty miles from the coast, Roosevelt and Kermit usually got in two or three hours of hunting each day. They were in elephant country on the morning of the twelfth of December when they struck camp with information that a herd was nearby. Not much later, they heard four or five of them feeding in the thick jungle. The sounds indicated that they were about half a mile away. Presently, one of the natives crouched and beckoned to Roosevelt. Peering through dense foliage, Roosevelt "caught the loom of the tusker." Evidently catching the scene of humans, the elephant "assumed the offensive." With huge ears cocked at right angles to his head and trunk hanging down, he charged "full tilt." Coming on steadily, silently, and at a great pace, his feet swishing through the long grass, he looked to Roosevelt like a "formidable monster." At forty yards Roosevelt aimed at the huge head and let loose with one barrel of the Holland rifle. As the elephant stopped, a bullet from Kermit's Springfield slammed into its head. When the elephant wheeled, Roosevelt emptied the second barrel between neck and shoulder. Three more shots by Kermit struck, but the elephant spun around and crashed away. Because there was not much daylight remaining, the trail was difficult to follow. When the elephant's lumbering in the jungle thicket gave him away, Kermit crept forward and Roosevelt slipped within a dozen feet of the elephant as he stood on the other side of a group of small, twisted, vine-matted trees. Father and son fired together. The mighty bull threw up his trunk, crashed over backward, and lay dead on his side among the bushes. "A fine sight he was," Roosevelt wrote, "a sight to gladden any hunter's heart, as he lay in the twilight, a giant in death."

The scene was memorialized by a camera that captured Roosevelt in a pith helmet and khakis, left hand in a pocket, the right arm bent by his side as Roosevelt leaned on the carcass.

After leaving the elephant camp the safari journeyed in country that was mostly covered with open forest, chiefly acacia trees. At one place the woods reminded Roosevelt of regions of Texas and Oklahoma. It was a pleasant ride along the road in early mornings, with the safari coming behind, but noontime became very hot under the glare of a brazen equatorial sun. When it moved lower, they sallied forth to hunt in jungle so thick that without the guidance of natives there was little success. Ten days out of Kampalla they crossed the little Kafu River and entered a native kingdom, under British protectorate but separate from Uganda, named Unyoro. In its main settlement, Hoima, Roosevelt was greeted by British officials, a few missionaries, and the Christian king, to whom Roosevelt served five o'clock tea.

After a pause to hunt, the safari continued into a new year. At noon on January 5, 1910, it reached Butiaba on the shores of Lake Albert Nyanza. To get from the lake named for Prince Albert's wife, Queen Victoria, they'd marched 160 miles. The landscape around Butiaba and Lake Albert Nyanza shimmered in the white, glaring heat, but when the sun went down, the land to the west, Roosevelt wrote, "was kindled in ruddy splendor."

Boats took them to the Lado country and the saffron-hued river Zaire and northward to the Victorian Nile, "alive with monstrous crocodiles, and its banks barren of human life because of the fly whose bite brings the torment which ends in death."

As Roosevelt began this final phase of his expedition he took from the Pigskin Library *Tales of Mystery and Imagination* by Edgar Allan Poe.

As the safari sailed northward, the waters of Lake Albert Nyanza stretched "beyond the ken of vision," Roosevelt observed, "to where they were fed by streams from the Mountains of the Moon." On his left hand rose the frowning ridges on the other side of which forests of the Congo lay like a shroud over the land. Entering the White Nile, they steamed past many hippos that roared from reed beds, then snorted and plunged beside the boat. Arriving at Koba, they were met by six professional elephant hunters who made a living poaching ivory in the Congo. Still in British territory 48 hours after leaving Butiaba on Lake Albert Nyanza, the safari left its small flotilla of boats and set up a permanent camp in good game country with no native villages in the region. Roosevelt and Kermit usually went out together with gun-bearers to shoot a buck for food. Roosevelt wore his customary khaki outfit while Kermit strode along in front in short trousers and leggings, but knees bared.

The purpose of making this camp was a search for the so-called "white," or "square-nosed," rhinoceros. Almost exterminated by hunting in South Africa, and unknown north of the Zambezi River, it was even scarce in the narrow ribbon of territory on the left bank of the Upper Nile. Conceding that "it would certainly be well if all killing of it were prohibited until careful inquiry has been made as to its numbers and exact distribution," Roosevelt believed that he had an obligation to science to collect an example of the rare species.

He got his chance. Along with Kermit and native trackers after hours of seeking signs of the rhino under burning sun in grass that was higher than their heads, one of the natives pointed toward a thorn tree about sixty yards away. Mounting a low anthill, Roosevelt saw the rhino, "rather dimly through the long grass." Lying asleep on its side, the female rhino looked like a giant pig. Evidently sensing peril, it lurched to a sitting position with its big ears turned forward. With a shot from the Holland, Roosevelt "knocked it clean off its feet." Squealing loudly, the rhino staggered ten yards, then collapsed. But with Roosevelt's shot, four other rhinos appeared out of the grass. As they fled in panic, Kermit wounded a bull and followed it a long way, but couldn't overtake it. (The body was found ten days later.) Meanwhile, Roosevelt killed a calf that was apparently that of the cow that he'd killed with the one shot.

No longer the hunter, but a naturalist, he observed and recorded the unique aspects of the white rhinoceros. It stood higher than the common rhino and was shorter in length. The most interesting difference to Roosevelt was a huge "ungainly, square-mouthed head" lacking the "curved, prehensile development which makes the upper lip of a common rhino look like the hook of a turtle's beak."

At night in the riverside camp Roosevelt listened to the grunts and brays of venturesome hippos splashing and wallowing among the reeds. During one unforgettable night, in addition to the hippo chorus came the roaring of lions and elephants, driving home to Roosevelt that he was, indeed, "in the heart of the African wilderness."

He was also no longer in healthy East Africa. Although he and Kermit continued to be in robust health, others in the party suffered with dysentery, fever, and sun prostration. While in Uganda, one of the gun bearers had died, and on a march from Koba to Nimule four porters had succumbed to dysentery.

On February 17, 1910, the safari left the tiny village of Nimule on a ten-day march across a barren and arid land to Gondokoro, during which the Roosevelts hunted game for meat and the collections of their sponsoring museum. Awaiting them at Gondokoro was a boat that had been sent by the British head man in that region of the Sudan, Major-General Sir Reginald Wingate. The boat was provided to Roosevelt for a Nile River voyage to the storied city of Khartoum.

But before going down the Nile Roosevelt intended to collect the handsomest, largest, and least known of African antelopes, the giant eland. Because all the other white men in the party were down with dysentery and fever, the hale and hearty Roosevelt father and son went out with sixty Ugandan porters, a dozen pack mules, and several little riding mules. Also part of the entourage were seven native soldiers of the Belgian Congo, led by a corporal. The weather was very hot, and the landscape a waste of barren desolation. There was ample game to supply meat for the campfires, but the quarry crowding Roosevelt's imagination was the giant eland. For two days he left camp before sunrise with gun bearers and a guide, only to spend a day of tracking with glimpses of eland but no opportunity to shoot.

At eight in the morning on the third day the tracker found the spoor of a lone bull. By half-past noon Roosevelt knew he was "close on the beast." Then he glimpsed the eland. The tense excitement that ensued is vivid in his account of the hunt:

> Taking advantage of every patch of cover I crawled toward it on all-fours, my rifle too hot [from the sun] to touch the barrel, while the blustering heat of the baked ground hurt my hands. At a little over a hundred yards I knelt and aimed at the noble beast; I could now plainly see his huge bulk and great, massive horns, as he stood under a tree. The pointed bullet from the little Springfield hit a trifle too far back and up, but made such a rip that he never got ten yards from where I was standing; and great was my pride as I stood over him, and examined his horns, twisted almost like a koodoo's, and admired his size, his finely modeled head and legs, and the beauty of his coat.

On the first two days Kermit had killed two eland, a cow on the first day and a bull on the second. With pride in his son, Roosevelt wrote, "Kermit could see game, and follow tracks, almost as well as his gun-bearers, and in a long chase could outrun them. On each day [of the hunts] he struck the track of the eland, and after a while left his gun-bearers and porters, and ran along the trail accompanied only by a native guide."

Returning to the camp on that third day, Roosevelt found R.J. Cuninghame in better health, while Alden Loring and others remained seriously sick. But by the last day of February they were able to join Roosevelt and Kermit as they started down the Nile.

17

★ ★ ★

Reunion at Khartoum

GLIDING NORTHWARD on the Nile, with stops now and then for hunts, Roosevelt spent time seated on the foredeck of the steamer gazing at the long, glistening river and recalling a boy called Teedie heading up the Nile from Cairo 37 years before. Looking back over the past year, he felt proud and satisfied with his accomplishment. In the company of Smithsonian scientists, 15 native soldiers, 260 porters, and a handful of white hunters, he and Kermit had claimed 512 animals, including 17 lions, 11 elephants, 20 rhinos, 8 hippos, 9 giraffes, 47 gazelles, 20 zebras, and thousands of specimens of birds and other small creatures for the enlightenment of perhaps millions of Americans who could never see them in the wild.

He also felt heartened by improvement in the health of his companions. He credited their rebounding from fever and dysentery to a case of champagne that he had opened at Gondoroko. Evidently remembering the disastrous effects of a bottle of whiskey on his guide during a hunt in the West, he had decided that on the African trip the only liquor he would carry for emergencies would be brandy and champagne. But in the eleven months of hardgoing in difficult terrain he'd sipped only six ounces of brandy, believing that hot tea would do him more good. In that time Kermit had been ill once, and only for three days, and Roosevelt for five days. He attributed his own fever not to Africa, but to a recurrence of a fever he'd contracted in Cuba. The attacks he had in Africa were "very slight" and nowhere near as severe as a fever he'd experienced while bear hunting early one spring in the Rockies.

Much worse than any fever was a longing for home that became more pronounced as the end of the African year approached. In mid-February 1910 he'd written to Andrew Carnegie, "I am homesick for my own land and my own people! Of course it is Mrs. Roosevelt I most want to see; but I want to see my two youngest boys [Archie and Quentin]; I want to see my house, my own books and trees, the sunset over the sound from the window in the north room, the people with whom I have worked, who think my thoughts and speak my speech."

In November 1909 he'd written to Edith, "Oh, sweetest of all sweet girls, last night I dreamed that I was with you, and that our separation was but a dream, and when I waked up it was almost too hard to bear."

As the Nile steamer neared Khartoum, he eagerly looked forward to seeing Edith in the flesh. She would be there to welcome him, along with her mother and daughter Ethel. Archie and Quentin would not be present because they'd had to go back to the United States to school. Nor would Ted be there. While his father and brother had been adventuring in Africa, the love for Eleanor Alexander that had kept him from joining the expedition had been formalized by their engagement, with the wedding in abeyance until the groom's father returned home.

When Edith gave Roosevelt this news, he thought about his own marriage and wrote to Eleanor, "There is nothing in the world that equals the happiness that comes to lovers who remain lovers all through their wedded lives, and who are not only devoted to each other, but wise and forbearing and gentle, as well."

To Ted he wrote of the wife who had let him go off to Africa for a year, "Greatly tho I have Mother I was at times thoughtless and selfish, and if Mother had been a mere unhealthy Patient Griselda, I might have grown set in selfish and inconsiderate ways. Mother, always tender, gentle and considerate, and always loving, yet when necessary pointed out where I was thoughtless and therefore inconsiderate and selfish, instead of submitting to it. Had she not done this it would in the end have made her life much harder, and mine very much less happy."

But going back to the bliss of life at Sagamore Hill was not to be an immediate thing. The voyage to the United States with Edith, Kermit, and Ethel would include a lengthy passage through the cities of Europe that would announce to Americans and the world that Teddy Roosevelt had emerged from the wilderness just as he'd entered it—brash, daring, and ready to speak his mind.

It became "a grand tour" that one writer said was "rich months, with emperors and kings, presidents and cheering thousands." When in Rome, he turned down an audience with Pope Pius X after the Pope demanded that he not agree to see a group of American Methodists, one of whom had offended His Holiness by calling him "the whore of Babylon." Roosevelt then snubbed the Methodists with equal pleasure.

Warmly received in Paris, he spoke at the Sorbonne on the "Duties of Citizenship." In the speech he voiced a philosophy which had characterized his life:

> It is not the critic who counts, not the man who points out how the strong man stumbled or whether the doer of deeds could have done better. The credit belongs to the man who is actually in the arena; whose face is marred by dust and sweat and blood; who errs and comes up short again . . . who knows the great enthusiasms, the great devotions, and spends himself in a worthy cause; who at least knows in the end the triumph of high achievement; and who, at worst, if he fails, at least fails while doing greatly, so that his place shall never be with those cold and timid souls who know neither victory nor defeat.

Visiting the country of his Dutch ancestors, he marveled at the tulips of Holland's annual flower show. Moving northward to Stockholm, Sweden, he donned a suit of white-tie-and-tails to accept the Nobel Peace Prize, a ceremony belatedly held in recognition of his mediation of a treaty of peace that had ended the Russo-Japanese War of 1905. His acceptance speech called for the limitation of naval armaments by the European Powers, and formation of a "League of Peace," that would be backed by force if necessary. "The ruler or statesman who should bring about such a combination," he predicted, "would have earned his place in history for all time and his title to the gratitude of mankind."

Going on from Sweden to Germany, the former president paid a call on a ruler who was busily building battleships. Kaiser Wilhelm was so impressed by his illustrious guest, and with himself, that he gave TR a photograph that was taken as they met. The inscription read, "When we shake hands we shake the whole world."

The penultimate stop en route home was England, where Alice joined him, Edith, Ethel, and Kermit. He arrived in time to be designated by President Taft to represent the United States at the funeral of King Edward VII. A week and a half later he was given a rare honor for an American of giving an address at London's historic Guildhall. In the speech the man who'd helped end Spanish sovereignty in Cuba, and who had recently been a visitor to British East Africa and British-dominated Egypt, lectured the government of the new king, George V. He told the astonished, assembled dignitaries in their regal robes, "Now, either you have the right to be in Egypt or you have not; either it is or it is not your duty to establish and keep order." If they were not prepared to rise to their responsibilities they should get out, but he hoped that in the interest of civilization, and with "fealty to your own great traditions," that they would not.

After delivering the Romanes lecture at Oxford University, he took some ribbing from the Archbishop of York. "In the way of grading which we have at Oxford," he said, "we agreed to mark the lecture 'Beta Minus,' but the lecturer 'Alpha Minus.' While we felt that the lecture [on the subject "Biological Analogies to History"] "was not a very great contribution to science, we were sure that the lecturer was a very great man."

On June 18, 1910, "the great man," as Ted called his father, returned to New York City and a tumultuous welcome. As the steamer *Kaiserin Auguste Viktoria* sailed into the harbor, she was saluted by the battleship *South Carolina* and a flotilla of destroyers and yachts decked with banners and blowing whistles." When the ship docked at the Battery it was to a roaring reception by the people on the wharf. Following the welcoming speeches and a parade of horse-drawn carriages, marchers, and five hundred Rough Riders who had come to New York from all over the country, the Roosevelts gathered for lunch at 433 Fifth Avenue in a house built by Ted's fiancee's great-grandfather. After the meal, they took a ferry and train to Oyster Bay. Two days later, at the Fifth Avenue Presbyterian Church, Ted and Eleanor were married.

Speaking to the welcoming crowd on the day he set foot on American soil for the first time in a year, Theodore Roosevelt had declared that it was peculiarly the duty of a man who had been president of the United States to be nothing more than a private citizen. But before he had sailed for home he had a visit in Europe from an ally in his years as a politician. Gifford Pinchot had rushed across the Atlantic in a veritable panic to report that Roosevelt's heir in the White House, President William Howard Taft, had not only abandoned Roosevelt's progressive policies, but was acquiescing in everything Congress was doing to uproot everything Roosevelt had done as president.

Roosevelt listened, then renounced the implication of Pinchot's visit that he rescue the Progressive Party by getting back into the political fray. But his dockside pledge that he intended to be only a private citizen fell on deaf ears. He found himself besieged by old friends and allies to ride to the rescue of the Progressives. For reasons known only to him, but widely speculated upon by allies, old enemies, and Roosevelt biographers, he changed his mind about going quietly into private life. In pondering Roosevelt's reversal, Wall Street tycoon J.P. Morgan, who knew a thing or two about human nature, expressed a not untypical Morgan view that a man always has two reasons for what he does, "a good one and the real one."

The explanation for Roosevelt's abrupt turnaround in the minds of his foes was that he, like Julius Caesar and every ruler since, was ambitious. On the contrary, wrote Roosevelt's old and steadfast friend and veteran of the West, novelist Owen Wister, Roosevelt's change of plans demonstrated "the strongest element of his character," both a sacrifice to obvious duty and the performance of a plain obligation to his ideals. In a memoir, *My Friendship with Roosevelt,* published 30 years after Roosevelt's death, Wister wrote that the "real reason" for his change of mind "was the same reason that a duck takes to water." He explained the Roosevelt character this way:

> Among all his bents, historical, zoological, whatever, he was the preacher militant perpetual, and to be in a fight for his beliefs was his true element. In the appeals made to him [before his decision to get back into politics] the water had not come quiet so close to the duck. [Then he had been dragged] to the edge of a definite pond, and into the pond he plumped. . . . And then, the pond flowed steadily into a brook, and the brook speedily into a river, and down the river he went toward a sea that neither he nor friend nor enemy dreamed of.

On September 21, 1910, Roosevelt wrote to Henry Cabot Lodge, "The fight is very disagreeable. Twenty years ago I would not have minded in the least . . . but it is not the kind of fight into which an ex-President should be required to go. I could not possibly help myself."

One thing led to another—the pond into a brook, the brook into a river, and the river into a sea—and by 1912, Theodore Roosevelt was the nominee of a revitalized Progressive Party for president of the United States.

As a third-party candidate he would run against Taft and the Democratic standard-bearer, Woodrow Wilson. Acknowledging that "the great bulk of my wealthy and educated friends regard me as a dangerous crank," the old warrior asserted that he wanted to find a remedy for evils which, if left unremedied, would in the end do away not only with wealth and education, but with pretty much all of civilization. "It is a fight that must be made, and it is worth making, and the event lies on the knees of the gods."

For the now grown-up and mostly independent bunnies of Sagamore Hill the tumult of Big Bear running for office was a familiar phenomenon. But for Ted's wife, and mother of little Grace Roosevelt as they set foot in the house in the summer of 1912, the scene encountered was a shock. Eleanor wrote in her autobiography:

> It was the first time I had been there when the entire family was at home. Before twenty-four hours passed I realized that nothing in my bringing up as an only child had in any way prepared me for the frenzied activity into which I was plunged. Something was going on every minute of the day. The house was full of people. Conferences went on all day. The telephone never stopped ringing. In the evenings my father-in-law received the newspapermen. At first I thought everyone would be tired when the day was over and would go to bed early, but I soon found out that nothing of the kind could be expected. The Roosevelt family enjoyed life too much to waste time sleeping. Every night they stayed downstairs until nearly midnight; then, talking at the top of their voices, they trooped up the wide uncarpeted stairs and went to their rooms. For a brief moment all was still, but just as I was going off to sleep for the second time they remembered things they had forgotten to tell one another and ran shouting through the halls. I tried going to bed with cotton in my ears, but it never did any good.

The Roosevelt family had weathered other campaigns, and no matter how this contest came out, they were certain everything would be fine. However, their confidence was shaken on October 12 with horrifying news that as Roosevelt left the Hotel Gilpatric in Milwaukee for a speech at a campaign rally, a man wielding a pistol had lurched out of a crowd of well-wishers and fired a shot into Roosevelt's chest. The terrifying report was quickly followed by word that he not been killed, or even seriously wounded, but had actually delivered his speech. He began by saying to the audience, "I shall ask you to be as quiet as possible. I don't know whether you fully understand that I have just been shot; but it takes more than that to kill a Bull Moose." The speech went on for an hour and a half with Roosevelt repeatedly brushing aside appeals that he stop and get himself to a hospital. His survival was attributed to his good physical condition and to the fact that the text of his speech had been tucked into an inside pocket and had blunted the impact of the bullet.

Expressions of admiration for this latest demonstration of courage by the hero of San Juan Hill by the American people did not translate into sufficient votes to enter the Roosevelt name in the annals of American history as the first president to serve a third term. "We have fought the good fight, we have kept the faith," he said to an old friend a few days after losing to Wilson, "and we have nothing to regret."

Seven months later from Sagamore Hill, Roosevelt announced that he was in receipt of an invitation from the governments of Brazil, Argentina, and Chile to visit those countries for the purpose of delivering a series of lectures. Anticipating a chance for yet another adventure, he said, "I have to go. It's my last chance to be a boy."

PART FOUR

★ ★ ★

To Be a Boy Again

18

★ ★ ★

Merely Deferred

I F ANYONE could get Theodore Roosevelt to take a break from his presidential activities for a few minutes in the waning months of 1908 it was John Augustine Zahm. Roosevelt and the vigorous, rosy-cheeked, blue-eyed, fifty-five-year-old Roman Catholic priest with a mane of white hair had been, as Roosevelt put it, "cronies for some time, because we were both of us fond of Dante and of science." The president was such an admirer of Zahm's book, *Evolution and Dogma,* that he'd regularly commended it to other theologians. He also liked that Zahm had gotten his early education in Ohio in "old-time American fashion in a little log school."

Discovering that he had a religious calling, Zahm chose to enter the priesthood. He was ordained in the Congregation of the Holy Cross in 1875. Two decades later, as Teddy Roosevelt garnered fame in leading the Rough Riders to glory, Father Zahm found himself elected head of the order's American province's hospitals, orphanages, and schools, including a small seminary named Notre Dame in the little Indiana town of South Bend.

Determined to make it equal to any "community of saints and scholars" in the United States, he spent money so freely to modernize the schools facilities that his superiors feared he would bankrupt the order. At their urging, and on the advice of doctors who said he was having a nervous breakdown, he left Notre Dame in 1906. Instead of resting and recuperating in the Caribbean, he threw himself into almost a frenzy of explorations in

Venezuela and Colombia. The expedition encompassed the daunting heights of the Andes Mountains and the mysteries and dangers of the Amazon River.

Toward the end of 1907 when he was planning another such expedition, he returned to the United States with the intention of finding as a companion for the odyssey a man who had "made nature study a predominant part of his life-work." Recognizing that the only man who qualified was Theodore Roosevelt, he arrived at the White House to propose that Roosevelt enlist in the venture, once he was "free from presidential cares." In addition to scientific aspects of the journey that Zahm knew would appeal to Roosevelt, he was prepared to stress that such a trip by the ex-president would have political and diplomatic benefits for the United States in its often touchy relations with Latin America. To help sell this idea he brought along John Barrett, whom Roosevelt knew as the director-general of the Pan-American Union.

It was not so much the prospects of improving U.S. south-of-the-border relations that appealed to Roosevelt as he listened to Zahm and Barrett, but Zahm's colorful, exciting accounts of South America's wildlife. At some point Roosevelt exclaimed that he had always wanted a chance to hunt the South American jaguar. Unfortunately, he informed his guests, he was at that very time engaged in planning a post-presidency year-long African safari.

Disappointed, Father Zahm left the White House with every indication from Roosevelt that the South American adventure wasn't being abandoned, but "merely deferred."

Back from Africa in 1910, and hailed for the accomplishment by his always-admiring countrymen, Roosevelt found that his published accounts of the safari had made him better off financially than at any time since he'd lost a large part of his wealth in the Dakota ranching enterprises. Royalties from his two-volume *African Game Trails,* compiled from the magazine articles for *Scribner's,* were expected to garner him $40,000. Compensation as a contributing editor for *The Outlook* magazine came to $12,000 a year. Other funds flowed in for lectures and other writings. Among the latter was a monumental monograph (40,000 words) on "Revealing and Concealing Coloration in Birds and Animals." While drafting it, he confided to Ted that he expected the work to "attract frenzied dissent and tepid assent among obscure zoological friends here and abroad."

Following his second-place finish in the 1912 presidential race, Roosevelt received a note from Father Zahm. It wished him "every blessing for 1913," then went on to exclaim that Roosevelt "made history as you probably never did during the year just closing." Zahm expected him to "make more during the years to come."

The adventuresome priest certainly had his finger firmly on the American pulse. A poll by *Independent* magazine in the spring of 1913 discerned that five years after Roosevelt left the White House he was, in the opinion of the public, "America's most useful citizen." If requests that Roosevelt make speeches were a measure of popularity, Theodore Roosevelt had nothing to worry about. In February 1913 alone he had to turn down 171 such invitations simply because his engagement calendar was already filled. Edith worried that he was "working like a steam engine" and looked "tired and jaded—having far too much to do."

One of the matters on his mind was an invitation that had come near the end of the 1912 campaign. It arrived on the letterhead of the Historical and Geographical Society of Rio de Janeiro. The Brazilian group proposed a series of Roosevelt lectures in the spring and summer of 1913. Accompanying the solicitation was an offer from the president of Brazil of a hunting trip in his country. These enticements were followed in January by a letter from the Museo Social of Argentina stating that if Roosevelt should go to South America, he would find a warm welcome from a population that had "heard so much about you, your public career and the high ideals you stand for." And if he came, said Dr. Emilio Frers, president of the Museo Social, he would, of course, be paid a honorarium. For three speeches Frers proposed a fee of $6,000, to be paid in U.S. gold dollars.

Although disinclined to give "merely an ordinary speech or to go on an ordinary trip," Roosevelt saw in the invitation an opportunity to visit his intrepid companion in Africa. At that time a supervisor for the Anglo-Brazilian Iron Company in Sao Paulo, Kermit had gone to Brazil after graduating from Harvard. With the idea of a South American adventure percolating in his thoughts, Roosevelt received a letter from Kermit in April 1913 about a hunting trip Kermit had made. Roosevelt replied, "The forest must be lovely. Sometime I must get down to see you, and we'll take a fortnight's outing, and you shall hunt and I'll act as what in the North Woods we used to call 'wangan [wagon] man' and keep camp."

There now occurred an amazing coincidence. With the fires of a new adventure rising like a wolf in a warrior's heart, Roosevelt remembered his friend Father Zahm and wondered if the time had come to rekindle the "merely deferred" idea of a Roosevelt-Zahm expedition in South America. Always a man to be sure he had his ducks in a row, and appreciating the value of having the assistance of the professional naturalists of a distinguished museum for what he saw as a scientific undertaking, he contacted Frank Chapman of the American Museum of Natural History in New York City.

When they met for lunch in early June, Chapman informed Roosevelt that a few days earlier he had gotten the same request for the museum's advice on choosing a naturalist. The query had come from Father Zahm. The priest had also told Chapman that he was planning to go to Sagamore Hill to tell Roosevelt of his intention of at last launching the South American expedition, in the hope that Roosevelt was now prepared to join it. Chapman told Zahm that he could save himself the trip to Oyster Bay. "Colonel Roosevelt is going to take luncheon with me here tomorrow," he explained, "and I shall be glad to have you join us."

As Roosevelt entered the museum's dining room just before one o'clock in the afternoon of June 6, 1913, he was astonished to find Zahm with Chapman. Striding toward Zahm, he said, "You are the very man I wished to see. I was just about to write you to inform you that I think I shall, at last, be able to take that long-talked-of-trip to South America."

With the expedition approved by museum president Henry Fairfield, Chapman prepared a list of professional naturalists who were ready to enlist in the expedition, subject to Roosevelt's approval. He gladly accepted the recommendations of George K. Cherrie and Leo E. Miller. "No two better men could have been found," Roosevelt wrote. "Both were veterans of the tropical American forests."

Miller was young, but he was enthusiastic and had good literary as well as scientific training. Working in the Guiana forests at the time, he would join Roosevelt and the others in Barbados. Cherrie was older. After twenty-two adventurous years of collecting in the American tropics that included the birth of his second of six children in a South American jungle camp, three months in a South American prison, and a brief career as a gun-runner during a revolution, he had achieved immortality as a naturalist by naming a new species of ant-thrush for the chief who'd been the beneficiary of the illicit trade in weaponry.

To arrange the expedition's equipment Chapman proposed Anthony Fiala. A former Arctic explorer, he was well known to Roosevelt as a member of the New York squadron in the Spanish-American War. Another army veteran, Jacob Sigg, had experience as a hospital nurse and a cook. A major part of his duties would be to serve as personal attendant to Father Zahm. Roosevelt's secretary, Frank Harper, was also enlisted in the party.

In composition, Roosevelt noted, the expedition was typically American. He meant that its members symbolized the wide variety of people from all over the world who had formed the ingredients for a unique stew in what was called the American melting pot. Roosevelt noted that he and Kermit were "of the old Revolutionary stock, and in our veins ran about every strain of blood that there was on this side of the water in colonial times." Cherrie's father was Irish, his mother a Scot. Father Zahm was part Alsacian, part Irish. Leo Miller's father had emigrated from Germany and his mother from France. Fiala's parents were Bohemian. Harper was born in England, and Sigg in Switzerland. Just as varied as these men's ethnicity were their religions. Zahm and Miller were Roman Catholic; Cherrie a Presbyterian; Sigg, Lutheran; Fiala a Baptist; and the Roosevelts belonged to the Dutch Reformed Church.

Except for 16-bore shotguns belonging to each of the naturalists, the weaponry for the sojourn was furnished by the Roosevelts. Kermit brought two Winchesters, a pair of shotguns (his 12-gauge and a 16-gauge), and two pistols (Colt and Smith & Wesson). Roosevelt brought his beloved and trusty Springfield rifle. Equipment consisted of canvas canoes, tents, ropes and pulleys, light cots and hammocks, and "plenty of cheesecloth" for screening the tents and making protective nets for hats to fend off mosquitoes. The choice of clothing was "to each his own." Roosevelt packed the kind of khaki gear he'd worn in Africa: U.S. Army flannel shirts, a couple of silk ones for dressing to be received by South American officialdom, a pair of hob-nailed boots with leggings. A pair of laced leather boots that came nearly to his knees were the recommendation of the naturalists for protection against snake bites. Although the intention was to live off the land, provisioner Anthony Fiala packed U.S. Army emergency rations and 90 cans of victuals for the subsistence of five men for five days.

The official purpose of the venture, beginning after Roosevelt's lecture tour, was to be the collection of specimens of fauna and flora in the region between the Paraguay River and the Amazon. The starting point was to be at Asuncion in Paraguay. To prepare for the trip, as he had done prior to going to Africa, Roosevelt immersed himself in the geography and topography of "the most extensive stretches of tropical forest to be found anywhere." His intention was to go up the Paraguay as far as it could be navigated, trek overland to one of the sources of the mighty Amazon, build canoes "on the spot," and descend the world's longest and most perilous river.

With customary Rooseveltian zest, he wrote to Father Zahm, "I don't in the least mind risk to my life, but I want to be sure that I am not doing something for which I will find my physical strength unequal." A letter to Kermit brimmed with excited anticipation. "I cannot tell you how I am looking forward to seeing you," he wrote, adding that he hoped that Edith would go with him, "but it is possible she may not." The letter continued, "It won't be anything like our African trip. There will be no hunting and no adventure so that I will not have the pang I otherwise would about not taking you along—which of course would never do."

Perhaps as a test of his stamina, he set out in the summer with Archie, age nineteen, and fifteen-year-old Quentin for a hunting excursion in the Arizona desert, hoping to shoot mountain lions. And no trip into the Southwest could be taken without taking time for a nostalgic reunion with men who had been with him as Rough Riders in Cuba. The journey included sightseeing at the Grand Canyon, the nearby Painted Desert, and exploration of a Hopi Indian village, where he was given the honor of admission to a sacred room to witness a tribal snake dance. While on the cougar-hunts he carried no gun and left the shooting to the boys. On the way back east from his last hunting trip in the West he stopped in Chicago to meet with leaders of the Progressive Party, but his mind was already far ahead of him, fixed on the challenges that awaited him in the jungles of South America. The date for his departure was to be October 4, 1913. En route to his last chance to be a boy he would mark his fifty-fifth birthday. He carried more than 200 pounds on a five-feet-eight-inch frame. Because of a blow while boxing in the White House, he had lost sight in the left eye. The vigorous life he encouraged in everyone had resulted in his own body being scarred, battered, and plagued with rheumatism that provoked him to complain that he felt like "a worn-out and crippled old man." Also a plague were lingering effects of having been hit by a trolley car in Pittsfield, Massachusetts, in 1902 in which doctors had to cut down to the shin bone, permanently damaging it. The injury remained so troubling that in 1908, the year before the start of the African safari, he told Kermit that if anything happened "there is always a chance of trouble which would be serious."

In South America, Kermit would recall the words with a chilling sense of having been given a grim prophecy.

19

★ ★ ★

A Difficult Trip Ahead

W HEN ROOSEVELT told people who speculated about what he would do as an ex-president that he had no intention of sitting in a rocking chair on the piazza at Sagamore Hill and letting the rest of the world get along as best it could without him, no one in the United States was less surprised, and none happier, than newspaper reporters, whom Roosevelt delighted in calling "idiots of the press"; their editors; and photographers (Roosevelt's term was "Kodak creatures").

Acutely conscious of having been regarded as "a great story" from the autumn of 1880 when he had plunged into the decidedly ungentlemanly arena of politics to his astonishing African safari and then his presidential bid in 1912, he'd hoped to avoid pestering from the press about his next great adventure by keeping it a secret until the very last minute, and possibly until he had already sailed away. But four days before the embarkation date of Saturday, October 4, 1913, the *New York Times* announced in bold headlines:

ROOSEVELT SAILS SATURDAY
Heads Exploring Expedition of Amazon

Consequently, what had been planned as a Progressive Party political dinner in the roof-top "Garden of Dance" of the New York Theater in Manhattan, with a speech by the party's once-and-possibly-future (1916) presidential candidate, became a raucous send-off to the ever-surprising and apparently tireless exponent of the strenuous life. A *Times* reporter gushed, "The Colonel has had many a great ovation, but never so boisterous and hearty as this one." Although he denied rumors that his hat would be in the ring three years hence, he promised that when he came back from South America, he would devote himself "with whatever strength I have to working with you for this [Progressive] cause."

The hat on Roosevelt's freshly barbered head on October 4 was not his political one. It was a buff-toned, stylish complement to a gray business suit with a carnation in the lapel. As he stepped from an automobile onto Pier 8 in Brooklyn, a dock worker appreciated that it was not a politician, but a man with a boyish heart who rushed toward the gangplank of the Lamport and Holt steamer *Vandyck*. "Good boy, Teddy," the docker yelled, "shoot 'em in the eye." A reporter covering the departure for the *New York Tribune* thought that the hero of San Juan Heights and recent intrepid African big-game hunter was not "the same strenuous Roosevelt of 1909."

As if determined to prove that he was up to the challenge physically, Roosevelt proved to be an exuberant and energetic voyager as the *Vandyck* headed south. On one memorable night he amused the other passengers by dancing the hornpipe. In a tug of war between married men and bachelors he anchored the husbands' end of the rope with his 220 pounds. Hoping to bring down his weight, he took daily brisk walks around the promenade deck. When he played shuffleboard and other deck games with people half his age, Edith was pleased to observe him thoroughly enjoying himself. She wrote to his sister Anna, "I haven't heard him laugh for years."

When he wasn't playing, he dictated articles for the *Outlook,* read several books at once, and conducted daily conferences on the expedition. In a letter to Ted's wife Eleanor he wrote, "It is not exploration work exactly, but it is pioneer work, and the collection of birds and mammals ought to be of some value."

Six days out of New York the ship arrived at Bridgetown, Barbados, where Leo Miller came on board. At age twenty-six, he brought his reputation as an expert naturalist with the American Museum. It was said that his exploits in the remotest part of southern Venezuela so impressed Sir Arthur Conan Doyle, best-known as the creator of Sherlock Holmes, that Conan Doyle patterned a mysterious, dinosaur-populated land in his non-Sherlockian novel *The Lost World* on Miller's account of a "country, and of the people and the animal life inhabiting its virgin fields" about which very little was known.

After a shipboard conference on October 11, Miller reported to his museum boss, Frank Chapman, "Our trip promises to be a great thing, and we are eager to start work."

Roosevelt sent a message to the Foreign Minister of Brazil, Lauro Muller, concerning the expedition's needs when the party landed in Rio de Janeiro. "My hope is to make this trip not only an interesting and valuable one from a scientific viewpoint," he said, "but of real benefit to Brazil, in calling attention to the ease and rapidity with which the vast territory can be traversed, and also to the phenomenal opportunities for development which she offers."

With a demonstration of a lifetime of caution, if not outright pessimism about what the future held, he advised Frank Chapman, "We have a difficult trip ahead of us. We will have all kinds of troubles, with waterfalls, showers, shallows, fevers, and the like, and we may not be able to get beyond the Amazon Valley." He added, "When we will get home I have no idea."

Before he could throw himself into the challenge, however, he had commitments in the form of the daunting schedule of speaking and public appearances that had provided the impetus for the sojourn to South America. He would have the much-anticipated happy reunion with his second son in Bahia, the oldest city in what was then Brazil, but later part of the future Salvador.

When Roosevelt laid eyes on Kermit, now twenty-four, he thought Kermit didn't look as healthy as he would have liked. This appearance was the result of a fall. A few months earlier, he'd plummeted forty feet from a suspended ninety-foot steel beam that was part of a bridge-building project. Landing on rocks, he had suffered two broken ribs, several broken teeth, and a dislocated knee. Although he had not expected to accompany Roosevelt on the venture into the wilderness, his mother had asked him to go along to "take care of Father." Therefore, instead of a fortnight of hunting, as Roosevelt had planned, Kermit found himself delaying marriage to Belle Willard (daughter of the U.S. ambassador to Spain and owner of Washington's Willard Hotel), and taking a leave of absence from the Anglo-Brazilian Iron Company.

Two days after leaving Bahia, the Roosevelt expedition reached Rio de Janeiro to find a welcome by the Brazilians that Father Zahm described as having "all the wild enthusiasm of a national holiday." Among the greeters was Lauro Muller. The government official informed Roosevelt that he had arranged that on the headwaters of the Paraguay River, at the town of Caceres, Roosevelt would be met by a Brazilian army officer, Colonel Candido Mariano de Salva Rondon. Recalling this turn of events, Roosevelt wrote, "My exact plan of operations was necessarily a little indefinite." Now he found that Muller's offer of help made it possible for the trip to be "of much more consequence" than he'd originally planned. Roosevelt wrote:

> He told me that he would cooperate with me in every way if I cared to undertake the leadership of a serious expedition into the unexplored portion of western Matto Grasso, and to attempt the descent of a river which flowed nobody knew whither, but which the best-informed men believed to be a very big river, utterly unknown to geographers. I eagerly and gladly accepted, for I felt that with such help the trip could be made of much scientific value, and that a substantial addition could be made to the geographical knowledge of some of the least-known parts of South America. Accordingly, it was arranged that Colonel Rondon and some assistants and scientists should meet me at or below Corumba, and that we should attempt the descent of the river, of which they had already come across the headwaters.

This abrupt change of plans did not sit well with the expedition's official sponsor. When Henry Fairfield Osborn of the American Museum of Natural History learned of the alteration in the itinerary, he had a horrible vision of the beloved icon of American heroism lying dead in a South American jungle. He shot off a threat to Roosevelt that the museum would not "assume part of the responsibility for what might happen in case he [Roosevelt] did not return alive."

The return message, sent to Frank Chapman, was a sample of Roosevelt bravado: "Tell Osborn I have already lived and enjoyed as much of life as any nine other men I know; I have had my full share, and if it's necessary for me to leave my bones in South America, I am quite ready to do so."

With the museum's backing intact, Roosevelt would first have to travel through Brazil, Uruguay, Argentina, and Chile for six weeks of speaking engagements. Consequently, Cherrie, Miller, Fiala, and Sigg left him at Rio de Janeiro to wait for him at Corumba. Father Zahm saw it as "a continuous ovation as well as a triumphal march." Roosevelt would write, "In all the South American countries there is more pomp and ceremony in connection wth public functions than with us, and at these functions the liveried servants, often with knee-breeches and powdered hair, are like those seen in familiar European functions; there is not the democratic simplicity which better suits our own habits and ways of thought. But the South American often surpasses us, not merely in pomp and ceremony but in what is of real importance, courtesy; in civility and courtesy we can well afford to take lessons from them."

During the two months before starting from Asuncion, in Paraguay, for the journey into the interior, he complained that he was kept so busy that he had little time to think of natural history. "But in a strange land a man who cares for wild birds and wild beasts," he noted, "[he] sees and hears something that is new to him and interests him."

As the time neared when he and Kermit would again brave the wilds, Edith Roosevelt prepared to leave husband and son and return to Sagamore Hill. "We're both feeling quiet and sad," Kermit wrote to his fiancee about Edith's leaving. She sailed on the steamer *Orcoma* from Valparaiso on November 26. Ten days later, Roosevelt, Kermit, Father Zahm, and Frank Harper took a train to Asuncion, Paraguay.

On the afternoon of December 9, 1913, they left behind "the attractive and picturesque city of Asuncion to ascend the Paraguay" on a gunboat-yacht of Paraguay's president. It was a "most comfortable river steamer" on which the food was good and the quarters clean. From its deck during three days of steaming northward toward the Tropic of Capricorn Roosevelt saw "fairly well-settled country, where bananas and oranges were cultivated and other crops of hot countries raised."

With him on the boat was an old Western friend, Tex Rickard, but now the owner of a sprawling cattle ranch near Concepcion. When the boat docked there at daybreak on the third day, Rickard accompanied Roosevelt ashore for a walking tour of a town that had been founded by Spanish conquistadores three-quarters of a century before the English and Dutch landed in North America. With sightseeing and official receptions completed, it was back to the gunboat. At noon on the twelfth it crossed the Brazilian border and the eagerly anticipated rendezvous with Colonel Rondon. On December 15 in Corumba they were greeted by George Cherrie, Leo Miller, Anthony Fiala, and Jacob Sigg. The naturalists informed Roosevelt that they had already collected eight hundred specimens of animals and birds.

* * *

Roosevelt's planning for the expedition included a deal with *Scribner's Magazine* for a series of articles. Like those he'd provided about his African adventure the essays would then be compiled into a book (*Through the Brazilian Wilderness*). By the time he arrived at Corumba he'd sent off the first, titled "The Start." With the second, "Up the Paraguay," went a letter to his editor, Robert Bridges. Roosevelt wrote, "This is all so different from my African trip!" He also expressed some doubt whether what he'd written in the essay "is satisfactory or not." The task that faced Bridges as he read the dispatches was not the quality of Roosevelt's prose, but the challenge of correctly interpreting Roosevelt's handwriting. Transposed to typeface, the series would begin running in the magazine in April 1914.

When "Up the Paraguay" appeared it gave readers an introduction through Roosevelt's eyes to "the piranha or cannibal fish, the fish that eats men when it can get the chance." There is no way of knowing how many people shivered with horror in snug American homes as they read:

> They are the most ferocious fish in the world. Even the most formidable fish, the sharks or the barracudas, usually attack things smaller than themselves. But the piranhas habitually attack things much larger than themselves. They will snap a finger off a hand incautiously trailed in the water; they mutilate swimmers. In every river town in Paraguay there are men who have thus been mutilated; they will rend and devour alive any wounded man or beast; for blood in the water excites them to madness. . . . Most predatory fish are long and slim, like the alligator and pickerel. But the piranha is a short, deep-bodied fish, with a blunt face and a heavily undershot or projecting lower jaw which gapes widely. The razor-edged teeth are wedge-shaped like a shark's, and the jaw muscles possess great power. The rabid, furious snaps drive the teeth through flesh and bone. The head with its short muzzle, staring malignant eyes, and gaping, cruelly armed jaws, is the embodiment of evil ferocity; and the actions of the fish exactly matches its looks.

Along with the second essay went 80 photographs taken by Kermit. The captions were written by Roosevelt. The one for a picture of a piranha said, "Maneating fish: see his teeth!"

These hungry, swarming inhabitants of the waters in the vicinity of Corumba continued to fascinate Roosevelt as he and the other explorers prepared for the next leg of the expedition. If someone dropped something of value in the water and waded in to retrieve it, he did so "very slowly and quietly, avoiding every possibility of disturbance, and not venturing to put his hands into the water." Nobody could bathe because scrubbing hands with soap "immediately attracted the attention of the savage little creatures, who darted to the place, evidently hoping to find some animal in difficulties."

Menacing piranhas aside, Roosevelt, Colonel Rondon, and other members of the party left Corumba by boat on December 17 to venture down the Paraguay River to one of its many tributaries, this one called the Taquary. The "noxious creatures" that attracted Roosevelt's eyes were cayman crocodiles, known locally as "jacares." They sometimes darted into the stream, looking like "miniatures of the monsters of the prime," and oblivious to the bullets fired at them by Roosevelt and the others. When a cayman was hit by a long .22-caliber bullet, it slid into the water and "at once forgot everything except its greedy appetite." Roosevelt observed it seizing "fish after fish, holding its head above water as soon as its jaws had closed on a fish" until a second bullet killed it.

Almost as interesting to Roosevelt as the cayman was the "giant antbear," known in the region as the "tamandua bendeira." They were easy game. Out in the open marsh the animal "could neither avoid observation, nor fight effectively, nor make good its escape by fight." It was "curious" to Roosevelt to "see one lumbering off at a rocking cantering, the big bushy tail held aloft," and on one occasion battling hunting-hounds by suddenly throwing itself on its back, evidently hoping to grasp the dog with its paws, or rearing to strike its assailant.

But none of these unique animals tempted Roosevelt's hunter's nature as much as the jaguar. Setting out to get one at three in the morning, Roosevelt was accompanied by Kermit, Colonel Rondon, two native jaguar hunters, dogs, and a boy carrying the saddle bags containing lunch. "As our shabby little horses shuffled away from the ranch-house," Roosevelt wrote of the start of his quest, "the stars were brilliant and the Southern Cross hung well up in the heavens, tilted to the right. The landscape was spectral in the light of the waning moon."

Hour after hour the hunters "shogged along" as night gave way to an overcast day, but with the sun breaking through here and there to light fields of papyrus that were a reminder of Africa. At last, on the edge of a patch of jungle, they found fresh jaguar tracks. With the hounds loosed, the party followed through ponds and long, winding bayous and islandlike stretches of tree-covered land. As the pace quickened, the dogs led the hunters through a marsh toward a taruman tree. Among its forked limbs, Roosevelt saw "a beautiful picture." The spotted coat of the big, lithe, formidable cat fairly shone as the jaguar snarled at the dogs below.

Fearing that if the jaguar descended, the hounds would be unequal to the challenge, and the jaguar would get away, Roosevelt raised the little Springfield rifle that had never failed him in Africa, sighted the jaguar from 70 yards, and fired. The jaguar fell from the tree "like a sack of sand through the branches, and although it staggered to its feet it went but a score of yards before it sank down." To Roosevelt the jaguar was "the king of South American game, ranking on an equality with the noblest beasts of the chase of North America, and behind only the huge and fierce creatures which stand at the head of the big game of Africa and Asia."

Roosevelt's jaguar was an adult female, "heavier and more powerful than a full-grown male cougar, or African panther or leopard." As Roosevelt knelt behind its carcass, holding its head erect in his right hand and grasping the Springfield in the left, Kermit snapped a picture that would be captioned "Colonel Roosevelt and the first jaguar."

The next day it was Kermit's turn. Around ten in the morning they were at a long, deep, winding bayou when they found tracks. After a long pursuit, they found a huge male jaguar high in the branches of a fig tree. They later learned that it was "a well-known" jaguar that had been raiding cattle herds and had killed a few cows and a young steer. A bullet from Kermit's 405 Winchester ended its cattle-killing career. With all the keenest of observations made by Teedie Roosevelt when he examined the body of the seal laid out on ice in front of a Broadway fish store, Theodore Roosevelt noted Kermit's prize for the record:

He was heavier than the very big male horse-killing cougar I shot in Colorado, whose skull Hart Merriam reported as the biggest he'd ever seen; he was very nearly double the weight of any of the male African leopards we shot; he was nearly or quite the weight of the smallest of the adult African lionesses we shot while in Africa. He had the big bones, the stout frame, and the heavy muscular build of a small lion; he was not lithe and slender and long like a cougar or leopard; the tail, as with all jaguars, was short, while the girth of the body was great; his coat was beautiful with a satiny gloss, and the dark-brown spots on the gold of his back, head, and sides were hardly as conspicuous as the black of the equally well-marked spots against a white belly.

During this respite before launching the primary goal of the expedition, the exploration of the unknown river whose headwaters had been discovered by Colonel Rondon, Roosevelt exhibited his skills as a naturalist in observations of the birds, insects, and other wildlife around Corumba, from the noisy howler monkeys, the armadillo, and huge anthills to the blunt-nosed, short-eared, water-living, piglike rodents called the capybara. He also spent a delightful, and rather nostalgic, afternoon watching the South American version of the Wild West cowboy, "the gaucho." Riding into a big square corral near the ranch house where Roosevelt was a guest, they demonstrated the "agility, nerve, and prowess" of North American cattle herders as they drove a small herd of calves, yearlings, and two-year-olds in for branding. They differed from Dakotas cowboys only in skin color—the gauchos were mainly of Indian or Negro descent—and in a lack of boots. "Their bare feet must have been literally as tough as thorn," Roosevelt noted, "for when one of them roped a big bull he would brace himself [on bare feet], bending back until he was almost sitting down and digging his heels into the ground, and the galloping beast would be stopped short and whirled completely round when the rope tautened."

Roosevelt's stay at the ranch ended just before Christmas. He was back in Corumba on December 24. The plan for the expedition required that it reach the headwaters of the unknown river that was their destination by late February, before the rainy season.

Homesick for the love of his life, Kermit dashed off a reassuring letter to Belle Willard. "You must be sure to realize that there's not the slightest danger for me in this trip," he wrote, "for the tropics agree with me."

His father agreed with this assessment of Kermit's condition. In a Christmas Eve letter to "Darling Edith," he wrote:

> Kermit is now in first rate shape, and as tough as hickory, and I never felt in better health—in spite of being covered with prickly heat—so if you do not hear from me to the contrary you can safely assume that this condition of things is permanent. Of course we have not yet really begun the expedition proper as yet, and there will be many disagreeable experi-

ences; but we are being hardened under exceptionally unpleasant conditions, and so far have had no hardships whatever. Kermit, Harper, Miller and I, with some of the Brazilians, who are capital fellows and great chums of Kermit, are returning from a delightful week at a huge ranch in the marshes of the Taquary River. . . . We each killed a jaguar, [Kermit's] being an exceptionally large one and mine a good average one; and we were in the saddle eight or ten hours a day . . . Kermit is his own mother's son! He is to me a delightful companion; he always has books with him; and he is a tireless worker. He is not only an exceptionally good and hard hunter, but as soon as he comes in he starts at his photographs or else at the skins, working as hard as the two naturalists.

When Roosevelt, Kermit, and the entire party boarded the river boat *Nyoac* on Christmas day, the shallow little steamer was crammed with men, dogs, rifles, partially cured skins of the specimens that had been collected, scores of boxes of provisions, ammunition, tools, tents, cots, bedding, clothes, saddles, hammocks, and all the items deemed necessary by outfitter Anthony Fiala for a trip through the "great wilderness" for which the Brazilian term was "matto grasso."

The sky was brilliantly clear. The early morning was cool and pleasant. Roosevelt and his companions sat on the forward deck, admiring the trees on the brink of sheer riverbanks, the lush grass of the marshes, and seemingly countless water birds. The boat would be piloted by two men, one black and one white.

Colonel Rondon ignored the colorful scene, preferring to read Thomas à Kempis. Kermit, Cherrie, and Miller squatted on a deck above the boat's paddle wheel while putting the final touches on the curing of the two jaguar skins. Fiala checked and double-checked the piles of equipment and supplies. Only "good little Father Zahm," because of his age and physical frailty, was not working hard. And, Roosevelt had assured Edith in his letter, everything possible was being done for the comfort, in little ways that meant much "to a man of my age on a rough trip."

That evening on the afterdeck as the boat pushed against the current of the Paraguay, the explorers dined in the open amid decorative green boughs and rushes. On both sides of the river was a fertile land, pleasant to live in, and there to provide a living to any settler who was willing to work. In Roosevelt's view there was no doubt that the country would soon be opened up by railroads, just as the American West had been, with the result that ambitious people would flood in to exploit the land by farming and mining. Roosevelt believed, as he had felt in East Africa, that South America "has a great future."

It was possible that in his own future lay hardship, Roosevelt realized, but for now "the day was our own, and the day was pleasant."

The former president of the United States proposed toasts to the health of the present one, Woodrow Wilson, and to the ever-helpful and accommodating president of Brazil.

20

★ ★ ★

"I'm bully!"

O N DECEMBER 28, 1913, Theodore Roosevelt was a guest at the ranch of Joao de Costa Marques and his son, who was secretary of agriculture of the Matto Grasso. Another guest was the president of the region. As a welcome for Roosevelt a great rodeo was arranged, followed by a hunt. The event afforded Roosevelt a chance to realize his long-held dream of killing a peccary (a boar) in native fashion with a jaguar spear. Two days later, chased by dogs, the animal was at bay in a half-hollow stump when Roosevelt set aside a rifle, "borrowed" a spear, and "killed the fierce little boar therewith."

Continuing through jungle so thick that "machetes were constantly at work" to clear a path, Roosevelt, Kermit, Colonel Rondon, and Marques's son waded across hip-deep marshes while vexed by swarms of mosquitoes and stinging fire ants. But pestering of insects couldn't compare to the pain Roosevelt suffered when he discovered that a prized pocket watch which had kept reliable time in battles of the Spanish-American War and during the year-long trek in Africa "came to an indignant halt."

When the party failed to return to the *Nyoac* at the expected hour, the steamer's worried captain ordered the boat's whistle to be sounded again and again. As Roosevelt finally climbed aboard, Anthony Fiala gazed at the dripping-wet, mud-spattered, welt-reddened, portly figure and gasped, "Are you all right, Colonel?"

Beneath a droopy gray mustache, the world's most famous set of teeth was revealed by a satisfied grin as Roosevelt exclaimed, "I'm *bully!*"

Looking across the dinner table at Roosevelt's disheveled figure, Leo Miller thought, "Good heavens, there sits an ex-president of the United States, and I have never seen a more dilapidated individual."

Having marked the turning of the calendar from 1913 to 1914, the expedition proceeded up the Paraguay River toward the town of Sao Luis de Caceres and the beginning of the search for the route of a river that was so mysterious that Rondon has named it Rio du Duvida (River of Doubt). Writing to his mother on January 3, Kermit reported that, except for a hurt knee, gotten when he'd jumped off the boat, "Father's in fine shape." He added, "A little less to eat and drink won't hurt anyone, and will improve Father's figure. How long this trip will take seems to be getting more doubtful every day; tho I think Rondon is putting an outside estimate on everything so as to have Father prepared for the longest & worst."

The strategy agreed upon by Roosevelt and Rondon on reaching Caceres was to divide the expedition: Leo Miller and Father Zahm leading a party to chart Rio Gy-Parana; Roosevelt, Kermit, Rondon, Cherrie, and Fiala would enter the River of Doubt. The rendezvous point at the conclusion of these explorations was to be the city of Manaos.

Because Caceres was the last point at which collected specimens could be sent to New York, Cherrie and Miller packed up more than a thousand birds and mammals. Roosevelt was so impressed by their work that he wrote to Henry Fairfield Osborn suggesting that it would be "a matter of justice that the men who undergo the hardship and discomfort of work in the field should be permitted themselves to describe the animals they have collected" in their own book.

"The quaint old-fashioned little town" of Caceras, on the outermost fringe of the Matto Grasso, Roosevelt noted, was "the last town we should see before reaching the villages of the Amazon." Just as fascinated by the town's inhabitants as he'd been by the natives of Africa, he saw pretty faces of women, "some dark, some light," looking out lattice-shuttered windows in white or blue one-story, red tile–roofed houses that had "come down from colonial days and tracing back through Christian and Moorish Portugal to a remote Arab ancestry." But he also discerned "the spirit of the new Brazil." Symbolized by "a fine new government school and its principal, an earnest man doing excellent work," the school represented to Roosevelt "the new educational movement which will do so much for Brazil."

From Caceres the expedition would enter the region of explorations by Colonel Rondon that had resulted in the discovery of the existence of the River of Doubt. His original purpose, eighteen years earlier, had been to open telegraph lines through the vast wilderness known as the "matto grasso." In 1907 he'd been sent by the Brazilian government to explore the uncharted region and to map it for the first time. In carrying out this mission Rondon proved to be exactly the kind of man that appealed to Roosevelt's own concept of hardy, adventurous manhood.

They were laudable traits that Roosevelt had found in Kermit. As the Roosevelt scholar Edward J. Renehan Jr., author of a book about Roosevelt's four sons titled *The Lion's Pride,* wrote for the Theodore Roosevelt Association's Internet Web site, "It seemed it was always Kermit—the lucky one, his brothers called him—who got to go along with TR on his most splendid adventures." Like all the Roosevelt boys, Kermit "shared his father's love of the outdoors and physical activity." No one in the family had been surprised by Kermit's enthusiastic embrace of the African expedition, or that he'd enlisted for the Brazilian adventure.

But on the verge of beginning the thrust into the unknowns of the River of Doubt, Kermit became ill. Although he thought he was simply coming down with a bad cold, the illness was a recurrence of malaria, contracted soon after he'd arrived in Brazil to work for the iron company. Felled in Caceras by a raging fever that reached 102 degrees, he laid in a hammock for four days while Roosevelt felt "utterly miserable with worry." Kermit's fever broke on January 12. Four days later, Roosevelt wrote to his youngest son, Quentin, "So far there have been no hardships, although of course there has been some fatigue and some discomfort." Telling Quentin it was the last letter he would receive for a while, and that "I think it will take six weeks to two months in getting to you," he expressed the hope that "not long after that I will be able to send a telegram to Mother announcing that I have gotten out of the wilderness and am about to sail for home."

While Kermit rebounded from his malaria, Roosevelt was dismayed when his secretary, Frank Harper, suddenly exhibited all its symptoms. Worried, and aware that Harper hadn't been cut out for the arduous demands of wilderness living, Roosevelt proposed that Harper leave the expedition. He departed on January 18 for Caceres with five crates of specimen skins and Leo Miller's living trophy of the expedition, a giant turtle named Lizzie.

Roosevelt's account of this portion of the expedition made no mention of the reason for Harper's departure. He said only that at Tapirapuan, named for the River of Tapirs, "we broke up our baggage—as well as our party." He explained, "All the skins, skulls and specimens, and all the baggage not absolutely necessary, were sent back down the Paraguay and to New York, in charge of Harper."

As previously agreed, the expedition was split in two. The larger group left Tapirapuan on January 19. Roosevelt's party, including Kermit, Rondon, Father Zahm, Cherrie, and Anthony Fiala, departed two days later for an expected month-long march to the headwaters of the River of Doubt. In addition to Kermit's photographic record of the expedition, there would be pictures captured by a movie camera that equipment manager Anthony Fiala had thought to add to his list of necessities and creature comforts. Roosevelt's contingent surpassed the size of the African safari, but instead of using native bearers, it had 98 mules and 70 oxen to carry Fiala's outfittings and cans of food on a journey of nearly 300 miles.

While there was no problem with the mules, about half the oxen had to be "broken in." Observing this process, Roosevelt found a comparison between the pack-men and cowboys in the West. As the oxen "bucked like wild broncos" and scattered their loads over the corral, the pack-men "were not only masters of their art, but possessed tempers that could not be ruffled."

This was not true of Kermit. Infuriated by the delay in starting, he wrote in exasperation to his far-away and sorely missed bride-to-be, "I have been ready to kill the whole lot, and all the members of the expedition." But once they were on the move he was feeling better, emotionally and physically, so that when his indomitable father broke into recitations of the favorite poetry of the parent, the son happily joined him.

From Tapirapuan their direction was northward to and across a highland (Plan Alto) from which flowed the affluents of the Amazon to the north and the Plate River to the south. The level country was a great natural pasture that reminded Roosevelt of Texas and Oklahoma. He saw a future in the region for stock-raising and expected the river to ultimately become a source of electric power. The proponent of the manifest destiny of the people of the United States to fill up a continent said of the Plan Alto, "It is fine country for settlement."

On January 24, 1914, after a sixteen-mile trek over the plains, camp was set up on the banks of the Rio Perdiz. Having marched fourteen hours without a meal, Roosevelt recorded, the party "feasted royally on beans and rice and pork and beef, seated around oilskins spread upon the ground." A campfire that evening passed in a traditional Roosevelt fashion when surrounded by other outdoorsmen of swapping stories of their adventures. Always a great listener who would recount others' stories in his hunting books, he did so with many of the tales he absorbed around the campfires in Brazil. But during those evenings nobody surpassed his own spellbinding yarns of roughing it in the West and hunting big game in Africa. His enchanted audience of Brazilians had a word for him: *pandego.* Kermit translated it from Portugese to mean "life of the party."

When a camp was broken in the morning, Roosevelt found the activity a "picturesque sight." He also enjoyed the breakfasts of rice, beans and crackers, with canned corned beef, and salmon or any game that had been shot, all washed down by coffee and tea. While mules and oxen were being packed, he usually sat down somewhere to write for *Scribner's.* Kermit saw it as "paying for his fun."

With the expedition on the move again, Kermit left the line of march astride "a big, iron-mouthed, bull-headed white mule" to hunt pampas deer. When he rejoined the party late in the afternoon, he had two bucks behind his saddle. Roosevelt pronounced the venison "delicious."

Riding day after day across the seemingly endless flats of grass and low, open, scrubby forest, Roosevelt took in the scenery with a naturalist's interest. He noted the flowers ("the most beautiful being the morning-glories"), "bastard rubber trees," and dwarf palmetto, but saw very little bird or animal life. "Yet the desolate landscape had a certain charm of its own," he wrote, "although not a charm that would be felt by any man who does not take pleasure in mere space, and freedom and wildness, and in plains standing empty in the sun, the wind, and the rain."

The Plan Alto bore some resemblance to the country west of the White Nile, home of the giant eland. But these Brazilian plains offered no big game, "no chance of seeing the towering form of the giraffe, the black bulk of the elephant or buffalo, the herds of straw-colored harte-beests, or the ghostly shimmer of the sun glinting on the coats of roan and eland as they vanished silently in the gray sea of withered scrub."

There was one feature that the Plan Alto shared with the African landscape. It had an "abundance of anthills, some as high as a man." Known to the Brazilians as "carregadores," or porter ants, these "inveterate burden-carriers" toted bits of leaves and blades of grass to their underground homes. They also took an interest in gnawing off snippets of clothing, requiring Roosevelt and the others to guard their vulnerable belongings. Of great interest, also, were black ants that were an inch and a quarter long and "very vicious" with a poisonous bite; grasshoppers as large as sparrows; and praying mantises. Especially fascinating was "an extraordinary colony of spiders." Discovered at a camping sight one early afternoon, the colony was among some dwarf trees at the edge of a pool of water. Although it appeared to have been abandoned, its occupants suddenly emerged by the hundreds at dusk from daytime hiding places in tree leaves to repair old webs or spin new ones.

Roosevelt diligently recorded for his eventual readers, "Each spun his own circular web, and sat in the middle; and each web was connected on several sides with other webs, while those nearest the tree were hung to them by spun ropes, so to speak. The result was a kind of sheet of web consisting of scores of wheels, in each of which the owner and proprietor sat."

Roosevelt did not note how long he watched the spiders. But when darkness fell and rain began, he was in place to record that the spiders were "still out, fixing their webs, and pouncing on the occasional insects that blundered into the webs."

More than a century later, a reader of Roosevelt's account can only wonder that a former president of the United States, champion of "the square deal" for every American, advocate of a foreign policy of speaking softly while carrying a big stick, and believer that the white man had a duty to carry his civilization and the gospel of Jesus Christ to the remotest corners of the globe, could spend an afternoon transfixed by spiders.

It's reasonable to assume that Theodore Roosevelt did not expect his writings about the expedition to Brazil, the safari across East Africa, and his adventures in the West to be read by several succeeding generations. He was speaking, as Roosevelt biographer H.W. Brands wrote in an introduction to a reprint of Roosevelt's *Through the Brazilian Wilderness*, to the people who never would have seen most of what he described.

After a late start on December 29, the expedition marched for six hours to reach one of the most spectacular natural wonders of the world, a waterfall named Salto Bello. Near a small native village, the wide cataract was a sheer drop of forty or fifty yards. Vine-covered cliffs flanked it as the river, "after throwing itself over the rock wall," rushed off in long curves at the bottom of a thickly wooded ravine, the white water churning among the black boulders."

The men of the settlement operated a ferry across the Rio Sacre. Parecis Indians, they were "an unusually cheerful, good-humored, pleasant-natured people" with bad teeth, but who otherwise "appeared strong and vigorous." They demonstrated their vitality by playing a kind of soccer in which only their heads were allowed to touch the ball. "It is hard to decide," Roosevelt wrote of the unique sport, "whether to wonder most at the dexterity and strength with which it is hit or butted with the head, as it comes down through the air, or at the reckless speed and skill with which the players throw themselves headlong on the ground to return the ball if it comes low down. Why they do not grind off their noses I cannot imagine."

Having breakfast on benches set under trees by the waterfall, with its roar "lulled to a thunderous murmur," Roosevelt believed there could have been no more picturesque place to have his morning repast. He would soon find himself awed by an even greater spectacle in the form of the Falls of Utiariy. The site had been discovered on his earlier explorations by Colonel Rondon and named for a local breed of falcon.

"Lovely though we had found Salto Bello," Roosevelt wrote of the new vista, "these falls were far superior in beauty and majesty. They are twice as high and twice as broad; and the lay of the land is such that the various land-scapes in which the waterfall is a feature are more striking." Excepting Niagara, he doubted that there was a waterfall in North America outranking it "if both volume and beauty are considered." As Roosevelt and Kermit admired "one sunset of angry splendor," they contrasted "this going down of the sun, through broken rain clouds and over leagues of wet tropical forest, with the desert sunsets we had seen in Arizona and Sonora. and along the Guaso Nyiro north and west of Mount Kenya."

After days and nights of relentless rain, the weather improved enough on February 2 for Roosevelt to go hunting. But the only game he found was a "rather hairy armadillo." Back at the camp, he held it by its "flexible tail" and presented it to Leo Miller to add to their collection.

Two events at the falls plunged Roosevelt into unusual sadness. The first was receipt of a telegram notifying him that his niece, Margaret Roosevelt, who had been a traveling companion for Edith to and from South America, had died of typhoid fever shortly after returning to New York. The second unsettling occurrence involved Father Zahm. The elderly, ailing priest who had been the impetus for Roosevelt's venture into the Brazilian wilderness announced that if he were to continue on the expedition, he would need a special chair that would be carried by four Parecis men. When Rondon heard of the idea, he rejected it. He told Zahm that the idea went against the democratic principles of the Parecis. Roosevelt sided with Rondon. He ordered Zahm back to Tapirapuan. Zahm replied that leaving was "the greatest disappointment of my life." As in the earlier departure of Harper, Roosevelt's published account of Zahm's leaving did not give the reason. He wrote, "From here Father Zahm returned to Tapirapuan, accompanied by Sigg." But in a memorandum that was signed by all the remaining men of the expedition, Roosevelt noted for the record, "Every member of the expedition has told me that in his opinion it is essential to the success and well being of the expedition that Father Zahm should at once leave it and return to settled country."

On February 4 the diminished party arrived at the Burity River. As the new encampment was being established, Roosevelt wrestled with another personnel problem. This one concerned Anthony Fiala. The veteran of explorations in the Arctic had proven to be, in the opinion of Leo Miller, "incompetent to do a single thing" on an expedition in the Brazilian tropics. Much of the equipment he'd brought from New York had turned out to be useless. But in deciding that Fiala should also leave the expedition, Roosevelt could not bring himself to send Fiala home. Instead, Fiala was assigned to a secondary expedition down the Papagaio River and into the Juruena and Tapajos. Roosevelt explained it as "performing a necessary part of the work of the expedition." It was a feeble attempt at all-around face-saving, and everyone recognized it. That night George Cherrie confided to his journal, "I think his going had a saddening effect on all of us."

In addition to Roosevelt, the remaining North Americans were Kermit, Cherrie, and Miller. Roosevelt later justified the trimming of the party by writing, "We have weeded out everyone unfit for exploration." Also left behind on orders from Colonel Rondon were "all luxuries" and half the party's baggage. Kermit wrote to Belle Willard, "We've been going through a regular course of shedding men and provisions." Roosevelt's account of the process needed only two sentences: "Here we had to cut down our baggage and rearrange the loads for the mule-train." And "Each of us got rid of everything above the sheer necessities."

After traveling 230 arduous miles in nineteen days, the greatly trimmed and lightened venture in exploration arrived at the banks of the upper Rio Juruena. One of the five known tributaries of the Amazon, it flowed only 150 miles from Roosevelt's goal—the unknown and enticing waterway with a name that was ominous in both languages of the expedition: "Rio du Duvida" in Portugese and "River of Doubt" in English. But the Brazilian government had given its pledge that should Roosevelt and his companions succeed in finding where the river went, it would be given a new name in honor of its illustrious explorer: "Rio Teodoro."

21

★ ★ ★

All Well and Cheerful

TRAVELING THROUGH a tropical wilderness in the rainy season on a journey of discovery and scientific observation, when the amount of baggage must be strictly limited, Theodore Roosevelt mused as his pared-down expedition rested by yet another Brazilian river, "entails not only a good deal of work, but also the exercise of considerable ingenuity if the writing and photographing, and especially the preservation, if the specimens are to be done in satisfactory shape."

Just how difficult the going could be was reinforced for Roosevelt in a message waiting for him at a station of the Brazilian telegraph service for whom Colonel Rondon had worked in extending lines into the Matto Grasso. In doing so, Roosevelt believed, Rondon had founded "the Brazilian school of exploration" in an enterprise that previously had been left to foreigners. The telegram read by Roosevelt was from Anthony Fiala. It contained the disturbing news that in going down the Papagaio there'd been a "misadventure." In rough rapids a few miles below a waterfall, two of the party's canoes had been upset at the cost of half the party's provisions, all of Fiala's baggage, and, most distressing of all, Fiala had nearly drowned.

The incident provided Roosevelt an opportunity to educate the eventual readers of his articles for *Scribner's Magazine* of the hazards of descending a "swift, unknown river rushing through uninhabited wilderness." Failure to remember this fact, he counseled, "is one of the obstacles in the way of securing a proper appreciation of the needs and the results of South American exploration."

Assessing how well his expedition had done in under three months, Roosevelt noted that more than 300 mammals had been collected, and about five times that number of birds. But now they stood on the verge of the most exciting part of the odyssey.

To be starting the last leg of the trip was for Kermit "a great relief." Since leaving Rio de Janeiro five months ago, he wrote to Belle, he had been continually afraid that the hard-working pack train might give out completely, or at least cause a very long delay. But now, he wrote, "we're here and ready to start down the river, and each day brings me nearer to you, my own dearest dearest Belle."

Writing to Edith, Roosevelt announced:

> Here we are ready to start down the Duvida, all well and cheerful. No one has an idea, or at least every body has half a dozen,—which comes to the same thing—,as to where the Duvida goes. . . . It is almost impossible even to guess at the amount of time it will take to go down it. If things go in the best way possible I think we may be in Manaos in a month and a half; two months is really the most probable, tho three or four is possible.

The assertion "all well and cheerful" was not true concerning Kermit. Roosevelt had been worried enough about Kermit's health that since the stop at Tapirapuan he'd suggested to Kermit that he go "straight on out" of the expedition. The idea certainly proved to be a temptation. Longing to be with Belle, Kermit confessed to her in a letter, "I have hated this trip." But the love and loyalty of a son, and his promise to Edith to take care of Father, had persuaded him that quitting "would be far worse than never to have come at all."

Making him more miserable were a recurrence of malarial fever and saddle sores that developed into boils. They were so painful that he couldn't get a good night's sleep and had to stand in the stirrups when he rode. He complained to Belle, "We keep crawling along, gradually cutting down the distance to the Duvida, but oh so slowly." He confessed, "I'm afraid I'm not very much of an explorer at present." While everyone else was hoping that the River of Doubt would turn out to be long and important, all he asked was that it "be short and easy to travel."

An obvious result of the nineteen-day trek from Tapirapuan to Rio

Juruena on Roosevelt that Kermit welcomed was a diminished waistline. The weight loss was a legacy not only of the physical demands of such an arduous trip, but the consequence of a limitation to two meals a day, breakfast and dinner. When the expedition arrived at Juruena station and Colonel Rondon declared that the mid-day repast could be restored during the brief respite, the announcement was greeted with delight by the expedition, with one notable exception. As Roosevelt insisted on continuing the twice-a-day policy, the only person who dared to confront him on the matter was Kermit. If Father chose to limit himself to two meals, said the son, "there was no reason why he should force fasting upon the rest of us."

Already at the Juruena station was a segment of the expedition that had continued on from Tapirapuan while Roosevelt's contingent took a longer route to carry out explorations and specimen collections. Led by two officers of the Brazilian army (Captain Amilcar and Lieutenant Lyra), the train of ox-drawn wagons carried material that would be needed going down the River of Doubt. Roosevelt was relieved that Amilcar reported the loss of only three oxen and their loads. After a short rest, Amilcar and his men and animals were off again, heading for the point at which the expedition planned to enter the unknown river.

In addition to meeting Amilcar at Juruena, Roosevelt found himself introduced to a few of the local natives. Members of the Nhambiquara tribe who'd met Rondon during his earlier explorations of the region, they had a reputation for ferocity. But Roosevelt found them "very friendly and sociable." He attributed their present peaceable demeanor to the civilizing effect of Colonel Rondon's "unwearied thoughtfulness and good temper, joined with his indomitable resolution." Roosevelt also noted that Rondon had never killed one of the Nhambiquaras.

"Nowhere in Africa," Roosevelt observed, had he and Kermit "come across wilder or more absolutely primitive savages, although these Indians were pleasanter and better-featured than any of the African tribes at the same stage of culture." Both sexes were "well-made and rather good-looking, with fairly good teeth, although some of them seemed to have skin diseases. They were a laughing, easy-tempered crew, and the women were as well-fed as the men, and were obviously well-treated, from the savage standpoint."

Accustomed to beholding naked natives, Roosevelt was fascinated and amused to see that the only raiment on most of the men was a string worn around the waist, while the women "did not wear a stitch of any kind any-where on their bodies." The men had holes in their lips into which decorative reeds were thrust.

Roosevelt wrote, "It seems like a contradiction in terms, but it is never-theless a fact that the behavior of these completely naked women and men was entirely modest. There never was an indecent look or a consciously inde-cent gesture."

Roosevelt soon discovered that some of the picturesque visitors were thieves. On the morning after a night of native dancing and singing for the entertainment of the white explorers, Colonel Rondon found that a native had made off with one of Rondon's dogs. "Probably the temptation had proved irresistible to one of their number," Roosevelt noted forgivingly, "and the others had been afraid to interfere, and also afraid to stay in or return to our neighborhood. We had not time to go after them; but Rondon remarked that as soon as he came again to the neighborhood he would take some sol-diers, hunt up the Indians, and reclaim the dog."

While the natives were in the camp, Kermit made good use of his camera to photograph them in their "Adam and Eve" attire, but when the negatives were bundled up to be sent in the next packet of Roosevelt's writings for *Scribner's,* Kermit made sure that the pictures went with a note stating that he wanted the negatives returned.

Roosevelt's article, "Across the Nhambiquara," dealt with the natives in the preachy tone he'd adopted when writing about African natives. "In spite of their good nature and laughter," he declared, "their fearlessness and famil-iarity showed how necessary it was not to let them get the upper hand."

On the afternoon of February 15, 1914, the expedition reached Campos Novo. It was in a large basin, several miles wide, and crossed by several brooks; the grassy land surrounding the small outpost provided food for the expedition's pack animals, and for a variety of farm animals, including goats, pigs, turkeys, and milch cows, allowing Roosevelt to have a drink of refreshing "delicious" milk, his favorite beverage after coffee. (That he always enjoyed a cup of coffee had been made known to the American people by the makers of Maxwell House coffee. After he'd finished a cup of that brand at a famous hotel, a waiter asked if he wanted another. Roosevelt asked the name of the coffee company. Told that it was Maxwell House, he said not only that he would like another cup, but that the coffee was "good to the last drop." This off-hand accolade immediately became the motto of Maxwell House coffee, and remains so.)

Cooking accommodations at Campos Novos consisted of two kitchens. One was in the open air. The other was under a shelter of ox hide. Roosevelt found the view over surrounding hills "lovely." He was pleased that as he ate he wasn't bothered by insects. Always interested in the birds of a region, he thought "the most conspicuous" species was a huge oriole that was the size of a small crow, with a naked face, a black-and-red bill, and variegated plumage of green, yellow and chestnut. There were also "a tiny soft-tailed woodpecker, no larger than a kinglet; a queer humming-bird with a slightly flexible bill; and many species of ant-thrush, tanager, manakin, and tody." Very interesting to him was the "false bell-bird, a gray bird with loud, metallic notes" that explained its name.

After a hunting-outing from the camp one day with a small Luger belt-rifle, Kermit came back with "a handsome curassow, nearly as big as a turkey" from which the cook made a thick Brazilian soup with rice. Of this "delicious canja" Roosevelt declared "there is nothing better of its kind." The uncooked remains of the curassow went into the specimen collection. Looking back on that afternoon's work, Roosevelt noted that it had produced "nine species new to the collection, six new genera, and a most excellent soup."

On the march again, the expedition arrived at Vilhena, another telegraph station, near a small river that Colonel Rondon had named "Twelfth of October," because he'd reached it on the date known as the day Christopher Columbus discovered the "New World." What is amazing about Roosevelt's recording of these facts is that one of the most well-read and history-minded Americans, and arguably the most intellectual president to that time, with the possible exception of Thomas Jefferson, confessed that until Rondon explained the naming of the river Theodore Roosevelt "had never known" what day it was that Columbus had landed in America.

From Vilhena the trek turned northward across a grassy plateau, a region of forests, and after three days, a beautiful open country on either side of a little brook that was known as one of the headwaters of the River of Doubt. With a camp established, Kermit ventured out alone and came to a small settlement inhabited by twenty or thirty men, women, and children of the warrior-like Nhambiquaras. Kermit rode into their camp with a manner that his father described as that of all "honest folk in the wilderness," meaning that Kermit "advanced ostentatiously in the open, calling out to give warning of his coming." In the land of the Nhambiquras, Roosevelt advised, it was considered not only against etiquette, but might prove "very unhealthy," to come through the woods toward them "without loudly announcing one's presence."

The naked Nhambiquaras greeted Kermit as a friend while plying him with pineapple wine. When time came for Kermit to return to his own camp, half a dozen men and boys went with him. Welcomed hospitably, they were invited to join Kermit, Roosevelt, and the others for a meal. Because Nhambiquara males adorned themselves with long reeds that pierced their lips, Roosevelt suggested that they might eat more comfortably if they removed them. The suggestion was answered with laughter. Roosevelt concluded that a Nhambiquara man taking out the reed "would have been bad manners—like using a knife as an aid in eating ice cream."

After supper, the guests danced beside the campfire, impressing Roosevelt with the rhythm and "weird, haunting melody of their chanting." While most of the Americans and Brazilians enthusiastically joined in the dancing, Roosevelt and Rondon watched appreciatively and applauded enthusiastically.

Again on the move, through alternate spells of drenching rain and blazing sunlight, the expedition came to a telegraph station at Bonofacio. It was a collection of thatched one-room cabins connected by a stockade. After breakfast a group of Nhambiquaras strolled in; the men put on an exhibition of archery that Roosevelt judged "not very good." From Bonofacio the expedition traveled about seven miles, crossing rolling prairies dotted with trees and clumps of shrub, to a brook that flowed into the River of Doubt, only a few miles away. On a page of his journal dated February 23, 1914, an exultant George Cherrie wrote, "At last we have arrived at the end, or rather the virtual end, of our long overland journey. Thirty-three days in the saddle since leaving Tapirapuan. We now have only two short marches of 7 or 8 miles each to the banks of the Duvida, where we begin the canoe journey down its unknown length."

22

★ ★ ★

The Oxford Book of
French Verse

ON FEBRUARY 24, 1914, Roosevelt's expedition kept its rendezvous with Captain Amilcar by a brook that flowed into the River of Doubt. Six miles from the stream, the party divided. Amilcar and Leo Miller would march three days to Gy-Parana River and descend it. Roosevelt, Kermit, Cherrie, and Rondon would head for the Duvida with a doctor and sixteen paddlers for the party's seven canoes. If they found within a few days that the Duvida fed into the Gy-Parana, the Madeira, or into the Tatpajos, they would know that it was not a river worth exploration and turn their attention to another mysterious waterway. The Ananas, its outlet was also unknown. The group would carry provisions for fifty days, but not full rations. On the way they would live primarily on fish, game, nuts, and palm tops. Their kit consisted of tents, bedding, medicines, instruments for determining their geographical position, and an assortment of books.

Should the party run into trouble, such as losing men or canoes in the rapids, or if any of the men got sick, Roosevelt noted coldly, "the loads would lighten themselves." Everyone was armed. The guns were intended for shooting game for food and self-defense. Demonstrating his capacity for always anticipating disaster, Roosevelt allowed that if the expedition were to lose its boats in falls or rapids, or have to make "too many and too long portages, or were brought to a halt by impassable swamps, then we would have to reckon with starvation as a possibility." Anything might happen. They were about to go into the unknown.

No one could say what the future held. "That was why," he wrote, "the river was rightly christened the Duvida."

Shortly after mid-day on February 27, they started down the river. The point from which they departed was about 12 degrees 1 minute south and 60 degrees 15 minutes longitude west of Greenwich. Their course was northward toward the equator. Of the seven canoes, one was small, one was "cranky," and two were old, waterlogged, leaky, and lashed together. The other three were good. Kermit went in the smallest of these. Rondon, Lieutenant Lyra, and three men to paddle took the next largest. Roosevelt, Cherrie, and a doctor, Alexander Lambert, took the largest with three men as paddlers. The rest of the boats carried the baggage.

A "strapping set" of expert river-men and men of the forest, the paddlers were as "lithe as panthers and brawny as bears" and "swam like water-dogs." "Equally at home with pole and paddle, with axe and machete," they reminded Roosevelt of pirates in pictures by Howard Pyle or Maxfield Parrish. He later learned that one of them really was a pirate and that another was "worse than a pirate," although why this was so Roosevelt did not explain.

Surveying of the river was done by Rondon and Lyra, with Kermit assisting by using a sighting rod. Lyra had a device to establish distance. Rondon recorded the data. Because of the twists and turns of the river, Kermit had to land nearly a hundred times in only nine and one-third kilometers in just half a day. Riding ahead of them, Roosevelt assumed the role of naturalist and found it "interesting work, for no civilized man, no white man, had ever gone down or up this river or seen the country through which we were passing." With all the diligence that had been shown by Teedie Roosevelt in keeping his notebooks on the subjects of a dead seal and the birds of the Nile River when he was ten, the grown-up veteran of warfare in fetid Cuban jungles and leading a great safari over game-rich African plains and down rivers teeming with hippos and crocodiles recorded the flora of the banks of the River of Doubt:

> The lofty and matted forest rose like a green wall on either hand. The trees were stately and beautiful. The looped and twisted vines hung from them like great ropes. Masses of epiphytes grew both on the dead trees and the living; some had huge leaves like elephants' ears. Now and then

fragrant scents were blown to us from flowers on the banks. There were not many birds, and for the most part the forest was silent; rarely we heard strange calls from the depths of the woods, or saw a cormorant or ibis.

When Roosevelt's party halted after a couple of hours to wait for the surveyors to catch up, their canoes were moored to trees. Axemen hacked out a clearing for a campsite. Tents were pitched, the luggage brought ashore, and fires kindled. Kermit and the others arrived just before nightfall. The stars of Roosevelt's first night on the river of his quest were brilliant and a new moon hung in the west. "It was a pleasant night, the air almost cool," Roosevelt wrote, "and we slept soundly."

In the morning as the surveyors pushed off, Cherrie went collecting birds in the woods. The most interesting to Roosevelt of those brought back were a brilliant turquoise-blue cotinga with a magenta-purple throat, and a big woodpecker, black above and cinnamon below with an entirely red head and neck. Leaving camp at noon, Roosevelt saw more birds and heard howler monkeys from the depth of the forest. Noting again the nature of the surrounding trees, he saw places where palms stood close together, "towering and slender, their stems a stately colonnade, their fronds an arched fretwork against the sky." The say was overcast, with rain showers, but when the sun broke through rifts in the clouds, its light "turned the forest to gold." In mid-afternoon the explorers in their canoes came to the mouth of a large, swift stream that Roosevelt thought was undoubtedly the known Bandeira whose headwaters they had crossed ten days before. According to Nhambiquaras, Roosevelt recalled, the Bandeira flowed into the Duvida. The expedition camped beside it that evening, and in the morning they dove into its depths to bathe. In two days going down the Duvida, they'd covered sixteen and a half kilometers.

March 1, 1914, dawned rainy. Moving somewhat west of north, they made more than twenty kilometers and camped close beside the river so that their "swimming-bath was handy." When one of the barefoot paddlers stepped on a poisonous coral snake, Roosevelt stomped on it with a booted foot. The snake bit it harmlessly. The incident provided Roosevelt an opportunity to note the dead snake's coloring, and that in the dark and tangled woods "anything motionless, especially if partially hidden, easily eludes the eye."

Always interested as much in the sounds of a forest as he was in its birds and animals, Roosevelt did not hear "such a chorus of birds and mammals" as he had occasionally heard on the overland trek across the Brazilian high-lands, when more than once he'd been awakened by the howling, screaming, yelping, and chattering of monkeys, toucans, macaws, parrots, and para-keets. But in this river-edging forest in the daytime there was mostly silence. And at night the strange cries and calls came from frogs and insects that died away at midnight, leaving the land silent again.

In this encampment the expedition experienced its first crisis. During the night an army of carregadores ants took a liking for the doctor's undershirt and devoured it. The also ate holes in his mosquito netting, and even partook of the strap of Lyra's gun case. But morning dawned with little rain, allowing Roosevelt and the others to drift and paddle delightfully down the river. Until mid-afternoon the current was not very fast, but then its flow quickened. "Faster it went, and faster," Roosevelt noted, "until it ran like a mill-race."

Hearing the roar of rapids ahead, the rowers made for the shore on their right. After going twenty kilometers that day, Roosevelt and his companions assessed the situation and agreed that the rapids were "a serious obstacle." About a mile of the river had many curls and a number of falls, some six feet high. They would be impossible to run in the canoes. This meant that they would have to be carried around the mile-long rapids. Doing so took all day on March 3 and 4 and the morning of the fifth.

Dragging the heavy dugout canoes, Roosevelt said with unusual under-statement, "was labor." To get around the obstacle a road had to be chopped through the jungle and a bed of hundreds of cut tree trunks laid to function as rollers, placed about two yards apart. The boats were lifted from the river with block and tackle. The men then harnessed themselves two by two on a drag rope while another used a hewn log as a lever to coax the boat along. "Bumping and sliding," it was "twitched through the woods."

In describing the portage for his *Scribner's* readers, snug in their comfort-able American homes, the proponent of the strenuous life could not resist a lecture. He wrote:

> Looking at the way the work was done, at the good-will, the endurance, and the bull-like strength of the camaradas [the Brazilian boatmen], and the intelligence and the unwearied efforts of their com-manders [Kermit and Lyra], one could but wonder at the ignorance of those who do not realize the energy and the power that are so often pos-

sessed by, and that may be so readily developed in, the men of the tropics. Another subject of perpetual wonder is the attitude of certain men who stay at home, and still more the attitude of certain men who travel under easy circumstances, and who belittle the achievements of the real explorers of, the real adventurers in, the great wilderness. The imposters and romancers among explorers or would-be explorers and wilderness wanderers have been unusually prominent in connection with South America (although the conspicuous ones are not South Americans, by the way); and these are fit subjects for condemnation and derision. But the work of the genuine explorer and wilderness wanderer is fraught with fatigue, hardship, and danger. Many of the men of little knowledge talk glibly of portaging as if it were simple and easy. A portage over rough and unknown ground is always a work of difficulty; and of some risk to the canoe; and in the untrodden, or even in the unfrequented, wilderness risk to the canoe is a serious matter.

In the times when Roosevelt set up his portable table and laid out sheets of foolscap and carbon paper to keep his writing commitment to *Scribner's*, Colonel Rondon enjoyed observing him. "I used to love to watch him think," he recalled. "A person could watch Roosevelt think! It was a very amusing sight, for he always gesticulated. He would be alone, not saying a word, yet his hands would be moving, and he would be waving his arms and nodding his head with the greatest determination, as though arguing with somebody."

In the portage of the rapids (called the Navaite Rapids) the canoe in which Roosevelt had been traveling was split in a way that raised grave doubts that it could be repaired. One of the already water-logged boats sank, requiring "more work in raising it."

After a lively debate among the explorers as to where each thought the River of Doubt would lead them, the expedition started downstream again on March 5. Their hands and faces were swollen from insect bites and stings. The current was swift, the water deep, as it meandered "hither and thither," but always in the general direction of east of north. The surveying canoes went first, while Roosevelt "shepherded" two pairs of lashed cargo canoes. At the end of half a day, they'd gone twelve kilometers.

Eight days on the river had left them where they'd started, in the sense that they still had no idea where they were going, and therefore no concept of how long the trip would take them. Roosevelt mused, "We did not know whether we had one hundred or eight kilometers to go."

Having completed the portage, they returned the boats to the river and made good time, covering nineteen kilometers, with a brief break to pillage a "bee tree" for honey. The tree was hacked open to reveal a nest built by the stingless bees in a hollow. Roosevelt noted that the honey was sweet yet with a tart flavor, and that the comb from which it was drawn differed from the combs he'd known elsewhere. Its honey cells were very large, while the brood cells were small and in a single row instead of a double row. Just as fascinating to him was a huge tree toad, the size of bullfrog, sitting upright— "not squatted flat"—on a rotten tree limb. When he stirred it up, it jumped to a small twig, catching hold with disks of its fingertips, and balancing itself with unexpected ease for so big a creature.

Back in his canoe at three o'clock, Roosevelt felt the current quicken. When the canoe passed over "decided ripples," he heard the roar of rapids ahead. With the river now racing, he directed the rowers into a bank. A quarter of a mile of reconnoitering revealed that there were big rapids that would certainly doom any canoe that ventured into them. With everyone in the expedition camped where Roosevelt had landed, Kermit, Rondon, and Lyra boated ahead as far as wisdom dictated, then returned to camp with their dismaying findings. The rapids continued a long way, with falls and steep pitches of roiling water.

At this point, Roosevelt calculated, the expedition had gone almost exactly 100 kilometers, but because of the snaking river, they were only about fifty kilometers north of their starting point.

After returning from a hunt which resulted in a jacu for dinner, Kermit reported that on this five- or six-kilometer venture downstream he'd found another steep rapids that would have to be gone around. This required three days of portaging (March 7, 8, and 9). To pass the time as the young men struggled to heave the heavy boats and all the cargo out of the river and up its banks Roosevelt read Kermit's copy of *The Oxford Book of French Verse*. Consequently, readers of his account of this interlude for *Scribner's* were treated to this:

> Eustache Deschamp, Joachim de Bellay, Ronsard, the delightful but appalling Villon, Victor Hugo's "Guitare," Madame Desbordes-Valmore's lines on the little girl and her pillow, as dear little verses about

a child as ever were written—these and many others comforted me much, as I read them in head-net and gauntlets [defenses against insects], sitting on a log by an unknown river in the Amazonian forest.

Happily and eagerly afloat once more on March 10, Roosevelt spotted a small cayman, known as a jacare-tinga. Progress was slow. Each set of rapids meant unloading the canoes and the camaradas carrying them past the turgid obstacle on their shoulders. At one point three canoes were paddled ahead by two naked rowers per boat. A pair of double, lashed-together canoes were let down the stream by ropes. When one of them was swamped, strenuous efforts were needed to rescue it. Working with the camaradas, Kermit came out of the water with his torso, arms, and legs blistered by insect bites.

The following morning brought "a serious misfortune." During the night, one of the old, leaky dugouts, one of the biggest cargo-carriers, had broken from its mooring and had dragged another boat downstream with it. A canoe was launched to retrieve them, but it struck boulders and was quickly smashed in a raging rapid. Fragments floated away. Roosevelt decided to give the site a name: Broken Canoe Rapids.

He wrote, "It was not pleasant to have to stop for some days; thanks to the rapids, we had made slow progress, and with our necessarily limited supply of food, and no knowledge whatever of what was ahead of us, it was important to make good time. But there was no alternative. We had to build either one big canoe or two small ones."

In heavy rain the men explored in different directions for good canoe trees. They found three suitable ones near the camp and the axemen immediately attacked them, supervised by Colonel Rondon. At the same time Kermit and Lyra went in opposite directions in search of game for food. Lyra bagged a jacu. Kermit shot two monkeys.

With the canoe-builders still hard at work on March 12, Roosevelt spent the day hunting in the silent forest. All went well until he burst through a tangle of foliage and disturbed a nest of wasps. Their "resentment was active," causing him to lurch into a tree containing a small party of carnivorous foraging ants. Grasping a branch as he stumbled, he shook down a shower of fire ants. The bite of one of the giant insects stung "like a hornet" and continued to hurt three hours later. Returning to camp, he found the canoe-builders still at work, rolling and shifting a huge, heavy tree trunk to position it for the axemen. After nightfall some of the men held candles as others chopped away to hollow out the wood, while the flicker of the lights showed the tropical forest rising in the surrounding darkness.

At mid-day on the fourteenth, in a torrential downpour, the finished dugout was dragged to the river and launched. The resumed expedition passed large whirlpools in the swollen, swift river. The heavily loaded canoes rode low so that when they raced through rapids they took on a great deal of water. In one set of big ripples Roosevelt's canoe was nearly swamped. Forging through the dangerous rapids was deemed necessary because no one knew where they were going or whether they had sufficient provisions to survive. Unless they made up time, it was likely that they would run short of food. At day's end they had gone nearly sixteen kilometers. Everyone's clothing was soaked by the river water, rain, and sweat. And when they put them on the next morning they were still wet.

The morning of March 15 began well. As usual, Kermit took the lead in a canoe that was the smallest and least seaworthy. With him were his dog, Tigueiro, and two black Brazilians, Joao, the helmsman, and Simplicio, the bowsman. While Kermit went ashore on an island to see what might be the best course to proceed, the Brazilians were to take the boat to the opposite bank. Before they'd gone a dozen yards, they found themselves caught in a whirlpool and pushed into rapids. Swept over them, but with the boat still upright and afloat, the two men fought to get it to land. They'd almost done so when another whirlpool dragged the boat to midstream where the dugout filled and turned over. Joao managed to swim ashore, but Simplicio was swept away, never to be seen again. Stranded on the island, with the 405 Winchester rifle that he'd carried through Africa and on hunts on the West, Kermit succeeded in reaching the overturned dugout, only to be swept off the rolling boat and whirled away. Losing his grip on the rifle, he barely kept his head above water. Weighted by his jacket, he tore it off. Gasping for breath, he fought the current and made it to shore. Safe on land, and seeing that his dog was also dripping wet, he realized that Triguiero had plunged into the river in an effort to save him.

The spot where Simplicio was lost was marked with a wooden post with an inscription in Portugese: "In these rapids died poor Simplicio." Because the man was unmarried, the money that he would have been paid at the end of the expedition was sent by Roosevelt to his mother. In recounting the tragedy in an article for *Scribner's* Roosevelt wrote, "On an expedition such as ours death is one of the accidents that may at any time occur, and narrow escapes from death are too common to be felt as they would be felt elsewhere. One mourns sincerely, but the mourning cannot interfere with the labor. We immediately proceeded with the work of the portage."

The next day brought two more calamities. The first involved a dog named Lobo that belonged to Rondon. While the colonel was supervising the portage of one of the new canoes, the dog wandered into the forest. When Rondom heard it yelping with pain, he rushed in the direction of the sound and found Lobo dead, shot with two arrows by Indians who'd fled. But this tragedy was eclipsed by a disaster with one of the new dugout canoes. Large and heavy, it had been made of wood that would not float. When its weight snapped a mooring rope, it sank in the rapids, taking with it the rope and a set of pulleys.

This "very bad thing," as Roosevelt called the loss, meant that it would be physically impossible to hoist the big canoes up even small hills. Worried about running out of supplies, he decided it was not wise to spend four days building a replacement canoe, especially since the murder of Lobo indicated the presence of possibly hostile Indians in the neighborhood. He also realized that the four remaining canoes could not carry all the loads and all the men, even if the loads were cut by leaving material behind.

The site of this disaster was named Broken Rope Rapids.

But the reality of the situation was truly grim. In eighteen days they had used more than a third of their food. They'd gone 125 kilometers, with the probability that they faced five or seven times that distance to go. Two weeks had been spent descending no more than seventy yards of rapids. Four canoes had been lost. And one man was dead. In a country of wild Indians who shot well with their bows and arrows, Roosevelt reasoned, it "behooved us to go warily, but also to make all speed possible, if we were to avoid serious trouble."

23

★ ★ ★

A River of Real Importance

THE IMMEDIATE RESULT of the loss of the rope and block and tackle was a convening of a late-night discussion of what George Cherrie called "ways and means" of continuing. It ended with agreement that only vitally needed baggage and supplies would be floated on four canoes lashed together to form a balsa (raft), each with three paddlers. Roosevelt and Doctor Cajazeira would travel on the raft. The others (thirteen) would walk along the shore.

The expedition's position, wrote Cherrie that night in his journal, "is really a very serious one." Provisions were decreasing daily. It was not possible to go back. "The journey ahead is undoubtedly *a very long one*," he continued. "The difficulties to overcome can only be judged by what we have passed through!"

Almost sixteen years earlier on a steamy July day in 1898, Colonel Theodore Roosevelt had led his Rough Riders and other Americans in a race to the summit of Kettle Hill in the San Juan Heights of Spanish Cuba. With the wolf rising in his heart, he'd known his "crowded hour." On March 17, 1914, about three hours after sunrise on the River of Doubt, he found himself on an overloaded raft as a trio of straining paddlers struggled to maneuver it around a raging and roaring stretch of water. Unwieldy and clumsy, the lashed-together canoes were hard to handle. As they came to a sharp bend they were caught by the swift current. With no alternative but to run a string of crashing, boulder-strewn rapids, Roosevelt and the doctor helped the laboring camaradas by paddling hard. The raft went "scraping and bumping" through one rapid after another in a frenzied attempt to guide the careening canoes toward the nearest riverbank.

Watching with horror in a single file from the shore were Kermit, Colonel Rondon, Cherrie, and Lyra, with nine camaradas, Unable to help, they saw their leader's raft swept along and slammed into a boulder. How it survived the crash no one could explain, but it did, and after a few minutes Roosevelt was on land, safe but soaked. Roosevelt would write of his brush with death that he'd been "within an ace of coming to grief," that they had "got through by the skin of our teeth," and "It was a narrow escape from grave disaster."

With all the loads taken out, and the empty canoes run through less dangerous channels between a cluster of islands, the party made camp by a small river with a low waterfall and many fish that were "delicious eating." Because the stream was a discovery, Rondon gave it a name that thrilled Roosevelt and surprised his son: Rio Kermit. Convinced that this newly named waterway was evidence that the Duvida had no connection with any other river, Rondon said, "There was no longer any question that the Duvida was a big river, a river of importance."

Before camp was broken the next day (March 18), Rondon had a bugler summon everyone around him to hear him declare that henceforth the River of Doubt would be known as "Rio Roosevelt." That said, he called for three cheers for President Roosevelt, three cheers for the United States of America, and three cheers for Kermit. Roosevelt responded by waving his hat and leading a chorus of "hip, hip, hurrah" for Rondon, Brazil, the Brazilian Telegraph Commission, Doctor Cajazeira, Lieutenant Lyra, and the camaradas. When Lyra pointed out that the cheers had omitted Cherrie, the naturalist promptly received his due.

Although Roosevelt wrote that naming the river after him "was a complete surprise," he had known all along that if the Duvida turned out to be, indeed, an unknown river, it would be named the Roosevelt. Yet in his story of the re-naming, he said he believed "River of Doubt" was "an unusually good name; and it is always well to keep the name of this character." But, he wrote, because his "kind friends insisted otherwise," it would have been "churlish" of him to "object longer."

That a river or stream would be named for Kermit had also been decided long before the expedition began was evidenced by Rondon producing a plaque bearing the name "Rio Kermit" to be nailed to a marker post.

When the expedition resumed, the explorers found signs that they were not the only people in the region. Indian villages were seen along the river, but no inhabitants. Assuming that they'd retreated to the forest, Rondon left peace offerings of an axe, knife, and glass beads. The gesture was fine with Roosevelt, but worried about the presence of Indians that might be hostile, and concerned about the state of supplies, he insisted that the expedition proceed as quickly as possible. His anxiety over Indians was soon reinforced by the finding of footprints and a few more abandoned settlements. He also heard voices of unseen people coming from the jungle.

While these concerns were genuine, it's arguable that Roosevelt was increasingly eager to go home. Having seen his beloved Kermit come close to being killed, he lived in dread that he might have to tell the mother of his children that her second son had died on an expedition that Kermit had never wanted to join, and had postponed his marriage to do so in order to keep his promise to his mother to watch over Father. Now, with lurking Indians on his mind, he confided to his journal, "I cannot accept the prospect of having my son's life threatened constantly by the presence of Indians, more than the life of any other member of the expedition, whenever his canoe goes out in front."

With the existence of the Rio de Duvida as an important river confirmed, he now saw no reason why the expedition should not move rapidly along, noting only the most significant of its features and leaving further exploration to others.

Kermit was also impatient. Frustrated by the pace on March 22, he wrote in his diary, "Off with a good many delays." At his father's insistence he was no longer the spearhead of the flotilla of canoes as it moved ahead. But if he shared his father's worries about hostiles in the forest, he did not show those concerns. When he had time on his hands, he ventured away on a hunt, with his faithful dog Trigueiro his only company. Whatever game he shot was certainly welcome, and needed. With half the expedition's provisions gone, either consumed or lost, Cherrie reckoned that they had rations for no more than twenty-five days.

The frustration Roosevelt felt about the slow progress was expressed in a diary note on March 24. They had come "only a trifle over 160 kilometers," and "thanks to the character and number of rapids," they had "three or four times the distance yet to go before coming to a part of the river where we might hope to meet assistance." The ordeal was also taking a toll on the camaradas. Kermit recorded, "Hard work; men disanimated."

On March 25 Cherrie noted, "There is a feeling of great depression in our camp tonight." But the following day, he cast aside his gloom and exulted in a startling archaeological find. On huge granite and quartzite rocks he discovered a series of carved concentric rings and three sets of what seemed to be the letter M, or perhaps inverted Ws. They were so unquestionably of ancient origin that Roosevelt mused about a moment "in a very remote past some Indian tribes of comparatively advanced culture had penetrated to this lovely river, just as we had now come to it." An even more rewarding discovery that day on the forest floor was a harvest of Brazil nuts that provided a welcome supplement to a dinner of cooked palm tops and two piranha that had been caught by one of the boatmen. Dessert was two tablespoons of honey for each man. "So we all had a feast," Roosevelt recorded, "and everybody had enough to eat and was happy."

After naming the stop "Camp of Indian Inscriptions," the expedition set out on March 27, 1914, and came to another rapids at a cost of two more destroyed boats. When paddlers became trapped in the debris, Roosevelt, Kermit, Cherrie, and others plunged into the treacherous current to rescue them. Up to his armpits and barely able to maintain his footing, Roosevelt slipped and stumbled against a boulder, re-injuring the knee that had been badly hurt in the 1902 carriage accident. While Dr. Cajazeira swabbed the gashed right knee with antiseptic and bandaged it, Roosevelt blamed the injury on clumsiness. Limping to his boat to resume the day's journey, he described the wound as "somewhat bothersome." Just ten minutes later, the expedition was forced to stop by another daunting rapids.

Plagued by torrential rains and swarming insects, and confronted with "all the unpleasant possibilities ahead," a decision was made to "cut to the bone" and throw away everything but the barest necessities. Two tents were kept, one for Roosevelt and a larger one for everyone else. In addition to the wet clothes on his back Roosevelt had a pair of pajamas, a spare pair of underwear, wash kit, a pocket medicine case, some adhesive plaster, needles and thread, his purse containing a letter of credit to be used at the end of the journey, and an extra set of eyeglasses. He also carried a cartridge bag, head net, and gauntlets.

Lightened to the limit, the expedition spent the final days of March getting to the foot of rapids in a gorge with walls too steep to be traversed, forcing the party to climb a rock-strewn, forest-clad mountain. Roosevelt's reward for making the ascent on his aching injured leg was "a beautiful view of the country ahead." Through an opening in the trees at the edge of a cliff he gazed at ranges of low mountains about the height of the lower ridges of the Alleghenies. "It was well worth seeing; but, beautiful although the country ahead of us was," he noted. "its character was such as to promise further hardships, difficulty, and exhausting labor, and especially further delay; and delay was a serious matter to men whose food supply was beginning to run short, whose equipment was reduced to the minimum, who for a month, with the utmost toil, had made very slow progress, and who had no idea of either the distance or the difficulties of the route in front of them."

As formidable as the challenge was, one of the main purposes of the expedition was not abandoned. Between navigating dangerous rapids and dealing with unexpected problems, the work of collecting specimens continued. Roosevelt noted with satisfaction that George Cherrie's "unwearied efforts" as the expedition's professional naturalist were rewarded from time to time by a species new to the collection. Roosevelt also found Cherrie to be a good man to talk to at the end of an arduous day. They chatted about their views of life, of a man's duty to his wife and children, responsibilities to humankind in general, duty to one's country in peace and war, and, of course, natural science.

Camped at the foot of the gorge on the last day of March, Roosevelt went to his tent in a thunderstorm and found his cot and bedding soaked. He had to sleep rolled up in a blanket. Except for the injured knee, he slept "comfortably enough" and awoke ready for whatever came next. Two mornings later, thinking he'd put his clothing out of reach of insects, he discovered that both termites and carregadores had chewed holes in a boot, the leg of one of his underpants, and a handkerchief. He noted, "I now had nothing to replace anything that was destroyed."

On the move on April 2, the expedition had spent "exactly a month going through an uninterrupted succession of rapids." In that time they had come only about 100 kilometers, and had descended nearly 150 kilometers from their point of departure. Four original canoes had been lost, along with the dugout built in the forest. A man was dead. And so was Rondon's little dog. "Most of the camaradas were downhearted, naturally enough," Roosevelt wrote, "and occasionally asked one of us if we really believed that we should ever get out alive; and we had to cheer them up as best we could."

Adopting the tone of a teacher as he wrote about the adventure so far, and assuming that someone would eventually read about it, he explained:

> Such an exploring expedition as that in which we were engaged of necessity involves hard and dangerous labor, and perils of many kinds. To follow downstream an unknown river, broken by innumerable cataracts and rapids, rushing through mountains of which the existence has never been even guessed, bears no resemblance whatever to following even a fairly dangerous river which has been thoroughly explored and has become in some sort a highway, so that experienced pilots can be secured as guides, while the portages have been pioneered and trails chopped out, and every dangerous feature of the rapids is known beforehand. In this case no one could foretell that the river would cleave its way through steep mountain chains, cutting narrow clefts in which the cliff walls rose sheer on either hand. When a rushing river thus "canyons," as we used to say out West, and the mountains are very steep, it becomes almost impossible to bring the canoes down the river itself and utterly impossible to portage them along the cliff sides, while even to bring the loads over the mountain is a task of extraordinary labor and difficulty. Moreover, no one can tell how many times the task will have to be repeated; or when it will end; or whether the food will hold out; every hour of work in the rapids is fraught with the possibility of the gravest disaster, and yet it is imperatively necessary to attempt it; and all this is done in an uninhabited wilderness, or else a wilderness tenanted only by unfriendly savages, where failure to get through means death by disease and starvation.

Such wilderness exploration, said the hero of the San Juan Heights, was as "dangerous as warfare" and the "conquest of nature demands the utmost vigor, hardihood, and daring, and takes from the conquerors a heavy toll of life and health."

Roosevelt found no more telling evidence of this reality than his wounded right leg. If it had been injured on an adventure in the pine woods of Maine or somewhere on the prairies of the West, rather than in the relentless humidity of the Brazilian jungle, healing would have been expected to be constant and complete. But each day as Dr. Cajazeira examined it and

changed the dressing he found little improvement. George Cherrie observed
Roosevelt and concluded that he was a very sick man.

Recovery had been complicated two days after Roosevelt's collision with
the boulder. On March 28 an attack of malaria resulted in his temperature
rising to 105 degrees. For Kermit it was a "particularly black night." His
account of those hours revealed why:

> The fever was high and father was out of his head. Doctor Cajazeira,
> who was one of the three Brazilians with us, divided with me the watch
> during the night. The scene is vivid before me. The black rushing river
> with the great trees towering high above the bank; the sodden earth
> under foot; for a few moments the stars would be shining, and then the
> sky would cloud over and rain would fall in torrents, shutting out the sky
> and trees and river.
>
> Father first began with poetry; over and over again he repeated "In
> Xanadu did Kubla Khan a stately pleasure dome decree," then he started
> talking at random, but gradually he centred down to the question of sup-
> plies, which was, of course, occupying every one's mind. Part of the time
> he knew that I was there, and he would then ask me if I thought Cherrie
> had had enough to eat to keep going. Then he would forget my presence
> and keep saying to himself: "I can't work now, so I don't need much food,
> but he and Cherrie have worked all day with the canoes, they must have
> part of mine."

At one point a few hours later, with Kermit and Cherrie standing by his
cot, Roosevelt said, "Boys, I realize that some of us are not going to finish
this journey."

He looked intently at Cherrie.

"I want you and Kermit to go on," he continued. "You can get out. I will
stop here."

Cherrie had no doubt that Roosevelt was contemplating suicide. From
that moment on both he and Kermit kept an eye on him to prevent him, in
Cherrie's words, "from carrying out what he felt was necessary," that he
must "relieve the party of what he considered a burden."

Years earlier in contemplating the heroic deeds of Rough Riders and
other soldiers in the jungles of Cuba on a mission to kick out Spain, Colonel
Theodore Roosevelt had witnessed a kind of bravery that he defined in his
autobiography, published just before he'd launched his quest to be a boy

again. He called it "three o'clock in the morning courage." It was, he said, "the most desirable kind." In an essay for *The Outlook* magazine in 1895 he'd written about the man "who is not frightened by the sweat and the blood, and the blows of friends and foes; who haunts not the fringy edges of the fight, but the pell-mell of men."

Certainly, no man had measured up to that Rooseveltian standard better than Kermit.

Like all the four sons of Theodore Roosevelt, he shared a love of the outdoors and physical activity. But the fair-haired boy (the only son with blond hair), he was also the most sensitive of the children for whom the best companionship was found in his imagination. His mother looked into Kermit's "big, dark eyes, full of poetry" and described him as "a good deal of a hermit" who "never need to retire to a cloister for a life of abstraction." Yet Kermit became a fierce defender of his controversial father as a young boy (he'd beaten up a boy who'd criticized Roosevelt), the valued companion in Africa and now the Amazon jungles of Brazil. To his older and younger siblings he was "the lucky one" who got to go along on Father's most exciting adventures.

Again and again, when it was touch and go whether the expedition could get around a rapids, Kermit's valor had often made the difference. He'd spent days stripped to the waist in water. His clothes were never dry. Bruises on his bare feet and scores of insect bites had become festering sores. What little he had for food he'd readily shared with camaradas, who emulated the gun bearers of Africa by adoring him. Frequently, it had been Kermit's Winchester rifle that provided meat for meals. And, Roosevelt could never forget, his second son had delayed his marriage to come along on a trip in the unknown to "look after Father."

That Kermit Roosevelt would now leave his father to die was, of course, as impossible as getting Theodore Roosevelt's permission to be carried. Rejecting the suggestion, he was on his feet as the battered and dispirited expedition dragged the five surviving canoes past yet another waterfall to find a new obstacle in the form of another portage that would require at least two more days of risking lives and canoes. At one point Kermit worried that the strain on Roosevelt was so great that his heart might give out.

"Men very disheartened," Kermit noted in his journal. "Hard work. Wet all day; half ration." The only smoker among the explorers then recorded the sad fact that he'd smoked his last pipeful of "Injus Bill" tobacco. But he had the consolation of a bottle of Scotch whiskey, the last of three. Watching

Kermit and Cherrie sipping the precious remainder, Roosevelt smiled and said, "I am sorry I can't enjoy that, but I wouldn't if I could. It would take too much away from your pleasure."

By April 1 Kermit and Lieutenant Lyra succeeded in hauling the expedition's five canoes around the last of the impeding falls. They had worked for four days to do so. Ahead of them lay other challenges, among them a chasm filled with rapids and falls. Forced to camp on April 2, they'd gone less than two miles. As the encampment was being organized, Kermit went hunting. He returned with a small turtle and a strange-looking fruit that was new to the naturalists. The turtle was boiled into a soup for breakfast.

But it wasn't the turtle soup and the sweet fruit that made the day remarkable for the discouraged, bedraggled, weary, and hungry men of the expedition. "Under such conditions," Roosevelt wrote, "whatever is evil in men's natures comes to the front."

The "strange and terrible tragedy" on this day was a homicide.

★ ★ ★

Murder in the Jungle

ONE OF THE CAMARADAS was "a man of pure European blood." Named Julio, he was "a very powerful fellow and had been importunately eager to join the expedition." Because he came with the reputation of being a good worker, Roosevelt had gladly enlisted him. But before long, Roosevelt recognized that Julio, "like so many men of higher standing," had no idea what such a venture really meant. Under the strain of toil, hardship, and danger his true nature emerged in which Roosevelt discerned "depths of selfishness, cowardice, and ferocity." He shirked all work and shammed sickness. Nothing could make him do his share, yet he was constantly begging for favors, so that after out of the goodness of his heart Kermit shared his rapidly dwindling supply of tobacco with him, Julio expected to receive more. Julio "threw all his tasks on his comrades," Roosevelt wrote, and, moreover, "he stole their food as well as ours." To Roosevelt this was "next to murder as a crime and should by rights be punished as such."

A dramatic contrast to Julio was a large black man named Paixao. A corporal and acting sergeant in the engineer corps of the Brazilian army, he had worked so hard that when his only pair of pants had become torn to tatters, Roosevelt gave him his spare trousers. One of the most admirable traits that the former commander of the Rough Riders found in Paixao was that he was a figure with military bearing. Also a stern disciplinarian, he was a man of action who stood ready to deal with miscreants by doling out appropriate punishment. Consequently, one evening when he caught Julio stealing food, he punched Julio in the mouth.

"Julio came crying to us, his face working with fear and malignant hatred," Roosevelt noted, "but after investigation he was told that he had gotten off uncommonly lightly." He spoke as a former deputy sheriff in the Dakota Badlands, veteran of two years as head of the New York Police Department, and an ex-president who frequently had to sit in judgment of men who had been convicted of federal crimes and appealed to him for executive clemency. One of them was a former member of the Rough Riders who had committed armed robbery. Roosevelt pardoned him and later appointed him to a high official position in which he rendered such good service that Roosevelt lauded him in his autobiography as a man whom, "as a soldier, as civil officer, as citizen, and as a friend, I valued and respected."

In the autobiography, published as the Brazilian expedition was being planned, Roosevelt wrote on the general subject of crime and punishment:

> Now I suppose some good people will gather from this that I favor men who committed crimes. I certainly do not favor them. I have not a particle of sympathy with the sentimentality—as I deem it, the mawkishness—which overflows with foolish pity for the criminal who cares not at all for the victim of the criminal. I am glad to see wrong-doers punished, The punishment is an absolute necessity from the standpoint of society; and I put the reformation of the criminal second to the welfare of society. But I do desire to see the man or woman who has paid the penalty and who wishes to reform given a helping hand—surely every one of us who knows his own heart must know that he too may stumble, and should be anxious to help his brother or sister who has stumbled. When the criminal has been punished, if he then shows a sincere desire to lead a decent and upright life, he should be given the chance, he should be helped and not hindered; and if he makes good, he should receive that respect from others which so often aids in creating self-respect—the most valuable of all possessions.

Hoping that Julio had learned a lesson from Paixao's punch in the mouth and that Julio would reform his ways, Roosevelt prepared himself for the next portage. But another member of the expedition, named Pedrinho, caught Julio pilfering some of the men's dried meat. Pedrinho reported this to Paixao. Because everyone was busy loading canoes, Paixao let the incident pass. But a while later, he upbraided Julio for lagging behind and slacking in his work. Paixao had just put down a load of cargo. As he departed to get another, he left his rifle on the ground.

Nearby, Roosevelt, Rondon, and Lyra were seated, waiting for the work to be completed. Engaged in conversation, no one paid any attention to Julio as he marched into camp, muttering to himself as usual, put down his load, picked up Paixao's carbine, and strode back to the trail.

A short time later, a shot rang out.

Rushing into camp from the trail, several of the men exclaimed in unison that Paixao was dead and that Julio had shot him and fled into the woods.

Roosevelt ordered a messenger to find Kermit and Cherrie and tell them to stay where they were and guard the canoes and provisions. Roosevelt, limping on his bad leg and with his revolver belted to a hip, and Dr. Cajazeira—"an absolutely cool and plucky man"—hurried as fast as possible to the scene of the crime. They found Paixao on the ground "in a huddle, in a pool of his own blood, where he had fallen, shot through the heart."

Roosevelt feared that Julio had run amuck and intended to take more lives, and that his next victim would probably be Pedrinho. With this dreadful scenario in mind, and worried that Julio might have returned to the camp to lay an ambush for Pedrinho, Roosevelt and the doctor returned to the camp and found no one there. Presently, the camaradas strode into the camp to report "the welcome news" that they'd found the carbine.

Relieved that abandonment of the rifle meant there would be no more killings, Roosevelt demonstrated a talent for deductive reasoning in a criminal investigation that readers of fiction had been relishing in American editions of short-stories and novels by Sir Arthur Conan Doyle concerning "the world's first private consulting detective," Mr. Sherlock Holmes of 221-B Baker Street, London, and his cohort in crime-solving, Dr. John H. Watson. A comparison of Theodore Roosevelt as sleuth in a Brazilian jungle to Sherlock Holmes is even more delicious because his investigative companion was also a physician.

Examining the clues, Roosevelt deduced:

> The murderer had stood to one side of the path and killed his victim, when a dozen paces off, with deliberate and malignant purpose. Then evidently his murderous hatred had at once given way to his innate cowardice; and, perhaps hearing some one coming along the path, he fled in

terror into the wilderness. A tree had knocked the carbine from his hand. His footsteps showed that after some rods he had started to return, doubtless for the carbine, but had fled again, probably because the body had then been discovered. It was questionable whether or not he would live to reach the Indian villages, which were probably his goal. He was not a man to feel remorse—never a common feeling; but surely that murderer was in a living hell, as, with fever and famine leering at him from the shadows, he made his way through the empty desolation of the wilderness.

As Roosevelt investigated and deduced, the expedition's cook quoted the melancholy proverbial philosophy of a native proverb: "No man knows the heart of any one." Then he said with deep conviction a ghostly belief that sent a shiver down Roosevelt's back of the kind that Edgar Allen Poe hoped to cause in readers of *Tales of Mystery and Imagination*, even if they read the stories in a Brazilian jungle. "Paixao is following Julio now, and will follow him until he dies," the cook declared grimly, pointing to the dead body. "Paixao fell forward on his hands and knees, and when a murdered man falls like that his ghost will follow the slayer as long as the slayer lives."

Roosevelt chose not to hunt for Julio. If he were captured, he would have to be guarded day and night on an expedition where there were always loaded firearms about. As a prisoner he might grab a weapon and kill someone else. He couldn't be shackled in a canoe that might overturn, dooming him to drowning. Nor could he climb cliffs with bound hands and feet. And standing watch over him would be an additional and severe burden on men already stretched to the limit. But neither could Julio be put to death legally, although he was a soldier who in cold blood had murdered another soldier. No one knew how many weeks of journeying remained. The food was running low. Sickness was appearing among the men. The first duty was to save them. Whether the murderer lived or died in the wilderness was of "no moment," compared to doing everything possible to secure the safety of the rest of the party.

Paixao was buried where he fell. This was in accord with Roosevelt's life-long belief that "where a tree falls there let it lay." The shallow grave was dug by the same men who had used their axes and skills to turn trees into dugout canoes. Reverently and carefully, the body "which but half an hour before had been so full of vigorous life" was in the ground beneath a mound with a rude wooden cross over him. A volley was fired in tribute to a brave and loyal soldier who had died performing the greatest and finest accomplishment in Theodore Roosevelt's lexicon: duty.

"Then we left him forever," he wrote, "under the great trees beside a lonely river."

Not knowing if Julio were alive, and if so, where he might be lurking to heave rocks down on the expedition, or to steal a canoe in the dead of night, the expedition remained on high alert for two days. On the morning of the third day, as the flotilla of four canoes floated down the river, Julio appeared on a bank from a thicket of trees. Waving arms and shouting, he begged to surrender and be taken aboard. Roosevelt gazed at him and saw "an arrant craven at heart, a strange mixture of ferocity and cowardice." The canoes passed by. At the first halt, Rondon explained that he hadn't picked up Julio because Rondon wished to consult with Roosevelt "as the chief of the expedition." Roosevelt gave his reasons against rescuing Julio, but because Rondon was the superior officer of both murderer and victim, he would not object to whatever Rondon chose to do out of his duty as an officer and according to the laws of Brazil.

At the next camp Rondon sent two expert woodsmen to look for Julio.

In perhaps the coldest line in Roosevelt's account of the trip down the River of Doubt, and possibly with righteous satisfaction, Roosevelt wrote, "They failed to find him."

Under way again, the expedition at first found no good place to camp, but eventually came to a place at the foot of a steep cliff that provided a narrow, boulder-covered slope where it was possible to sling hammocks and a "slanting spot" for Roosevelt's cot. Battered and sagging, the bed looked to Roosevelt like a broken-backed centipede. The next day, Kermit and Cherrie found a new location that was not much better. Despite Kermit suffering an attack of fever, and Cherrie and Lyra plagued by dysentery, the camp was arranged. Roosevelt's "bothersome" leg was tended by the doctor. The wound was inflamed. That night Roosevelt's temperature shot up. But because Roosevelt's teeth were chattering so much, the doctor had to measure it by placing the thermometer in an armpit. It registered 100.4 degrees. Cajazeira covered him with a blanket and insisted that he down half a gram of quinine salts in a cup of water.

When the expedition left a camp that the doctor termed a "disagreeable bivouac," the camaradas had to carry Roosevelt to his canoe and place him on a bed of crates. Readers of *Scribner's Magazine* would eventually be told,

"It is not ideal for a sick man to spend the hottest hours of the day stretched on the boxes in the bottom of a small open dugout, under the well-neigh intolerable heat of the torrid sun of the mid-tropics, varied by blinding, drenching downpours of rain."

He longed for "a big Maine birch-bark," such as that in which he once went down the Mattamakeag at high water. It would have slipped down the rapids "as a girl trips through a country dance."

On Palm Sunday (April 5, 1914) Roosevelt's fever was down and Kermit was feeling well enough to go with Rondon and Lyra to reconnoiter the river ahead. They came back to make the heartening announcement that "after these rapids we're out of the hills." Cherrie's diary notation that evening saw brighter prospects. "The mountains, that have so long hemmed us in," he wrote, "seem to be falling away from the river. The river seems to be broadening."

Five days later, Kermit had a recurrence of fever. It reached 104 degrees, requiring the doctor to inject him with quinine every six hours. Although Kermit declared himself "feeling better" in the morning, he had head and back aches and was too weak to work. He crawled into a canoe and covered himself with a tarpaulin. Ordinarily his dog would have settled next to him, but that morning Trigueiro evidently had other things on his mind. As the boats floated away, no one noticed the dog was not with them. When they did, there was no going back to look for him.

On Saturday, April 11, Kermit's continuing distress over the fate of the pet that plunged into a raging river in an attempt to help its master avoid drowning galvanized Roosevelt into action. As head of the expedition, he insisted that Rondon send out a party of camaradas to look for Trigueiro. This meant delaying the start of the next part of the journey, with very little likelihood that the dog would be found, or that he was alive. The expedition waited all day, but just as the sun was setting the searchers returned, preceded by Trigueiro, who greeted Kermit in dog fashion by licking his beaming face.

The reunion took place at the expedition's twenty-eighth camp. For the first time there were no roaring rapids. But even more exciting to the men of the expedition than the return of Kermit's dog was a report by one of the men who'd gone off fishing that he'd found that a vine had been cut by an axe or knife at a place reachable only by canoe. And a post at the spot had been carved with the initials A.J. Because the local Indians did not have boats, this discovery meant that the vine must have been cut by someone who had come up the river, and that the voyager was most likely looking for rubber trees to tap.

Venturing ahead with great excitement on April 12 (Easter), the expedition came to a newly built house in a planted clearing. No one was at home, except for a couple of watchdogs. Contents of the house suggested that it was occupied by a man, woman, and child, and that they had only just left. An hour farther downstream stood a house belonging to an elderly black man. He welcomed these surprising men who had come *down* the river with "the innate courtesy of the Brazlian peasantry" that Roosevelt had hoped Americans would emulate.

In mid-afternoon the voyagers stopped at a "picturesque" house of palm thatch, but its occupants appeared to have hastily evacuated in fear of an Indian raid. When they came back and discovered that white men were their guests, they were hospitable and communicative. They invited them to spend the night.

During forty-eight days, covering 300 kilometers of "absolutely unknown ground," Roosevelt and the others had seen no other human being. Six weeks had been spent slogging their way through a seemingly interminable series of rapids on a river about the size of the Rhine or Elbe, of which no geographer had any idea of its existence.

With deserved pride, Roosevelt wrote, they were putting on the map a river that appeared on no map published in Europe, or the United States, or that any map of Brazil recognized.

"I esteemed it a great piece of good fortune to be able to take part in such a feat," he said while acknowledging that it was an achievement that represented "the capping of a pyramid" which during the previous seven years had been guilt by Colonel Rondon and the Brazilian Telegraphic Commission.

The expedition had passed the period of peril and possible disaster.

There might still be risks ahead to individuals, and some difficulties and annoyances for everyone, but there was no longer the least likelihood of calamity for the expedition as a whole.

Its triumphant leader wrote, "The wearing work, under very unhealthy conditions, was beginning to tell on everyone. Half the camaradas had been down with fever and were much weakened; only a few of them retrained their original physical and moral strength. Cherrie and Kermit had recovered; but both Kermit and Lyra still had bad sores on their legs, from the bruises received in the water work. I was in worse shape."

The aftereffects of the fever still hung on. The leg which had been hurt while working in the rapids with the sunken canoe had developed an abscess that "the good doctor" had cut open to insert a drainage tube. He credited Cajazeira for "unwearied care and kindness" and praised Kermit, Cherrie, Rondon, and Lyra for taking care of him without mentioning (perhaps because he didn't remember, or chose not to recall) the night when the doctor's patient pleaded to be left behind in order not to jeopardize the welfare of the others. He chose instead to assert that it was such a man's "duty to go forward, if necessary on all fours, until he drops."

He minimized his perilous situation, and his heroism, by telling his readers, "Fortunately, I was put to no such test. When my serious trouble came we had only canoe-riding ahead of us."

Now the north was "calling strongly to the three men of the north—Rocky Dell Farm to Cherrie, Sagamore Hill to me; and to Kermit the call was stronger still," because of a wedding.

"In our home country spring had now come," he wrote movingly and with Rooseveltian romanticism, "the wonderful northern spring of long glorious days, of brooding twilights, of cool delightful nights. Robin and bluebird, meadow-lark and song sparrow, were singing in the mornings at home; the maple-buds were red; windflowers and bloodroot were blooming while the last patches of snow still lingered; the rapture of the hermit-thrush in Vermont, the serene golden melody of the wood-thrush on Long Island, would be heard before we were there to listen. Each man to his home, and to his true love! Each was longing for the homely things that were so dear to him, for the home people who were dearer still, and for the one who was dearest of all." His beloved Edith.

And the children he'd once again left behind, as so often during their growing up, save one, "the lucky one" named Kermit, in order to grab a last chance to be a boy again.

25

★ ★ ★

A Wedding in Spain

A MONTH BEFORE the men of the expedition discovered that the worst of their journey was behind them, the *New York Times* had published (on March 23) an alarming headline:

ROOSEVELT PARTY LOSES EVERYTHING
IN RAPIDS OF A BRAZILIAN RIVER;
MEMBERS OF PARTY PROBABLY SAFE;
MAY BE ON AN UNKNOWN RIVER

Five days later, Anthony Fiala was in the town of Santarem and able to send a cable to the newspaper: "The Roosevelt party is in good health, exploring the Duvida River." He added, "It is expected to reach Manaos early in April."

But on the very day when Fiala's confidence-instilling message was sent (March 28), Theodore Roosevelt was so despondent because of his crippling leg injury and malarial fever that he proposed to Kermit and Cherrie that for their sake and the expedition's they should "go out" and leave him to die in the jungle.

That he had come through that crisis and survived others during an arduous month of navigating a continually dangerous river had demanded of everyone a twenty-four-hour-a-day demonstration of "three o'clock in the morning courage," and the unflinching devotion of a son and an indomitable doctor. During the thirty days between Fiala's telegram to New York and the expedition's return to a semblance of civilization, there had been other crises. Rondon thought Roosevelt "never was himself again." Although the leg-wound had begun to heal, he suffered from an infection of cellulite tissue that was so painful he was often unable to sit. Cherrie noted that because he was unable to eat properly he'd lost one-fourth of his weight and become so thin that his clothes "hang like bags on him."

But now the end of the ordeal was near. With the help of a "first-class waterman, cool, fearless, and brawny as a bull," as a guide, the expedition passed that last of the dangerous rapids on April 26. The paddles were plied with hearty goodwill, with Cherrie and Kermit, as usual, working like the camaradas, as the canoes "went dancing down the broad, rapid river." At one o'clock in the afternoon the boats reached the mouth of the Castanho River and an army camp with flags of the United States and Brazil flying over it. Rifles fired a salute in welcome.

As the boats landed, the men of the expedition looked back on the two months they'd spent in canoes. From February 27 to April 26 they had traveled more than 750 kilometers on a river that could no longer be called "unknown." Now it was "Rio Roosevelt." (The name proved to be so cumbersome for the Portugese tongue that it was soon changed to "Rio Teodoro.")

Upon arriving at the "attractive camp," commanded by one of Rondon's lieutenants by the name of Pyrineus, Roosevelt learned that Anthony Fiala had gone home, but that Leo Miller was at Manaos, and that the camp was only four hours above the river hamlet of Sao Joao, a port of call for rubber steamers, from which he could travel to Manaos in two days. Roosevelt also rejoiced to learn that Captain Amilcar, the head of the party that went down the Gy-Parana River, was all right. After spending his last night under tent canvas Roosevelt boarded a steamer at Sao Joao for Manaos and a reunion with Leo Miller.

When the river steamer *Cidade de Mandaos* moored at half-past two in the morning of April 30, 1914, Roosevelt had to be taken ashore on a stretcher. Shortly after the boat docked, Kermit was handed a bundle of letters from his fiancee. Belle had sent them from London and Madrid, where, she informed him, she expected to marry him in June. Though very ill, Roosevelt cabled Edith, "Successful trip," without revealing how sick he was. He then marshaled enough strength to dictate a telegram to Lauro Muller. To the Brazilian official who more than any other had made the expedition possible he reported:

> We have had a hard and somewhat dangerous but very successful trip.
> No less than six weeks were spent slowly and with peril and exhausting
> labor forcing our way down through what seemed a literally endless suc-
> cession of rapids and cataracts. For forty-eight days we saw no human
> being. In passing these rapids we lost five of the seven canoes with which
> we started and had to build others. One of four best men lost his life in
> the rapids. Under the strain one of the men went completely bad, shirked
> all his work, stole his comrades' food and when punished by the sergeant
> he with cold-blooded determination murdered the sergeant and fled into
> the wilderness, Col. Rondon's dog, running ahead of him while hunting,
> was shot by two Indians; by his death he in all probability saved the life of
> his master. We have put on the map a river of about 1500 kilometers in
> length running from just south of the 13th degree to north of the 5th
> degree and the biggest affluent of the Madeira. Until now its upper
> course has been utterly unknown to everyone, and its lower course altho
> unknown for years to the rubber-men utterly unknown to all cartogra-
> phers. . . .
>
> My dear Sir, I thank you from my heart for the chance to take part in
> this great work of exploration.

When the last zoological specimen was noted for the record, the expedition's collection consisted of more than 2500 birds, nearly 500 mammals, and an assortment of reptiles and fish. Many of them were new to science.

Before Roosevelt could depart Manaos for the port city of Belen and then back to the United States he had to face the ordeal of an operation to treat his abscessed leg. With that done, and feeling better than he had in weeks, he was carried to the freighter *Dunstan* and placed in the captain's quarters at the skipper's insistence. On the fourth day he was able to get around with a cane. On May 5 he left the ship walking. Two days later, the Roosevelt expedition came to an end with a formal ceremony and a personal farewell to the camaradas. Kermit translated as his father told them, "You are all heroes." Each was given two gold sovereigns as mementoes.

Dr. Cajazeira lectured his patient about the importance of continuing to take his quinine.

When Roosevelt invited Colonel Rondon to visit Sagamore Hill some day, Rondon gave a reply that indicated he was not unfamiliar with the politics of Theodore Roosevelt's country. "I shall be there," he said, "when you are once again elected president of the United States."

When Colonel Roosevelt of the Rough Riders returned from his crowded hour in Cuba, he'd bounded down the gangplank of the ocean steamer *Miami* at Montauk, Long Island, on August 15, 1898, exclaiming, "I feel as big and as strong as a bull moose." He'd made the same boast on his return from Africa. On May 19, 1914, family, friends, and other welcomers, as well as newspaper reporters, saw a far different figure. Clothing sagged on an almost gaunt frame. His sunburned face showed fatigue. He favored his right leg, but when Ted offered an arm to lean on, it was brushed away as Roosevelt snapped, "I can take care of myself."

Asked if he planned to run for president in 1916, he said that the only plans he had were to go to Washington to address the National Geographic Society and answer any question on geography "from any reputable man," and to travel to Spain for the wedding of his second son.

In his talk to the nation's leading geographers, many of whom had expressed concerns about the truth of his claim to have explored an unknown river, he used the analogy of having put the cap on a pyramid that had been built by Colonel Rondon and the Brazilian Telegraph Commission. Charting the Duvida in chalk on a blackboard, he gave a detailed description of the expedition and its work that together dispelled the geographer's doubts. When reports of their embrace of Roosevelt's claims reached London, they were quickly followed by an invitation to present his findings to the Royal Geographical Society.

But first there was a wedding to attend in Spain.

Because Edith didn't feel up to an ocean crossing so soon after the death of her sister, and still emotionally drained by the ordeal of months of not knowing if she would ever see her husband and son again, Roosevelt was accompanied by Alice (now the wife of Congressman Nicholas Longworth). The nuptials of Kermit Roosevelt and Bella Willard were a civil ceremony on June 11. That night Roosevelt happily wrote to Edith, "I never saw two people more in love with each other."

On the evening of June 16, 1914, the man who had once told the English to do their duty to Egypt or leave that country spoke to English scientists about the River of Doubt. His audience were members of the same venerated society of geographers that in 1872 had at first rejected the claim by American journalist Henry Morton Stanley that he had found the "missing" explorer and missionary Dr. David Livingstone alive in an African village. When he entered the hall, he was given the kind of reception he would have received had he walked into a convention of the Progressive Party, prepared to announce his candidacy for president in 1916. Part of his warm welcome may also have been acknowledgment that he was the former president of the United States and Nobel laureate. Certainly the sustained ovation recognized the courage shown by a man of his age in venturing into unexplored Brazilian jungles. In introducing the guest of honor the president of the Royal Society recognized that "he must have overcome great difficulties."

Settled expectantly in the crowded, small hall, the geographers were taken into those jungles and onto the Duvida—400 miles by dugout canoe in relentless tropical heat, soaked by drenching rains and raging rapids, stung and bitten by voracious insects, bruised and battered in body and sometimes in spirit, with occasionally faltering courage, with no turning back and no idea where it all would end, whether dead or alive.

"It was," said one of the previous doubters to reporters after the Society adjourned, "a very good lecture."

Nagged by a recurrence of the jungle fever, Roosevelt sailed from England on June 18 on the German liner *Imperator.* Although tired and vexed by a hoarse throat, he genially accepted rounds of applause from his fellow passengers whenever he entered a dining room for a meal. One of the passengers was the world's most famous magician and escape artist, Harry Houdini.

What the passengers didn't know, and certainly Roosevelt didn't, was that Houdini had memorized a picture of a hand-drawn map by Roosevelt of the Duvida that had been obtained by a London newspaperman, and shown to Houdini. What he had in mind, in the certainty that at some point in the crossing the passengers would demand a performance of his famous mind-reading act, was inveigling Roosevelt to participate in the act by picturing in his own head the course of what was now the most famous river in the world. Unaware that a trick was being played on him and the audience, Roosevelt agreed to visualize the river's route. In a "trance," Houdini proceeded to draw the memorized map on a slate. Gazing at it in wide-eyed wonder,

Roosevelt exclaimed, "That was the most amazing thing I've ever seen."

In November 1914 the articles Roosevelt had written for *Scribner's* became a book, *Through the Brazilian Wilderness*. It was dedicated "with esteem, regard, and affection by their friend" to Lauro Muller, Colonel Rondon, Amilcar, Lyra, Dr. Cajazeira, and "our companions in scientific work and in the exploration of the wilderness."

"Throughout the body of the work," he said in the preface, "will be found reference after reference to my colleagues and companions of the expedition, whose services to science I have endeavored to set forth, and for whom I shall always feel cordial friendship and regard."

Roosevelt's book was followed in the spring of 1916 by Father Zahm's memoir of the expedition, titled *Through South America's Southland*. The valiant priest who had encouraged Roosevelt to make the trip informed him that he was thinking about another venture. This idea, an exploration of the Rio Negro into Venezuela, he said, "becomes more and more dominant from day to day."

Zahm was not alone in contemplating another adventure. In December 1914 Roosevelt inquired if Henry Fairfield Osborn and the American Museum of Natural History would be interested in sponsoring a six-month odyssey to the South Pacific. Offering to finance it by again writing a series of articles for *Scribner's*, Roosevelt wrote, "I believe I could make a trip that would be worth while, and that it would do credit to the Museum." His envisioned a journey to Polynesia in 1918. But world events scuttled the project. With European powers engaged in a war that Roosevelt expected to soon involve the United States, he turned his attention to what he might do to contribute to the defeat of Germany and her allies. With the wolf rising in his heart, he asked President Woodrow Wilson to allow him to raise a regiment, as he had done in 1898. Having promised American voters in 1912 that he would keep the country out of the war, Wilson greeted the idea of Teddy Roosevelt leading an army with horror.

Disappointed by the rejection, but not surprised by it, Roosevelt wrote to Kermit, "I had hoped that we might round out Africa and South America by a 'greater adventure' together."

A consolation that spring was the awarding to Theodore Roosevelt by the American Geographical Society of a new David Livingstone Gold Medal for exploration. In accepting it, he said it really belonged to Colonel Rondon. He was gratified that the same gold medal was given to Rondon, through the Brazilian ambassador to the United States, in August 1918.

By then, the United States was in "the Great War" to "save the world for democracy," and Roosevelt's sons, Kermit, Ted, Archibald, and Quentin, were in it. Kermit had gone to war even before American entry by serving with British forces in Mesopotamia, then switching to the U.S. Army to fight in France beside his brothers. Meanwhile, Ted had distinguished himself as the only Reserve officer to command a Regular unit in combat. Archie was so severely wounded that he was declared 100 percent disabled and sent home. The youngest, Quentin, had joined the fight as an Army Air Services pilot and been killed in action at the age of twenty.

Roosevelt wrote to an old Rough Rider comrade, "It is bitter that the young should die." But there were "things worse than death," continued the broken-hearted but proud father, "for nothing under Heaven would I have had my sons act otherwise than as they acted. They have done pretty well haven't they? Quentin killed, dying as a war hawk should . . . over the enemy's lines; Archie crippled, and given the French cross for gallantry; Ted gassed once . . . and cited for 'conspicuous gallantry'; Kermit with the British military cross; and now under Pershing."

As Americans welcomed Armistice Day, Roosevelt found himself in the hospital. He was there to be treated for anemia, vertigo (caused by an old ear infection), the leg troubles left over from his last chance to be a boy, and general signs of physical exhaustion. In the previous six weeks he had been on a whirlwind speaking tour. In Alliance, Nebraska, he had demanded a total American victory so that no nation would ever dare to "look cross-eyed at us."

Republicans attending a party rally held in Carnegie Hall on October 28 hoped that he would announce his candidacy for president in 1920. They were heartened by his attack on the conduct of the war by President Wilson. To his delight and relief Republicans swept to victory in congressional elections in what he considered a repudiation of Wilson's war policies, and therefore vindication of his own relentless criticism of it. To one of the doctors attending him in the hospital he said of Wilson, "I would like to be left alone in this room with our great and good president for about fifteen minutes, and then I would be cheerfully hung."

Informed that he would have to remain hospitalized for some time, he kept busy with correspondence, drafting magazine and newspaper articles, and greeting well-wishers who came to call. Informed by doctors that they could do no more for his condition, he was discharged. Offered a wheelchair, he shrugged off an assisting hand and snapped, "Don't do that. I am not sick, and it will give the wrong impression."

In a letter to Ted he said it would be "a couple of months before I am in any kind of shape." But it didn't matter, he added, because "this happens to be the very time when I do not care to speak or to take an active part in politics."

On the day of New Year's Eve came an envelope from France containing France's official commemoration in the form of a citation for Quentin's sacrifice for French freedom.

January 1, 1919, was passed sitting on a sofa in the old nursery of the Sagamore Hill house and looking out a south-facing window. On the third a rheumatic specialist came to look him over. The next day, Edith wrote Kermit that his father was "having a horrid painful time."

Roosevelt stated on the fifth that he felt a little better. That day he was visited by the British poet Alfred Noyes. He then dictated a letter to Kermit and spent eleven hours honing proofs of a *Metropolitan Magazine* article and an editorial for the *Kansas City Star* newspaper on the subject of the League of Nations.

That evening as Edith sat nearby, playing solitaire, he said to her, "I wonder if you will ever know how much I love Sagamore Hill."

When he complained to her of "a terribly odd feeling," as if his heart and breathing were about to shut down, she woke the nurse and later summoned a doctor. The physician gave him a shot of morphine. His valet, James Amos, put him to bed around midnight. As the servant settled into a chair to sleep, a lamp was on. Roosevelt said, "James, please turn out that light."

He died in his sleep of a coronary artery embolism.

Archie cabled Kermit and Ted at their camp near Coblenz: "The old lion is dead."

EPILOGUE

★ ★ ★

NEWS OF BWANA MAKUBA'S death reached Ted in the early evening while Kermit was not in camp. Ted found him later that night in his tent, sipping wine. "We sat up the rest of the night and talked," Kermit wrote to their mother. "Father somehow was very near, and as if he would never be far. I don't feel sorry for him; he wouldn't want it, that would be the last thing. There never was anyone like him, and there won't be. . . . [I]t is foolish to think of oneself, but you will know how the bottom has dropped out for me; at first it was complete, but comes the realization that father could never really die, and that even though I can't bother him about every little decision, when a really vital one comes he will be there as unfailing as ever."

Kermit organized and ran the Roosevelt Steamship Company. He was the father of Kermit Jr., Joseph Willard, Belle Wyatt, and Dirck. Among his circle of literary friends were his father's old pal Rudyard Kipling, the poet Edwin Arlington Robinson (Kermit had gotten Roosevelt to give him a government job), William Butler Yeats, Gertrude Stein, Alexander Woollcott, famed as founding member of the Algonquin Round Table wits of the 1920s, and other stars in the literature of the hard-drinking Jazz Age. Using his literary skills, he published his own memoir of Africa with Bwana Makuba and other adventurers in *The Happy Hunting Grounds*.

Taking a respite from his shipping firm, Kermit accompanied brother Ted in a hunting-exploring expedition to the Himalayan Mountains and later to China in a quest for a Giant Panda for display in Chicago's Field Museum. The brothers published their adventures in books titled *East of the Sun and West of the Moon*, and *Trailing the Giant Panda*. The outfitter for the first expedition was Anthony Fiala.

Increasingly, Kermit showed the same dark moods of his Uncle Elliott, who had become an alcoholic and died in an epileptic seizure. Some scholars of the Roosevelt family of Sagamore Hill theorize that Roosevelt had chosen Kermit as his confidante in an attempt to protect him from the demons that had plagued Elliott.

The hope proved unavailing. The dark side of Kermit recognized by his mother, and so feared by Father, emerged in bouts of heavy drinking and infidelity to Belle that threatened their marriage. With his business hit hard by the effects of the Great Depression, and unable to write because of drinking, he periodically left Belle for a woman named Carla Peters, just as his uncle had been alcoholic and had taken a mistress.

When the Second World War broke out in September 1939, Kermit sought the assistance of his friend, Winston Churchill, to obtain a commission in the British Army. Churchill knew of Kermit's valor under the Union Jack in fighting on the Near East front in the last war. But the man appealing to Churchill in 1940 was a shadow of the dashing hero who had captured Turks by waving an officer's baton at them. Churchill recognized Kermit's condition as the toll taken by alcohol on him physically and spiritually, and that by volunteering Kermit was expressing a no-longer-young man's need to prove that he could still be the heroic figure of the Great War, the "lucky one" who'd dared the wilds of Africa and Brazil with his father, and as the younger brother who'd conquered the Himalaya Mountains with Ted.

If Churchill saw Kermit as a man verging on the brink of doom, and hoped to aid him in getting a commission, he soon had reason to believe that his faith was justified. Kermit proved he still possessed the quality of valor by taking part in a plan of Churchill's to thwart an invasion of Norway by the Soviet Union. But before the mission could be mounted, Norway surrendered to Germany. When a second British attempt to get a hold in Norway in which Kermit took part failed and required evacuation of British commandos, Kermit helped to extricate the men and equipment. He carried some of the wounded on his back. He'd done this while staying sober.

Sent on a mission to North Africa in 1940, Kermit found German patrols, but none of the exciting action he desired. Bored, he resumed drinking and became ill. Sent back to England, he was diagnosed with a flare-up of malaria he'd contracted while on the Brazil expedition. He was also found to have an enlarged liver. Because of these illnesses he was discharged from the army in early 1941. Back in New York in June and reunited with Belle, he vanished almost immediately.

An appeal by Belle to President Franklin D. Roosevelt put the FBI on his trail. Agents found him in July, beaten up after a fight with a taxi driver. After two commitments to the care of a sanitarium, he went to California with Carla Peters in early 1942. When the FBI traced him again, agents reported finding him "stumbling drunk" and reciting Edwin Arlington Robinson's poem, "Richard Cory," about a young man who seemed to have everything but went home one night and put a bullet through his head.

Appeals by Belle and brother Archie to FDR and General George C. Marshall resulted in Kermit being sent to an army air corps base at Fort Richardson, Alaska. He had no specific duty, but he persuaded pilots to take him along on bombing missions against Japanese forces on small islands in the Aleutians. He also helped organize Eskimos and Aleuts into a militia, in case the Japanese attempted to overrun the islands. Sober and feeling good about himself, he wrote to Ted that the war was his "fountain of youth." But he was soon dropping in at Nellie's diner in Anchorage and drinking a few glasses of wine.

Years of hard liquor had left him severely weak, with his stomach distended and arms and legs shockingly thin. Almost any task left him exhausted.

On the night of June 3, 1943, he said to a friend, "I wish I could sleep."

Not long after saying goodnight to the friend, he emulated "Richard Cory" by closing the door of his quarters, placing his Colt Army .45 pistol under his chin, and putting a bullet in his head. In keeping with his father's maxim that where a tree falls, "there let it lay," he was buried at Fort Richardson in Grave 72, Plot A, marked by a plain white army headstone.

The enterprising outfitter of the Brazilian adventure, Anthony Fiala, outlived Theodore Roosevelt by thirty-one years. Well into his eighties, he died in 1950. Among his lifetime of treasures was one of the last letters written by Roosevelt. Dated three days before Roosevelt's death, it praised Fiala's work with a small arms maker during the war.

Jacob Sigg, the Swiss valet for Father Zahm, died at age 65 in Patino, Paraguay, where he'd settled into a quiet life of farming with his wife.

After nearly 40 expeditions in his beloved South America, and with more than 120,000 birds collected in his career as a naturalist, George Cherrie had been the American consul in La Guaira, Venezeula, when news came to him on January 6, 1919, that Roosevelt was dead. The intrepid scientist who refused to abandon Roosevelt in the Brazilian jungle lived until 1948. He died at age 83 in the same year that Edith Roosevelt passed away at Sagamore Hill.

Four years later, death claimed Leo Miller. He'd left his position with the American Museum of Natural History to go into business and lecture from time to time on "The Truth about the River of Doubt." When asked about Theodore Roosevelt, he usually answered, "For a long time it seemed that it could not be possible that a man like that could ever die."

Colonel Rondon became one of the most honored men in Brazilian history. Proclaimed "Civilizer of the Wilderness," made a marshal of Brazil, and with a city named for him, called Rondonia and located in the western part of Matto Grasso, he died at the age of 90 in 1958.

Roosevelt's secretary, Frank Harper, lived the longest after the expedition. He died in a nursing home in Santa Monica, California, in 1971.

As to the former River of Doubt, two attempts by expeditions sent out by the Brazilian government to follow Rio Teodoro met with failure. The first expedition never returned and was presumed to have been killed by Indians. The second was abandoned mid-way out of fear of meeting the same fate. Not until 1927 would there be a successful venture. Led by a British explorer, Commander George M. Dyott, at the request of the Roosevelt Memorial Association (later the Theodore Roosevelt Association), its purpose was to produce a film record of the route for a series of documentaries on Roosevelt's life. Finally, in 1992, the New Century Conservation Trust and the Theodore Roosevelt Association launched an expedition headed by Charles T. Haskell and Elizabeth C. McNight, with Roosevelt's great-grandson, Tweed Roosevelt, in the vanguard. A high-tech enterprise, it had sturdy inflatable rafts that were impervious to the pounding of rapids and crashes into boulders. Global positioning satellites eliminated any doubt as to where the expedition was at all times.

Tweed Roosevelt said of following his illustrious ancestor's route, "They were explorers, while we were merely adventurers, and there is a world of difference." In a foreword to historian Joseph R. Ornig's book, *My Last Chance to Be a Boy: Theodore Roosevelt's South American Expedition of 1913–1914*, published in 1994, Tweed noted that Roosevelt had been five years older than himself, and sixty-five pounds heavier, and "in much worse shape," but had survived with grace and humor.

He certainly had. On the day of his return to New York, May 19, 1914, he stood still for a photographer to snap a picture of him. Wearing a baggy coat and vest, necktie, and white shirt with a collar that was too loose, under a big soft hat with upturned brim, a cord dangling from his pince-nez glasses, and with droopy gray walrus mustache and tired-looking expression, he gazed intently at the cameraman and declared, "I am worth more than several dead men yet."

AUTHOR'S NOTES

★ ★ ★

TRYING TO GET TO KNOW Theodore Roosevelt, and in seeking to understand him, an author does not today, and never has, set off into unexplored territory. The trail was blazed and marked by the man himself. Very little of what Theodore Roosevelt did in his life went unrecorded in his own hand and spoken words. Historian Stephen E. Ambrose hit the Theodore Roosevelt nail squarely on the head by asserting that he "stands alone, unchallenged by any other twentieth-century president, as a writer and scholar." Certainly, he has no equal as a prodigious, prolific writer of letters, magazine articles, essays, monographs, biographies, histories, speeches, and books. Forty-two titles range in subjects from glorious sea battles in the War of 1812, jungle skirmishes in Cuba, the lives of a British reformer-turned-tyrant (Cromwell) and two American politicians (Thomas Hart Benton and Gouverneur Morris), his own hunting adventures, and the monumental *The Winning of the West,* to the thrills of a year-long African safari and his nearly fatal last chance to be a boy by chasing a river named Doubt.

Library and archive files bulge with his papers, photographs, and other memorabilia. They are found in the Theodore Roosevelt Collection of the Houghton Library at Harvard, the Library of Congress, American Museum of Natural History in New York, Scribner's Archives at Princeton, the University of Virginia Library in Charlottesville, Virginia, and at Sagamore Hill and the Theodore Roosevelt Birthplace national historic site where Teedie Roosevelt started his Roosevelt Museum of Natural Science. Many of his thousands of letters, official and to friends, family, and his beloved children, have been culled and published. Friends of his, colleagues, foes, critics, admirers, and companions on his hunts and other adventures wrote about him.

Countless accounts of the adventures of Theodore Roosevelt are found in newspapers and magazines from his time, and since then, along with innumerable Roosevelt biographies. He is one of literature's most fascinating and enduring subjects. His life has been attractive not just to writers about history, but to those who make it. Every subsequent president of the United States turned to him, either for inspiration and guidance, or to borrow a ringing phrase. In the eight decades since his death he has remained an icon of American culture and remains highly ranked as a leader and popular heroic figure.

No one cannot admire a president who could say about the Panama Canal, "While the Congress debated, the canal was built." And there's not a man of middle age, or older, who cannot understand Roosevelt's need to grab a last chance to be a boy again. Who but Theodore Roosevelt could have a cuddly stuffed toy bear named after him, and not be offended?

Yet few people who think they know all about Theodore Roosevelt realize that after he left the White House he went off to Africa for a year of exploration, big-game hunting in the name of science, and self-discovery. Or that he very nearly died in pursuit of the course of an unknown Brazilian river because he thought it would be fun. But surprisingly, except for brief summaries in biographies, a scholarly book by Joseph R. Ornig on the Brazilian expedition, and a greatly abridged *The Hunting and Exploring Adventures of Theodore Roosevelt Told in His Own Words*, edited by Donald Day, with an introduction by Elting E. Morison, there has been until now no single-volume, comprehensive telling of Roosevelt's life as explorer, hunter, and adventurer in the wilds of his own country, Africa, and South America.

My principle sources were Roosevelt's own accounts found in *Hunting Trips of a Ranchman*, *The Wilderness Hunter*, *Outdoor Pastimes of an American Hunter*, *African Game Trails*, *Through the Brazilian Wilderness*, *A Book-Lover's Holiday in the Open*, and his autobiography. Articles by him were published in the magazine *The Outlook* and the *Geographical Journal* of London. Other material appeared in many contemporary magazine and newspaper articles, essays, and interviews. There are also official reports and speeches made by Roosevelt's traveling companions.

The African safari was written about by Kermit Roosevelt in *The Happy Hunting Grounds*. Books touching on the exploration of the River of Doubt were published by Frank M. Chapman (with a Roosevelt introduction), Paul Russell Cartwright, Joseph L. Gardner, Edward J. Goodman, and Leo Miller.

I'm also grateful for the insights provided by Roosevelt biographers Lawrence F. Abbott, H.W. Brands, Hermann Hagedorn, William Henry

Harbaugh, William Draper Lewis, Nathan Miller, Edmund Morris, Sylvia Jukes Morris (a biography of Edith Roosevelt), Henry Pringle, Edward J. Renehan Jr. (*The Lion's Pride: Theodore Roosevelt and His Family in Peace and War*), Corrine Roosevelt Robinson (TR's sister), Roscoe William Thayer, R.L. and C.C. Wilson, and Owen Wister (*Roosevelt, The Story of a Friendship*).

Thanks, too, to Jake Elwell and Olga Wieser of Wieser & Wieser Literary Agency for their steady encouragement and always-wise counsel.

Photographs and cartoons in this book are from my collection, assembled throughout a lifetime of admiring Theodore Roosevelt, and in the course of gathering material for my other books on him: *Commissioner Roosevelt: The Story of Theodore Roosevelt and the New York City Police, 1895–1897; Colonel Roosevelt: Theodore Roosevelt Goes to War, 1897–1898; The Bully Pulpit: A Teddy Roosevelt Book of Quotations*; and my first mystery novel, teaming a young Theodore Roosevelt and incipient detective named Sherlock Holmes, *The Adventure of the Stalwart Companions*.

Being enamored with Roosevelt has also resulted in the only biography of his namesake, *Theodore Roosevelt Jr.: The Life of a War Hero*, a large portion of which deals with Ted's Asian explorations with the "lucky one" of the Roosevelt "bunnies," the indomitable, heroic, and ultimately tragic Kermit.

On February 18, 1918, lying in a bed in New York's Roosevelt Hospital (built by one of his cousins), suffering with the "old Brazilian trouble," Roosevelt had written to his "Dearest Kermit" with the U.S. Army in France and provided a fitting way to end this book. "Well, old side partner," he said, "your letters are perfectly delightful and surely you must know how my heart thrills with pride whenever I think of you."

SELECTED BIBLIOGRAPHY

★ ★ ★

Abbott, Lawrence F. *Impressions of Theodore Roosevelt*. Garden City, N.Y.: Doubleday, Page & Company, 1920.

Brands, H. W. *TR: The Last Romantic*. New York: Basic Books, 1997.

Chapman, Frank M. *Autobiography of a Bird Lover*. New York: Appleton Century Co., 1935.

Cutright, Paul Russell. *Theodore Roosevelt the Naturalist*. New York: Harper & Brothers, 1956.

Day, Donald, editor. *The Hunting and Exploring Adventures of Theodore Roosevelt Told in His Own Words*. New York: The Dial Press, 1955.

Gardner, Joseph L. *Departing Glory: Theodore Roosevelt as Ex-President*. New York: Charles Scribner's Sons, 1973.

Goodman, Edward J. *The Explorers of South America*. New York: The MacMillan Co., 1972.

Hagedorn, Hermann. *The Roosevelt Family of Sagamore Hill*. New York: The MacMillan Co., 1954.

Harbaugh, William Henry. *Power and Responsibility: The Life and Times of Theodore Roosevelt*. New York: Farrar, Straus and Cudahy, 1961.

Harlow, Alvin F. *Theodore Roosevelt: Strenuous American*. New York: Julian Messner, Inc., 1943.

Jeffers, H. Paul. *The Bully Pulpit: A Teddy Roosevelt Book of Quotations*. Dallas, Texas: Taylor Publishing Company, 1998.

———. *Colonel Roosevelt: Theodore Roosevelt Goes to War, 1897–1898*. New York: John Wiley & Sons, Inc., 1996.

———. *Commissioner Roosevelt: The Story of Theodore Roosevelt and the New York City Police, 1895–1897*. New York: John Wiley & Sons, Inc., 1994.

———. *Theodore Roosevelt Jr.: The Life of a War Hero*. Novato, CA: Presidio Press, Inc., 2001.

Miller, Nathan. *Theodore Roosevelt: A Life*. New York: William Morrow, 1992.

Miller, Leo E. *In the Wilds of South America.* New York: Charles Scribner's Sons, 1918.

Morris, Edmund. *The Rise of Theodore Roosevelt.* New York: Coward, McCann & Geohegan, 1979.

Morris, Sylvia Jukes. *Edith Kermit Roosevelt: Portrait of a First Lady.* New York: Coward, McCann & Geohegan, 1980.

Pringle, Henry F. *Theodore Roosevelt: A Biography.* New York: Harcourt, Brace & Co., 1931.

Roosevelt, Kermit. *The Happy Hunting Grounds.* New York: Charles Scriber's Sons, 1920.

Roosevelt, Theodore. *African Game Trails: An Account of the African Wanderings of an American Hunter-Naturalist.* New York: Charles Scribner's Sons, 1910; Cooper Square Press, 2001.

———. *A Book-Lover's Holiday in the Open.* New York: Charles Scribner's Sons, 1919.

———. *Hunting Trips of a Ranchman.* New York: The Modern Library (reprint) 1998.

———. *Letters.* Edited by Elting R. Morison and John Blum. 8 vols. Cambridge: Harvard University Press, 1951–54.

———. *Outdoor Pastimes of an American Hunter.* New York: Charles Sribner's Sons, 1902.

———. *Ranch Life and the Hunting Trail.* New York: Charles Scribner's Sons, 1925.

———. *Theodore Roosevelt: An Autobiography.* Charles Scribner's Sons, 1913.

———. *Through the Brazilian Wilderness.* New York: Charles Scribner's Sons, 1914; Cooper Square Press, 2001.

———. *The Wilderness Hunter.* New York: The Modern Library (reprint), 1998.

Wister, Owen. *Roosevelt, The Story of a Friendship.* New York: MacMillan, 1930.

INDEX

★ ★ ★

ABOUT THE AUTHOR

★ ★ ★

A broadcast journalist for more than three decades, H. PAUL JEFFERS has published over fifty works of fiction and nonfiction, including biographies; histories of the FBI, Scotland Yard, and the Great Depression; "true crime" studies; mysteries; historical westerns; and young adult non-fiction. His other Roosevelt books are *Theodore Roosevelt Jr.: The Life of a War Hero; Commissioner Roosevelt; Colonel Roosevelt;* and *The Bully Pulpit: A Teddy Roosevelt Book of Quotations.*

Other biographies include *An Honest President: The Life and Presidencies of Grover Cleveland; Diamond Jim Brady: Prince of the Gilded Age; The Napoleon of New York: Fiorello La Guardia;* and *Sal Mineo: His Life, Murder and Mystery.*

Before becoming a full-time author, he was a TV news producer and reporter in Boston, producer/writer/editor for the ABC and NBC radio networks, and the only person to hold the position of news director at both of New York City's all-news radio stations. He has taught writing and journalism at New York University, City College of New York, Syracuse University, and California State University at Long Beach.

He lives in New York City.